Teaching Movement & Dance

HIGH/SCOPE
EDUCATIONAL RESEARCH FOUNDATION
Ypsilanti, Michigan

Teaching Movement & Dance

A Sequential Approach to Rhythmic Movement

by Phyllis S. Weikart

THE
HIGH/SCOPE
PRESS

Published by
THE HIGH/SCOPE PRESS

High/Scope Educational Research Foundation
600 North River Street
Ypsilanti, Michigan 48197
(313) 485-2000

Lynn Spencer, Editor
Gary Easter, Designer/Photographer
Dianne Macut Kreis, Associate Designer
Linda Eckel, Cover Designer
Carolyn Ofiara, Typographer

Library of Congress Cataloging in Publication Data

Weikart, Phyllis S., 1931-
  Teaching movement & dance.

  Bibliography: p.
  Includes index.
  1. Movement education—Study and teaching. 2.
Folk dancing—Study and teaching. I. Title. II. Title:
Teaching movement and dance.
GV452.W44   793.307   82-6239

ISBN 0-931114-16-0 (pbk.)   AACR2

Printed in the United States of America

To my family

Contents

(continued)

Part Two:
Beginning Folk Dances

Preface

It has been a distinct pleasure to have had the opportunity to work with persons of all ages and share my love of the music and movement which is embodied in international folk dance. I have learned a great deal about people and about the teaching/learning cycle in my three decades as a teacher of movement and dance. Helping students succeed has always been an important goal for me and when I encounter students who aren't successful, I want to know *why* they are having problems. Am I not presenting the material clearly? Is the material too difficult for the learners? Are students not trying as hard as they could? These and similar questions have guided my teaching and research over the years. At first, I attempted to answer these questions by simplifying and modifying the rhythmic movement teaching/learning process. But I discovered, after numerous trials and errors, that unless beginners master the basic skills needed to achieve rhythmic movement (the ability to walk to music and to be comfortable with movement) they will not be able to execute dance steps and sequences successfully—no matter how clearly the material is presented, no matter what simplifications or modifications are made, and no matter how motivated the student might be.

Dancing and moving rhythmically are important and often undervalued skills in our society. Most of us, at least once in awhile, want to exhibit such skills. The difficult teenage years in high school are made more pleasurable if a boy or girl is comfortable on the dance floor and when participating in other rhythmic movement activities. Students I've had in university folk dance classes report feeling better about themselves when they learn to dance. I believe (and have preliminary

evidence to support the notion) that attainment of rhythmic competency helps the learner master physical skills found in sport and games, enhances a learner's ability in the music curriculum area with specific skills including pitch-matching, and helps the learner attain readiness skills for reading and language development. I plan to continue my work in these areas.

I wrote this book for all teachers of rhythmic movement activities who share my desire to assure success for their students—child or adult. Music and physical education teachers, dance teachers, preschool and elementary classroom teachers, special education teachers, curriculum coordinators and supervisors, as well as persons working with older adults, and parents, will find the book useful.

I certainly don't have all the answers, and my information will not guarantee universal success, but I believe the teaching steps and methods I outline in the book can help many individuals of all ages succeed, even if their previous attempts at rhythmic movement resulted in failure.

I wish to express sincere thanks to all the people who have helped me over the years as I prepared to write this book:

- The many folk dance teachers in this country from whom I have had the pleasure and privilege to learn. These include: Fred Berk, Sunni Bloland, Dick Crum, Andor Czompo, Eliahu Gamliel, Rickey Holden, Athan Karras, Martin Koenig, Atanas Kolarovsky, Judith and Kalman Magyar, Yves Moreau, Moshe Itzchak-Halevy, Bora Ozkok, Ken Spear, and Ron Wixman.

- The students of all ages who have been the recipients of my trials and errors.

• The "tiny teachers" in the first and second grades and their music teacher, Sue Lawson, with whom I had the pleasure of working for two years—a very special thanks.

• My friends and colleagues who have listened patiently to my ideas, reacted, advised, reviewed chapters, and tried out the teaching sequences, with special appreciation to my workshop assistant, Gloria Abrams, and to Esther Gray, Charles and Mary Hohmann, Mary Howell (who collected test data for me), Sandra Huron, Catherine Nadon-Gabrion, and Carolyn Tower.

In addition, I am most grateful to the many professionals at the High/Scope Press who have contributed their time and talents unselfishly to the production of this book. My editor, Lynn Spencer, has been tireless in her efforts. Her expertise, her patience, her good humor and her excellent advice have been most appreciated. Special thanks also are extended to the following people: Nancy Altman Brickman, Judy Clouse, Gary Easter, Linda Eckel, Millie Flory, Dianne Macut Kreis and Carol Ofiara.

And, most especially, I thank my husband, David, and daughters, Cindy, Cathy, Jenny, and Gretchen for the joy I've experienced dancing with them, and for their encouragement, support, and understanding over the years.

I hear and I forget
I see and I remember
I do and I understand

— *Proverb*

Introduction:
Rhythmic Movement—
Success or Failure

This book is written for concerned teachers who want their students of all ages to become more comfortable with and proficient in activities requiring rhythmic movement competency. Children and adults who experience success with rhythmic movement are more likely to join in and enjoy dance, musical activities, sports, and recreation. They learn to appreciate the meter and rhyme of spoken language. And they don't worry as much about "looking silly" or failing to perform "appropriately" in front of others.

Opportunities for rhythmic movement experiences abound: in elementary classrooms, in music and physical education classes, in competitive athletics, in dance, and in exercise and recreation programs for people of all ages. These types of activities are important for the broad development of the child and the continued well-being of the adult (including senior citizens).

The teaching methods and activities presented in this book allow individuals to experience success with rhythmic movement through a step-by-step, easy-to-follow sequence. The book also presents the theory behind the learning process for achieving rhythmic movement competency, thus giving teachers an in-depth understanding of *why* as well as *how* to teach movement and dance to all age groups.

Before describing this process, however, some definitions are needed. What exactly is meant by the term *rhythmic movement?* Used in a generic sense, rhythmic movement refers to *sequences or patterns of body movements that combine elements of time and space.* Dynamics of intensity, flow, and style are then

added to enrich the movement and feeling of the experience. "Rhythmic" denotes a *time* relationship, ranging from simply matching external steady beats to matching more complex subdivisions of the beat within groupings of beats. "Movement" denotes *kinesthetic* or *motoric* ability (motion in space). Movement of the body may occur in a very simple pattern (such as walking forward) or in very complex patterns (such as changing direction, level, and intensity throughout a specified duration of time).

The simplest rhythmic movement activities are those in which the individual is *not* asked to respond to a beat created by another person or group. For example, a teacher asks the class to "MARCH 8 steps, JUMP 8 times, and then HOP 4 times on each leg." Although the teacher gives the signal to begin, he or she does not create a group beat. Instead, the students perform the rhythmic movement to their *own* organization of time and space. In most sports activities, the athlete combines elements of time and space in a pattern of rhythmic movement keyed to his or her individual beat. To swim, for example, a person must combine the movements of the arms and legs in a coordinated pattern to his or her own organization of "time" or beat.

Next in the order of rhythmic movement difficulty are those activities which require an individual to move to an externally produced beat, either alone or in a group. For example, students who march, jump, and hop to a teacher's drum beat are performing fairly difficult rhythmic movements. Likewise, a group of persons performing exercise warm-ups, or a group of swimmers synchronizing a crawl stroke, are participating in fairly difficult activities because they must move to an external beat. Dancing in a group to a musical selection is another example of an activity requiring persons to match their movements to the external beat instead of to their own natural beat.

The most difficult rhythmic movement activities are those in which participants move to an external beat they themselves pro-duce—doing two things at once. The marching band is a perfect example of this type of activity. Singing while moving, speaking while moving (reciting a poem while doing a movement sequence to it), and singing while playing a hand-held or barred instrument are further examples of the most complex rhythmic movement activities.

It is clear that rhythmic movement describes many different activities in many different learning programs. In music programs, the term refers to musical activities that integrate various movement sequences; in physical education, to activities that use music, such as free exercise in gymnastics, figure skating, synchronized swimming, or warm-ups to a common beat; and in the classroom to language-based activities to which movement is added. Rhythmic movement also describes all types of dance activities. In this sense, the term is used in place of the word *dance* when *dance* denotes too narrow a concept, or when the teacher wants a less threatening term (for example, to present a rhythmic activity to boys and girls for whom the word *dance* has negative connotations). Rhythmic movement also is used in place of the term *creative movement* if a particular group is put off or threatened by the word *creative*.

Essentially, then, rhythmic movement combines two elements: (1) the element of rhythm employing *time,* and (2) the element of movement employing *space.* An individual must understand and be comfortable with each element if the whole is to be successful.

In this book, the capacity to utilize *time* in rhythmic movement is called *rhythmic competency*. The first teaching progression presented in this book *(Chapter II)* can be used by teachers to help both children and adults attain a **basic level of rhythmic competency**. An individual who is rhythmically competent is able to (1) accurately identify the beat in a musical selection or a language-based activity, and (2) match that beat through the physical task of walking to it. The second teaching progression presented in this book *(Chapter III)* can be used by teachers to help individuals develop their capacity to utilize *space* in movement activities. This capacity will be referred to as **basic comfort with movement**; that is, the ability of an individual to (1) move with the body free of tension in space, and (2) combine this movement with his or her own beat and tempo. These two teaching progressions should be presented concurrently.

Learners must become actively involved in the rhythmic movement learning process if they are to master movement sequences and function independently without a visual model. I use a language process—the **four-step language process**—to foster active learning. The **four-step language process** is introduced in *Chapter I* and is a necessary part of the teaching progression leading to the development of a **basic level of rhythmic competency** *(Chapter II)*. The language process recurs throughout the book as learners participate in rhythmic experiences ranging from simple coordination sequences to organized dance. The **four-step language process**, however, requires individuals to organize movement to an external beat and is therefore not part of the beginning movement experiences presented in *Chapter III*. Language is used in these beginning movement experiences, but in a different way—guiding the problem-solving activities presented in the chapter to promote the learners' aural and visual discrimination and their understanding of movement concepts.

I originally developed the teaching progressions leading to a **basic level of**

rhythmic competency and **basic comfort with movement** for elementary school children to help them succeed in music and physical education programs and in classroom activities that employ movement. But the audience for these progressions has expanded over time to include all age groups (preschool* to senior citizens). Many adults, including senior citizens, are returning to rhythmic activities, such as exercise to music, fitness dance, and ballroom dance, but they often lack the rhythmic coordination and relaxation needed to succeed. Beginners are beginners at any age when it comes to rhythmic movement. And all beginners need to develop similar

basic competencies in order to be successful with more complicated rhythmic activities. Therefore, I have modified the activities in this book so they can be used with adults as well as children, although the primary focus is on the younger population.

The focus is still on elementary-age children because, while it is never too late to teach rhythmic movement, it is much easier and more natural to work with children before they become resistant to movement activities than to overcome all their feelings of inadequacy after lack of success has become apparent. Children who, by age eight or nine, have experienced repeated failures in group situations involving rhythmic movement will be difficult students, as will adults who have

---

*It should be noted that preschoolers will benefit from activities and teaching progressions presented in *Chapters I, II,* and *III*, but should not be expected to perform the activities presented in the rest of the book.

had even more unsuccessful experiences. In either case, teachers must contend with a damaged sense of self, a pattern of misbehavior to cover up the failure, lack of interest in trying for fear of repeating past failures, tension, insecurity, and the "I don't want to do it" syndrome. Because these attitudes are very difficult to overcome in group learning situations, I offer in this book teaching techniques I have found to be effective in dealing with such problems at the elementary-age level (with additional techniques for older populations).

Why do people experience failure so often in rhythmic movement activities—whether adult or child? I have wrestled with this question for years. We can all identify family members, friends, casual acquaintances and strangers who refuse to participate in rhythmic movement activities such as dance and athletics. Think of all the "wallflowers" you've seen standing on the edge of a dance floor watching others enjoy the music, movement, and fellowship of dancing.

Perhaps the answer to this question lies in the activities a child experiences in his or her earliest years. Parents often overlook or are not aware of the importance of providing appropriate, developmentally sequenced rhythmic activities for infants at their earliest stage of development (for example, patting or stroking babies to the underlying steady beat of music or songs sung, rocking babies, bouncing babies on the knee to a beat, or playing "pat-a-cake" with them). Then, too,

preschool teachers often are not aware of the importance of providing developmentally appropriate activities for their students which reinforce the concept of beat and promote comfortable movement in space. In addition, significant changes have occurred over the last two decades in children's play activities. Television viewing consumes children's valuable play time as well as time that parents and/or older siblings could spend playing with or reading to them. Passive forms of play, as with popular electronic games, often take the place of more vigorous physical activity, such as jumping rope, swinging, using the teeter-totter, playing hop scotch, or playing language-based rhythmic games (for example, "one potato, two potato, three potato, four"). And finally, many of the movement activities designed by early childhood educators (grades K-4) of all disciplines are too difficult for children of this age and result in repeated failures.

In order to test some of my assumptions, I developed a **Rhythmic Competency Analysis Test**. The test was designed as an informal tool to help me gather information in a systematic and careful manner. (*Appendix A* contains a complete copy of this test.) Initially, the test was used to determine how many students in a group of first through third graders could identify an underlying beat in a musical

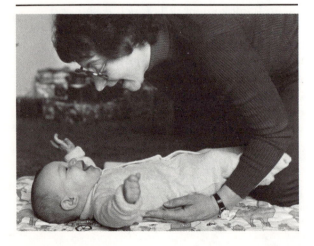

selection and how many could walk to that same beat. Three tasks were developed to determine at what level the breakdown in a child's rhythmic ability occurs: (1) identifying the beat; (2) organizing and repeating two motions to the beat; and (3) walking to the beat. The test was administered to 464 children in grades 1-3 over a two-month time span.

Table 1 presents the results of the test for first through third graders on the three tasks, by grade level. Results show that 61% (60% male, 63% female) of the first grade children

beat (Task 1); 55% (55% male, 56% female) were successful with Task 2; but only 37% (41% male, 33% female) could walk to it (Task 3). With third graders, 74% (72% male, 76% female) were able to identify the underlying beat (Task 1); 70% (67% male, 73% female) were successful with Task 2; but only 51% (45% male, 58% female) were able to walk to it (Task 3). These results suggest two things. First, if walking to music is one of the simplest rhythmic movement tasks, then many of the most commonly used movement activities presented in the early elementary grades are too difficult for children to perform

Table 1

Results of *Rhythmic Competency Analysis Test* Administered to Children in Grades 1-3

GRADE	NUMBER	TASK 1[a]			TASK 2[b]			TASK 3[c]		
		Total %	M %	F %	Total %	M %	F %	Total %	M %	F %
1	186	61	60	63	43	37	49	34	26	43
2	165	59	57	61	55	55	56	37	41	33
3	113	74	72	76	70	67	73	51	45	58

[a] Task 1: Child identifies underlying steady beat and matches that beat by patting the top of the head with both hands.

[b] Task 2: Child identifies underlying steady beat and matches that beat by patting the top of the head and then the tops of the shoulders with both hands (one pat to each body part in a double coordinated motion).

[c] Task 3: Child walks to the underlying steady beat.

tested were able to accurately identify the underlying beat of music used (Task 1); 43% (37% male, 49% female) were able to coordinate two motions to the beat (Task 2); but only 34% (26% male, 43% female) were able to walk to that same beat (Task 3). When a second piece of music with a different tempo was played to double-check these findings, the results were the same. Test results for second graders indicate that 59% (57% male, 61% female) could identify the

successfully. Second, boys probably will have more difficulty than girls with rhythmic movement tasks.

Is rhythmic competency attained "naturally" by youngsters through maturation? To answer this question, a modified form of the **Rhythmic Competency Analysis Test** was administered to 301 students in grades 4-6, and to 90 teenagers (ages 13 to 18). Table 2 illustrates the results of this test, which point

Table 2

*Results of Modified[a]
Rhythmic Competency Analysis Test
Administered to Children in Grades 4-6
and Teenagers*

GRADE	NUMBER	TASK 1[b]			TASK 3[c]		
		Total %	M %	F %	Total %	M %	F %
4	78	73	64	82	73	59	88
5	119	84	78	90	78	69	87
6	104	81	77	86	76	72	80
Teens #1[d]	45	96	92	100	71	62	81
Teens #2[e]	45	97	94	100	75	66	85

[a]Task 2 was eliminated for this age group.

[b]Task 1: Child identifies underlying steady beat and matches that beat by patting the legs with both hands.

[c]Task 3: Child walks to the underlying beat.

[d]Participants in four-week camp program, May.

[e]Participants in seven-week camp program, June-August.

to differences in male/female success rates. (The modification omitted Task 2, which was the assessment of the double coordinated motion. It seemed unnecessary to include this step because I already had enough evidence to support my contention that the younger children would experience an increasing lack of success as the coordination tasks became more difficult. In addition, I did not want to include this activity for the older children because "touching the head, touching the shoulders" might result in a "turn off.")

I plotted the results of the **Rhythmic Competency Analysis Test** for all age groups to illustrate the overall performance pattern (see Table 3). Results show that the children tested in the early elementary grades had not experienced sufficient opportunities to identify a beat or to match the beat with simple body coordinations. Fewer than two-thirds of the first and second graders tested could identify the beat (Task 1); of those successful with the beat identification, only about half of them could walk to the beat (Task 3). The third graders show a slight improvement; the boys and girls are similar in their ability to identify the beat and walk to it, but the girls are beginning to pull ahead. In the fourth and fifth grades, the girls move well ahead of the boys on Task 3 and remain approximately 20 percentage points ahead in the teenage years. Although more than 90% of the teenage males could identify the beat (Task 1), only 62% (group 1 males) and 66% (group 2 males) could walk to the music (Task 3). In contrast, all the teenage girls could identify the beat (Task 1), and over 80% could walk to the music (Task 3). These male/female statistics have been duplicated in all the adult populations I have informally assessed over the past two years.

Why is the female success rate so high and the male success rate so low? Experience with rhythmic coordination activities is certainly a major factor. By fourth grade, girls have participated in many activities that use beat—jumping rope, disco dance, hand-jive—whereas boys have not engaged as much in such activities. The suggestion from the data collected on all groups is clear: boys will have more difficulty with rhythmic tasks than girls. Without assistance, one out of three boys will lack basic rhythmic coordination and approximately one out of five girls will lack these skills.

I wanted to help teachers assess their students' rhythmic competency. But I realized that the **Rhythmic Competency Analysis Test** would not be practical to administer in most classrooms because it only tests one student at a time. I wanted to give teachers a quick and simple measure they could use to predict an individual's ability to be successful with rhythmic activities. Therefore, I devised the **Rhythmic Coordination Screening Test.** (A complete description of this test appears in *Appendix B.*) To assess the test's accuracy, I administered it to the previously mentioned students in grades 4-6 and to the two groups of teenagers before I gave them the **Rhythmic Competency Analysis Test**. In 95% of the cases, those who had difficulty with the **Rhythmic Coordination Screening Test** could not walk to music. Because of its accuracy as a predictor of success, experienced teachers who will be presenting rhythmic activities to their class, or teaching physical education, or teaching dance, can use the **Rhythmic Coordination Screening Test** for a quick assessment of the student's or the group's rhythmic coordination ability.

To test the assumption that teaching progressions providing an ordered series of experiences will help youngsters succeed in rhythmic movement activities, I arranged for students in a combined first and second grade class to be given the **Rhythmic Competency Analysis Test** as part of their regular music class. When I first tested the class in early October of the school year, I found that only 55% of the students could identify the underlying beat in a musical selection by using a single tapping motion of both hands on top of the head, and only 22% could walk to the same piece of music. Three months later (January), however, after the class had experienced the teaching progressions I had designed, I retested them: every child could identify the underlying beat, and 77% of the students in class could walk to the beat. By May, every child in the class could walk to the beat of several musical selections. Table 4 illustrates these findings. This pattern of success was repeated in another first-grade classroom in which the teacher presented the sequenced tasks to students in short activity sessions each day during the times when the children seemed to need activity.

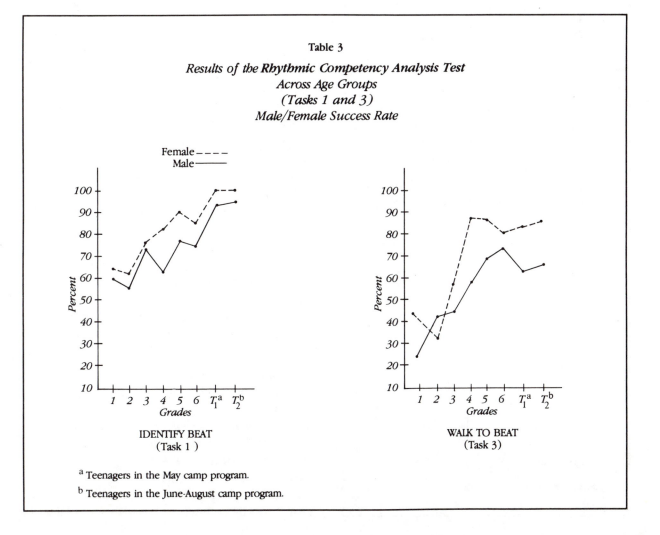

Table 3

Results of the Rhythmic Competency Analysis Test
Across Age Groups
(Tasks 1 and 3)
Male/Female Success Rate

Female – – – –
Male ———

IDENTIFY BEAT
(Task 1)

WALK TO BEAT
(Task 3)

[a] Teenagers in the May camp program.

[b] Teenagers in the June-August camp program.

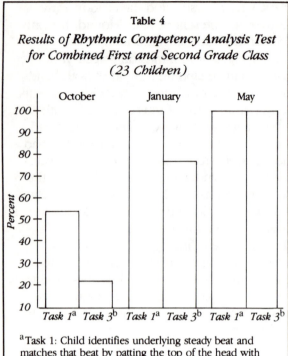

Table 4

*Results of Rhythmic Competency Analysis Test
for Combined First and Second Grade Class
(23 Children)*

^aTask 1: Child identifies underlying steady beat and matches that beat by patting the top of the head with both hands.

^bTask 3: Child walks to the underlying beat.

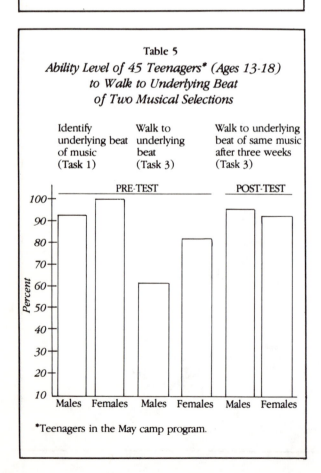

Table 5

Ability Level of 45 Teenagers (Ages 13-18)
to Walk to Underlying Beat
of Two Musical Selections*

*Teenagers in the May camp program.

In a related experiment, I asked the first group of teenagers who had taken the **Rhythmic Competency Analysis Test** (see Table 2) to take part in an ordered series of movement experiences consisting of 20 minutes of rhythmic coordination tasks which were divided into five four-minute blocks of "follow-the-leader" experiences and about 12 hours of beginning folk dance activities. I conducted the activities over the first three weeks of a four-week camp session. As illustrated in Table 5, the pre-test results of the modified **Rhythmic Competency Analysis Test** showed that all the girls could identify the underlying beat (Task 1), and 81% of the girls could walk to the underlying beat (Task 3). Of the teenage boys, 92% could identify the beat, but only 62% of the boys who experienced the same musical selection as the girls could successfully walk to it. The post-test, administered three weeks later (see Table 5), demonstrated that 95% of the boys and 92% of the girls could walk successfully to the music. (This experiment was replicated with the second group of teenagers.) It should be noted that none of the groups tested heard the music used for either the pre- or post-test outside of the testing sessions.

These findings indicated to me that rhythmic coordination does not develop naturally in many individuals by the adult years. However, most children and adults can be successful with rhythmic movement activities if they experience a sequence of interrelated and increasingly complex rhythmic coordination activities. Since I felt that the learning experiences available to foster these skills were not sufficient, I designed the teaching progressions and methods presented and described in this book to meet these needs.

This book is divided into two parts. The first part (*Chapters I* through *VI*) presents information and techniques for teachers to use when introducing rhythmic movement and dance to beginners. *Chapter I* contains a description of the **four-step language process** teachers can use as a framework within which to teach beginners how to become rhythmically competent. *Chapter II* contains

the teaching progression that leads to the development of a **basic level of rhythmic competency**, with suggested teaching activities. *Chapter III* contains the teaching progression designed to help learners achieve **basic comfort with movement**, with suggested teaching activities. *Chapter IV* presents ways for teachers to link together elements of time and space to help learners achieve rhythmic movement competency. In *Chapter V,* I give my rationale for focusing on international folk dance and present introductory folk dance experiences, the final step in achieving rhythmic movement competency. *Chapter VI* focuses on the actual delivery system for teaching folk dance—how teachers should proceed when learners are ready for beginning folk dance. *Part Two* of this book contains the folk dance descriptions.

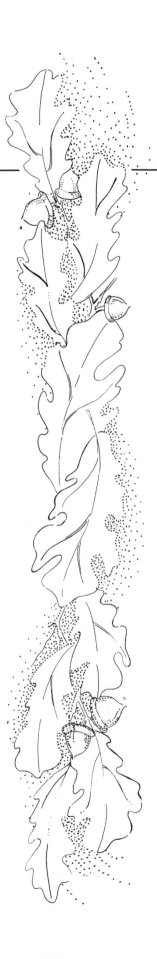

Part One

A Sequential Approach to Teaching Rhythmic Movement

I.

Language as the Bridge to Movement

Most children and adults are required to master physical skills and movement activities throughout their lives. In school, for example, teachers may suggest movement problems and ask their students to watch and follow them as they demonstrate the activity or skill. The demonstration is wasted, however, for many students because they cannot "decode" the visual sequence of movement as it is demonstrated. I make this statement after observing many individuals of all ages who could not perform basic rhythmic coordination activities.

It is important for students of all ages to understand fully the movement activity in which they are participating, whatever its complexity. Language is a natural bridge to movement—making the learning process an active experience for the participant, a cognitive experience. In the **four-step language process**, explained in this chapter, the learner uses language to prepare for the movement sequences and then combines language with movement. Language thus becomes the organizer for movement.

Teachers of elementary-age children will find that the language process provides an excellent framework for presenting bilingual experiences to their students (translating names of body parts, contrasting movements, counting in the dance sequences). Colleagues who have used the language process with special populations of mentally and physically handicapped report success. Special education teachers will find that the language-to-movement activities work well with youngsters with special needs.

The four-step language process is the foundation for the teaching progression leading to a **basic level of rhythmic competency** (see *Chapter II*). In the simplest language-to-movement activity, the student matches the naming of a body part with a corresponding bilateral motion (using both hands), tapping the body part named. For example, the student chants "HEAD, HEAD, HEAD, HEAD" while tapping the head with both hands simultaneously. This activity can be extended with action words as the teacher explores with students the meaning in movement of TAP, PAT, TOUCH, THUMP, POUND, SWING, BEND, STRAIGHTEN—words and motions are brought together in simultaneous language-to-movement. As students gain more experience, they begin to sequence words and motion by twos and later by fours, for example, "KNEES, SHOULDERS" then "IN, OUT, UP, DOWN."

Teachers use language in a different way to help students achieve **basic comfort with movement**, a process described more fully in *Chapter III.* In one phase of this process, teachers use language in the form of verbal directions; students respond with movement as they listen to the directions. Because individuals today are very visually oriented,

they need opportunities to decode messages and directions aurally. Movement activities can assist them in this process. For example, the teacher asks students to "put your hands on your shoulders," "put your hands on your head," "take one hand and put it on your knee," "thump your chest with the other hand." The teacher does not demonstrate the activity, but supplies the direction in language only. As students process the spoken language, they further develop their listening skills.

In a related vein, my observations have indicated that individuals who can decode a visual demonstration often do not *understand* what they are doing; they are only copying the

leader's action. By using language as a bridge to movement, however, teachers can help students deepen their understanding of movement concepts. For example, in another phase of the teaching progression leading to **basic comfort with movement**, the teacher demonstrates a simple movement, such as bending and straightening the arms, and asks the students to describe with language the movement demonstrated. Since there are several ways to describe the movement, the teacher can ask students to provide many different descriptions of the same movements (for example, "IN, OUT"; "PULL, PUSH") rather than work toward an identification of the words "BEND, STRAIGHTEN." The latter definition is a very narrow "correct answer" while the former helps the student achieve a more complete understanding of the concept in a much more creative manner.

Teachers may at times choose to combine verbal directions with visual demonstrations. For example, the teacher swings the arms from side to side saying, "I am showing one way to swing my arms; can you do what I'm doing?" "Can you find another way to swing your arms? Another way? Another way?" "Can you swing any other parts of your body?" While it is important to occasionally combine aural and visual experiences in this way, teachers should primarily focus on one or the other.

In *Chapter IV,* I explain how the skills developed through the two basic teaching progressions can be combined by students to produce successful rhythmic movement. In these more complex activities, language again provides a natural bridge to movement. The learner sequences with language the movements to be executed. For example, before performing a movement, such as walking, jumping, or hopping, the learners chant the language pattern for the movement: "JUMP, 2, 3, 4."

The Four-Step Language Process

The language process is designed to bridge language and movement through a four-step

---

Figure 1

*Relationship Between Language and Movement
in the Four-Step Language Process*

LANGUAGE: *BODY-PART IDENTIFICATION*		MOVEMENT
SAY	HEAD, HEAD, HEAD, HEAD	No movement
SAY AND DO	HEAD, HEAD, HEAD, HEAD	Tap top of head while SAYING "HEAD"
WHISPER AND DO	Same as SAY AND DO, except whispered	Same as SAY AND DO
THINK AND DO	Language is repeated silently	Same as SAY AND DO

LANGUAGE: *ACTION WORDS*		MOVEMENT
SAY	TAP, TAP, TAP, TAP	Tap top of head while SAYING "TAP"
SAY AND DO	TAP, TAP, TAP, TAP	Same as SAY AND DO
WHISPER AND DO	Same as SAY AND DO	Same as SAY AND DO
THINK AND DO	Language is repeated silently	Same as SAY AND DO

LANGUAGE: *MOVEMENT IDENTIFICATION*		MOVEMENT
SAY	WALK, WALK, WALK, WALK	No movement
SAY AND DO	WALK, WALK, WALK, WALK	Walk while SAYING "WALK"
WHISPER AND DO	Same as SAY AND DO	Same as SAY AND DO
THINK AND DO	Language is repeated silently	Same as SAY AND DO

LANGUAGE: *DANCE STEP*		MOVEMENT
SAY	CROSS, SIDE, BACK, SIDE	No movement
SAY AND DO	CROSS, SIDE, BACK, SIDE	Execute dance steps simultaneously with language
WHISPER AND DO	Same as SAY AND DO	Same as SAY AND DO
THINK AND DO	Language is repeated silently	Same as SAY AND DO

sequence. The four steps in the language process are as follows:

STEP I	SAY
STEP II	SAY AND DO
STEP III	WHISPER AND DO
STEP IV	DO (THINK AND DO)

The language steps are used at all levels of movement activity—from the simplest (see next chapter) to the most complex (organized dance). Figure 1 illustrates the relationship between language and movement for each step. Teachers should follow STEPS I and II (SAY, SAY AND DO) when introducing a new rhythmic coordination activity to students, then present STEPS III and IV (WHISPER AND DO, DO) in the learning sequence, after which music is added (when the learners understand and are comfortable with the sequence). These steps should be followed no matter what movement activity is being taught—from the simplest to the most complex. Occasionally, STEP I (SAY) may be omitted if the sequence is very simple.

I recommend the **four-step language process** for teachers who are presenting rhythmic movement activities to any age group; it is an especially important and effective technique to use in teaching patterns of organized dance. Very often dance is taught by a "watch me and and do as I do" process. But problems in reversing and visually decoding movement are created when a circle formation is used and the teacher is across the circle from the learners. Rhythmically competent students may successfully learn dance steps if this visual teaching technique is employed, but will be unable to perform successfully when the visual model is removed. Those individuals lacking rhythmic competency will not be successful because they cannot "decode" the movements of the visual model.

Step I: SAY

In this first step, the teacher asks children or adults to use simple descriptive words to identify body parts or to indicate motions and stepping patterns which will be matched with movement in the second step (SAY AND DO). For example, ask your students to chant "HEAD, HEAD, HEAD, HEAD" or "TAP, TAP, TAP, TAP" or "WALK, WALK, WALK, WALK." The only external beat imposed is that created by the repetitive single-word language. No music is used when teaching this first step.

You may find that STEP I can be omitted in many cases if the STEP II: SAY AND DO sequence appears to be easy for a particular group of learners. It is more critical to follow STEP I when working with young children and with special populations because these groups must be comfortable with the chant *before* movement is added. Learning disabled individuals may have difficulty expressing the exact words, but you should encourage them to try to say the words as well as they can. A vocal utterance may be all they can produce; this is satisfactory. You also will find this step useful when teaching dance sequences that are longer than 4 beats (for example, SIDE, BACK, SIDE, CROSS, SIDE, LIFT, SIDE, LIFT).

Step II: SAY AND DO

The teacher asks children or adults to match the repetitious chant with body movements. As with STEP I, no singing or music is involved. The teacher begins the chant to establish a beat and tempo and then adds the accompanying movement so that both the chant and movement occur simultaneously.

For example, the teacher chants "KNEES, KNEES, KNEES, KNEES" and then accompanies the chant with action: both hands touching the knees simultaneously in rhythm with the spoken word. Later you may vary the language used in order to emphasize the nature of the movement and begin the development of a movement vocabulary. For example, in the case cited above, action words such as "TAP, TAP, TAP, TAP" can replace "KNEE." Ask different students to assume the role of leader (to create a beat and tempo change), and ask them to change the language and movement.

Step III: WHISPER AND DO

The teacher asks the students to repeat STEP II, but to whisper the chants. This activity is an important bridge to the next step, DO (when students just think the words). Be certain the students continue to verbalize the words to retain the thought process. In STEP III, music is added *after* the learners become proficient in performing the activity. Language helps the learners match the musical beat with movement.

Step IV: DO (THINK AND DO)

The teacher now asks the students to "think" the words while continuing the movement without music. When the students are able to retain the thought process of the verbal pattern, they will be able to maintain a consistent tempo and a steady beat. Otherwise, they will increase the tempo unconsciously, a phenomenon that is difficult to control once music is added. If students practice movements using their own steady beat and tempo, they are more apt to maintain this consistency when the external beat of music is added.

Adding Music to the Four-Step Language Process

Music, which creates the external steady beat, should not be added to the last two steps of the **four-step language process** until learners can successfully perform the entire sequence. When music is introduced, the beat to be matched must be strong enough to be clearly understood by the learners. Movement to music begins with STEP III (WHISPER AND DO); then the whisper is eliminated and replaced with STEP IV, DO (THINK AND DO), thus matching movement to the external beat. (At times, it may be useful to whisper the language sequence to the musical beat *without* movement before proceeding to STEP III, WHISPER AND DO.)

II.
Teaching Progression Leading to a Basic Level of Rhythmic Competency

Rhythmic competency, as defined in the *Introduction,* refers to an individual's capacity to utilize time in rhythmic movement. Simple identification and matching of an external steady beat with movement is at one end of the rhythmic competency continuum; using movement to match subdivisions of the beat within groupings of beats is at the other end. Anyone who wants to successfully participate in organized dance or successfully complete other motoric tasks that require accurate timing and coordinated movement must attain rhythmic competency.

A person who has developed a **basic level of rhythmic competency** is able to match an external beat through the physical task of walking to it. To achieve this level of competency, an individual must be able to identify the steady beat in a musical selection or language-based activity. Watch any group that is singing together, playing instruments, or participating in locomotor rhythmic movement activities—the greater the number of individuals who perceive the common beat, the more successful the group experience will be.

Beat is a very abstract concept: one must perceive (feel) the steady pulse which is externally created by the musical selection or language-based activity. I often have found, in my work with first graders* who do not understand *beat,* that using visual and aural methods to clarify this concept for them is not successful. The only method that has proved almost totally successful is a tactile (physical) one; interestingly, this method is identical to

the tactile stimulation many infants receive from adults and other children. Infants and very young children who have been patted and bounced on a parent's knee to the beat of external music or spoken rhymes, or who have been sung to, rocked, or stroked rhythmically, usually develop a kinesthetic feel for *beat* and subsequently achieve a **basic level of rhythmic competency** early in life.

Realizing that there might be a link between very early rhythmic experiences and early rhythmic competency, I created a tactile stimulation activity for a first grade music class that was similar to these early experiences: while a song was sung, a rhyme spoken, or a musical selection played, I asked the students to keep the beat with a patting motion on their legs. The music teacher and I then moved in back of the seated children and reinforced the beat by patting their shoulders to the beat. Later the children patted the teachers' shoulders to the beat, which gave us the opportunity to assist those children who were not exact with the beat. Almost immediately, this teaching method increased the percentage of children who achieved accuracy in beat identification from approximately 66% to 95% of the class. Listening to music or rhymes and having the teacher clap in time to the beat (an aural method), or looking at a chalkboard as the

---

*In this chapter, and in *Chapters III* and *IV,* my focus will be on the elementary-age child; I will, however, suggest activities that are appropriate for the older child and adult at the end of each chapter. Preschool teachers will find the activities in *Chapters I–III* most suitable for their young students.

teacher points to notes on the board (a visual method), does not seem to help children understand the abstract *beat*.

The teaching progression presented in this chapter is based on what I have learned from my experiences over the years teaching folk dance to adults, university students, and teenagers, teaching physical education, working in music classes and with music educators, and working with classroom teachers. In order to help students learn about beat, they must be given opportunities to respond to it in many ways. Physical education teachers can use this teaching progression to help their students develop awareness of the body in motion and to help them master the timing which is a necessary underpinning of sports and games. Elementary classroom teachers have many opportunities, through rhythmic movement activities, to introduce language and reading concepts to their students. Activities suggested in the teaching progression leading

to rhythmic competency may be used in the early elementary grades instead of other rhythmic movement activities which often require students to combine rhythmic patterns and movement sequences before they have had enough experience with them separately. The purpose of this teaching progression is to raise a child's competency level *before* movement activities (which often result in failure) are added. If 90% of the children in a class can successfully accomplish the activities presented, discipline problems (which may be the result of repeated failures) should decrease. The end result of this successful experience will be increased opportunities for teachers to design more challenging, exciting, and beneficial activities for children. And the pillars for supporting rhythmic movement competency will be anchored to a solid base. The teaching progression for the other component of rhythmic movement, **basic comfort with movement**, is described in *Chapter III*. Teachers should review *Chapter III* prior to presenting the activities in *Chapter II* since students should master both competencies during the same time span.

The Rhythmic Competency Teaching Progression: Activity Levels

The rhythmic competency teaching progression follows four activity levels; a fifth level of activity is employed *after* learners reach a **basic level of rhythmic competency**:

ACTIVITY LEVEL	MOTION	BEAT
LEVEL ONE:	Single Coordinated	1
LEVEL TWO:	Alternating Single	2
LEVEL THREE:	Double Coordinated	2
LEVEL FOUR:	Combined Double	4
Basic Level of Rhythmic Competency		
LEVEL FIVE:	Other Combinations	4-8

The first four activity levels are sequenced to build coordination through body movements that are executed rhythmically and combined with the **four-step language process**. Figure 2 illustrates this relationship. The fifth level consists of more complex combinations of movements and language for learners who have achieved a **basic level of rhythmic competency**. The first two levels of the **four-step language process** (SAY, SAY AND DO) and of the four-level teaching progression can be adapted to any age group to help learners achieve a **basic level of rhythmic competency**. Teachers who are working with children and adults who are classified as learning disabled or motorically uncoordinated should find all the sequences very useful in their total curriculum. STEP I of the language process (SAY) probably can be omitted with most populations of adults who are practicing activity LEVELS ONE and TWO; younger learners should also progress rapidly through these two levels. LEVELS THREE and FOUR will require much more time and practice for both children and adults; these activity levels seem to be the bridge to a **basic level of rhythmic competency**.

FOUR-STEP LANGUAGE PROCESS	RHYTHMIC COMPETENCY ACTIVITY LEVELS			
Figure 2 *Combining the Four-Step Language Process with Movement to Achieve A Basic Level of Rhythmic Competency*				
STEP	**LEVEL ONE** Single Coordinated Motion	**LEVEL TWO** Alternating Single Motion	**LEVEL THREE** Double Coordinated Motion	**LEVEL FOUR** Combined Double Motions
I SAY	"HEAD, HEAD, HEAD, HEAD" or "PAT, PAT, PAT, PAT"	"HEAD, HEAD, HEAD, HEAD" or "PAT, PAT, PAT, PAT"	"HEAD, SHOULDERS, HEAD, SHOULDERS" or "WAIST, KNEES, WAIST, KNEES"	"HEAD, SHOULDERS, WAIST, KNEES"
II SAY AND DO	Unite language and movement. Both hands *or* feet used together.	Unite language and movement. Alternate hands *or* feet.	Unite language and movement. Both hands *or* feet used together.	Unite language and movement. Both hands *or* feet used together.
III WHISPER AND DO	Continue STEP II using a whisper.	Continue STEP II using a whisper.	Continue STEP II using a whisper.	Continue STEP II using a whisper.
IV THINK AND DO	Think the language and do the movements.	Think the language and do the movements.	Think the language and do the movements.	Think the language and do the movements.

[1]Please note that LEVEL FIVE activities are introduced *after* a basic level of rhythmic competency is achieved; they are therefore omitted from this chart.

NOTE: When music is added, begin with STEP III, WHISPER AND DO, matching language and movement. If difficulty is experienced, WHISPER the words to the music *before* adding movement.

How to Introduce LEVELS ONE to FOUR

1. Students are seated to develop the time component of rhythmic movement in as limited a space as possible and to create a nonweightbearing position that makes it easier for them to coordinate leg movements. Standing, the weightbearing position, is more awkward for beginners—they feel much more visible.

2. As necessary, the teacher uses tactile stimulation (patting the students' shoulders) to insure that all students understand the meaning of beat. Students may also be paired to pat each others' shoulders.

3. Single-word language is used as the organizer for the movement; learners match a word with a motion ("HEAD" or "PAT").

4. An external beat, supplied either by a drum or other instrument or through instrumental music with an easily identified beat, is *not* added until students have mastered the language plus movement step, as evidenced by a number of successful executions.

5. No partners are used. No right or left foot is specified. No "CLAPS" or "STAMPS" are added to LEVELS ONE, THREE or FOUR, which require only bilateral movements.

6. Bilingual experiences may be added, as appropriate.

LEVEL ONE: Single Coordinated Motion

Have the students chant "HEAD, HEAD, HEAD, HEAD" while patting the top of the head with both hands. (This is the second step of the language process, SAY AND DO.) This bilateral body awareness activity may be varied by patting other body parts—shoulders, knees, ears—again using both hands. The children should be encouraged to suggest different body parts to pat and to take turns as the leader. Changing leaders creates a change in beat and tempo, as each will set the beat and tempo most comfortable for him or her. As children become more proficient, action words may be substituted for the body part names; thus, the children are actively exploring the differences between words such as "PAT," "TAP," "TOUCH," "THUMP," "POUND." This simple language-to-movement activity helps the children develop a movement vocabulary. Teachers should remember to provide rhythmic reinforcement when necessary for this single-beat-repeated-pattern by patting children's shoulders to the beat.

If child-size chairs are available that permit the children's feet to touch the floor, the seated position should be used in a variety of LEVEL ONE activities. (These seated activities are also appropriate to use with older children and adults.) If chairs are not available, learners can sit on the floor and practice the movement patterns. It is important to remember that *both* feet should be used at the same time while sitting. Ideas for bilateral LEVEL ONE feet and leg movements include: thumping the heels to the floor with legs extended, bouncing both feet to the floor in a modified jumping motion, putting the soles of the feet together (knees separated) to enable the sides of both feet to tap the floor. For beginners, moving the feet in LEVEL ONE activities while in a seated position is a helpful bridge to the weightbearing position.

Teaching Techniques for LEVEL ONE: Single Coordinated Motion

1. Have learners use both hands or feet simultaneously in a coordinated (bilateral) movement.

2. Do not ask students to "CLAP" or "STAMP," as these are not bilateral LEVEL ONE movements.

3. Introduce the activity with children (adults) in a seated position.

4. Use *single* words to name body parts or describe motions ("HEAD" or "PAT").

5. Repeat the word/motion (SAY AND DO) for a minimum of 8 beats (high repetition).

6. Ask children to suggest new patterns either by changing the body part or the action word. Children who make suggestions become leaders, initiating language and adding movement to their own beat and tempo. The teacher and other students become followers. This technique helps children develop independence.

7. The physical education teacher can use LEVEL ONE motions as warm-up activities and as body awareness activities. The elementary classroom teacher will find LEVEL ONE activities useful for channeling children's energies and extending the meaning of language (including bilingual experiences). The music teacher can use LEVEL ONE activities to help students learn about beat and to introduce echo patterns, accent, and the bordun on barred instruments.

8. Once students have successfully mastered the activity with language only, add an external beat using repeated single beats on a drum, single notes on a recorder, or a repeated chord on a piano. Children now execute the WHISPER AND DO step followed by DO as they match the external beat. The teacher then adds recorded musical selections that have a strong, easily identified beat. Learners need to listen to many different pieces of music and respond to the underlying beat. Ask your students to close their eyes while doing this activity—a useful teaching strategy to help learners function independently rather than copy you or other class members.

9. Ask students to execute the DO step at LEVEL ONE while they sing a song or recite a rhyme only after they can successfully identify the underlying beat of several musical selections, and after they can maintain a consistent beat and tempo with movement. Teachers place complex task demands on children when they ask them to generate language or sing a song while continuing a movement pattern with their hands or feet. This stage is another excellent time for teachers to move around behind the seated children and reinforce the beat by patting them on their shoulders.

10. Add bilingual experiences, as appropriate.

LEVEL TWO: Alternating Single Motion

Have students chant "HEAD, HEAD, HEAD, HEAD" while tapping one hand and then the other on top of their heads. Or ask them to choose other body parts for this body awareness activity. As in LEVEL ONE, you may substitute action words for names of body parts. For example, students may chant "PAT, PAT, PAT, PAT" while patting their thighs first with one hand and then the other. Or students may chant the word "PUNCH" while making a punching motion first with one arm and then the other. Or they may chant "WALK" while alternately moving their feet and legs in place (in the seated position). Elementary teachers can use action words found in reading materials to reinforce or define their meaning through movement.

Teaching Techniques for LEVEL TWO

1. Introduce activity with children (adults) in a seated position.

2. Have students move their hands or feet in alternating motions to their steady internal beat.

3. *Do not specify "right" or "left"* in alternating patterns as this introduces another thought layer into the process. When children are secure with "right" or "left" *and* with alternating movements, then the two may be combined.

4. Repeat the same word/motion (SAY AND DO) for a minimum of 8 beats (high repetition).

5. Move around behind children as they execute an alternating pattern and reinforce the alternating pattern by patting them on the appropriate shoulder. This rhythmic patting on the body reinforces beat as well as the alternating movement. Be certain to pat the same side of the body the child is using.

6. Ask different children to suggest body parts or action words and to lead the group by chanting the word and then adding the movement. This technique allows children to use the beat and tempo most comfortable for them.

7. Add an external beat when LEVEL TWO is mastered. Coordination to the music is begun with WHISPER AND DO.

8. *Do not add language-based activities or singing until students are very secure with beat and the alternating movement.*

9. Be certain to incorporate sufficient foot and leg movement patterns at this level to help children, while in a seated position, prepare for future walking activities.

10. Make sure the music and movements are strong and decisive enough to help the learner keep the beat.

11. Add bilingual experiences, as appropriate.

LEVEL THREE:
Double Coordinated Motion

Have the students match the language of two words ("HEAD, SHOULDERS, HEAD, SHOULDERS") with two coordinated motions (tapping the top of the head followed by tapping the shoulders). In this SAY AND DO step, students use both hands or feet in a coordinated bilateral movement. You or the students may choose other body parts (for example, "WAIST, KNEES, WAIST, KNEES") and follow the same sequence. Some children (or adults) may have difficulty with LEVEL THREE. In these cases, I recommend that you ask your learners to repeat the first patting movement four times ("HEAD, HEAD, HEAD, HEAD") and then to repeat the second patting movement four times ("SHOULDERS, SHOULDERS, SHOULDERS, SHOULDERS"). Once students can do this, ask them to repeat each movement twice ("HEAD, HEAD, SHOULDERS, SHOULDERS"), and finally just once ("HEAD, SHOULDERS").

As in the preceding levels, action words such as "THUMP" and "POUND" may be substituted for names of body parts, but should be added gradually as learners develop increased skill. As in LEVEL ONE, the "CLAP" and "STAMP" should not be added, as these are not bilateral movements.

Contrasting direction words such as "OUT, IN" or "UP, DOWN" or "OVER, UNDER" or "HIGH, LOW" may be used with accompanying movements for LEVEL THREE activities. These actions are more difficult for students to perform accurately because they do not involve physical contact on the beat. Therefore the *decisiveness* of the motion as a consistent tempo is maintained is very important for success; when the word "OUT" is chanted, for example, students thrust their arms forward or sideward and then return them toward the body with the word "IN." Likewise, in the SAY AND DO for "UP" students should thrust both arms overhead.

Teaching Techniques for LEVEL THREE

1. Use *both* hands or feet simultaneously (bilateral movement).

2. Do not add "CLAP" or "STAMP"; these are not bilateral movements.

3. Introduce activity with children (adults) in a seated position.

4. Execute each part of the double motion *once* in 2 beats ("HEAD, SHOULDERS" or "OUT, IN").

5. If several double motions are sequenced, repeat the same double motion enough times to insure success *before* changing motions.

6. If children have difficulty, move behind them, patting their "HEAD, SHOULDERS" as they say the words.

7. Accompany action words or contrasting direction words with decisive movements.

8. Use an "echo movement." Give children verbal commands and have them respond with SAY AND DO. Example: The teacher says "SHOULDERS, KNEES, SHOULDERS, KNEES" and the children SAY AND DO. Later the children may respond with echo movement only—the DO step.

9. Have children close their eyes as they SAY AND DO the double coordinated motions to help them concentrate on the beat and think about what they are doing.

10. Make sure students use leg movements in a seated position at LEVEL THREE, such as "APART, TOGETHER" or "RAISE, LOWER" or "HEELS, TOES."

11. Link LEVELS ONE, TWO, and THREE in a series of patterns to music. Be certain to begin with LEVEL ONE for at least one set of 8 beats, then proceed to LEVEL TWO, and finally on to LEVEL THREE.

12. *Do not try LEVEL THREE movements with singing or language-based activities* as the coordination is very difficult; combining singing or speaking with double coordinated motions should not be attempted by learners until they have reached a **basic level of rhythmic competency**.

13. Add bilingual experiences, as appropriate.

14. Evaluate the group. "Pass" the movement around the class. The teacher uses SAY AND DO for "KNEES, SHOULDERS, KNEES, SHOULDERS," then each student in turn repeats the SAY AND DO. Those who can't SAY AND DO the activity, or those who can't sustain the beat and tempo passed around the group, lack LEVEL THREE competency. Observe your class; if there are students who cannot follow new double coordinated motions with accuracy, the class is not ready to go on to the LEVEL FOUR.

LEVEL FOUR: *Combined Double Motions*

Have students chant four words, "HEAD, SHOULDERS, WAIST, KNEES" and then SAY AND DO while touching the appropriate body parts, using both hands simultaneously in bilateral sequence. Students should practice each double motion, "HEAD, SHOULDERS" and "WAIST, KNEES," separately as in LEVEL THREE *before* combining them.

Each time students attempt a new combined double motion, they should SAY the four words several times *before* attempting SAY AND DO. It also may help to SAY AND DO each word twice ("HEAD, HEAD, SHOULDERS, SHOULDERS, WAIST, WAIST, KNEES, KNEES"). The simplest words at this level are names of body parts; as in the previous levels, substituting action words for body parts will be more difficult for young students. Begin with movements which proceed in the same direction, such as "HEAD, SHOULDERS, WAIST, KNEES." "HEAD, SHOULDERS, KNEES, WAIST" would be more difficult. It is easier to move from "HIGH" to "LOW" than from "LOW" to "HIGH." After movements in the same direction are mastered by the students, have them combine sequences horizontally as well as vertically—"OUT, IN, UP, DOWN." Students usually need to master this final degree of complexity before they are able to achieve a basic level of rhythmic competency.

A basic level of rhythmic competency is reached when (1) children (or adults) can successfully perform new LEVEL FOUR sequences, and (2) children (or adults) can follow these LEVEL FOUR sequences when music is played.

Teaching Techniques for LEVEL FOUR

1. Use both hands or feet simultaneously (bilateral movement).

2. Do not use "CLAP" or "STAMP" as these are not bilateral movements.

3. Introduce activity with children (adults) in a seated position.

4. Execute each part of the combined double motion *once* in 4 beats. Repeat the same sequence enough times to insure success.

5. Watch for problems between beats 2 and 3 in the 4-beat sequence—"HEAD, SHOULDERS, WAIST, KNEES." If a problem arises, SAY AND DO "SHOULDERS, WAIST" a few times and then ask your students to do "HEAD, SHOULDERS, WAIST, KNEES" again.

6. Use body parts and the corresponding words before using action words or contrasting direction words.

7. Use the legs in 4-beat sequences ("APART, TOGETHER, TOES, HEELS; OUT, IN, RAISE LOWER.")

8. Use movements in one direction before combining directions.

9. Evaluate the appropriateness of the level for a class by giving verbal commands to which the children respond with SAY and then with SAY AND DO, or by using echo movements.

10. Add music after a combination is secure. The tempo of the music will need to be slower at this level. WHISPER the sequence to the music before using WHISPER AND DO.

11. Remember, LEVEL FOUR activities are very difficult to perform while singing or with language-based activities. Such combinations should only be attempted by upper elementary students and adults who are rhythmically competent.

Suggestions for the Older Child and Adult for LEVELS ONE to FOUR

LEVEL ONE and LEVEL TWO *arm* movements will need very little attention in most populations of older children and adults. *Leg* movements while seated, however, are very important LEVEL ONE and LEVEL TWO activities for these age groups, because they lead to successful locomotor movement sequences. LEVEL THREE and LEVEL FOUR arm and leg movement activities will help the older child or adult overcome any rhythmic coordination deficiency. Movements introduced and perceived more as exercise sequences (for example, "arms OUT, IN or UP, DOWN," "legs APART, TOGETHER") will be more acceptable to older students than "touch HEAD, SHOULDERS." The seated position is even more necessary for beginners who are older as these individuals are apt to be more self-conscious and fearful of failure as they begin the activity.

The sequences presented to older students must be challenging enough so they are not perceived as "dumb," yet simple enough to allow those for whom the activity is designed to be successful. In physical education classes, for example, ask older students to sit on the floor and perform coordination sequences—routines which will be perceived as exercise warm-ups. The same types of exercise routines which build rhythmic coordination in older children may be useful in adult exercise classes, and as warm-ups in dance classes.

LEVEL FIVE: Other Combinations (Executed While Seated)

Once a **basic level of rhythmic competency** has been achieved, you may present learners of any age with more difficult rhythmic coordination challenges. The learners' ability to execute these sequences will indicate their ability to perform more difficult 2-beat patterns in dance (as discussed in *Chapter V*). Following are several ideas for LEVEL FIVE combinations.

1. **Add the "CLAP" or "STAMP."** The student adds the "CLAP" or "STAMP" to movement sequences. Keep in mind that the person who does not possess basic rhythmic competency will find it very difficult to incorporate the "CLAP" or "STAMP" because neither is a bilateral movement.

2. **Combine LEVEL ONE with LEVEL TWO.** Example: Students "PAT" the thighs with both hands, "PAT" one thigh with one hand, "PAT" both, "PAT" the other. (This is a bridge to the "JUMP, HOP.")

3. **Alternate double motions (4 beats).** The student matches the language of the words "OUT, IN, OUT, IN" by straightening and bending one arm for 2 beats and then the other for 2 beats. On the surface, this activity may seem to be easier than the combined double motions described in LEVEL FOUR, but it isn't. It is difficult for a person to resist movement on one side of the body while moving the other side. Children who are rhythmically coordinated will not have difficulty with this task, but those who aren't will be very confused. Visual modeling by the teacher and other children only adds to their confusion. (This coordination is a necessary prerequisite to 2-beat foot patterns.)

4. **Alternate combined double motions (8 beats).** The student uses one arm or leg to perform the combined double motion (4 beats) before using the other arm or leg. For example, the student moves one arm "OUT, IN, UP, DOWN" and then repeats the sequence with the other arm. As in the preceding examples, it is difficult for individuals who are not rhythmically competent to work with one side of the body and then the other.

5. **Add the rest in a 2- or 4-beat sequence.** In a 2-beat sequence, the student "TAPS" a body part, or "CLAPS" or "STAMPS" then "RESTS" for a beat ("HEAD, REST, HEAD, REST" or "STAMP, REST, STAMP, REST"). The student says the word "HEAD" in the SAY AND

DO, then whispers "REST." Later on, the student thinks the word "REST." The student must have a word for the resting beat in order to remain conscious of the duration of the beat. In the 4-beat sequence, begin with the fourth beat in the sequence as a rest, then the second, before adding the third or first beats as silent (resting) beats:

"PAT, CLAP, SNAP, REST"

"PAT, REST, SNAP, CLAP"

"PAT, CLAP, REST, CLAP"

"REST, CLAP, SNAP, CLAP"

(Note: Repeat each sequence several times.)

6. **Combine arm and leg patterns while sitting.**

• Student BOUNCES the feet and PATS the thighs (or any other body part).

• Student alternates foot movements (while seated): "HEEL, STEP, HEEL, STEP" and, at the same time, executes a double motion with the arms ("KNEES, SHOULDERS").

• Student uses a double motion of both legs and arms. Example: Feet go "APART, TOGETHER" and arms go "OUT, IN."

• Student uses a double motion of the feet and a combined double motion of the hands. Example: Feet go "HEELS, TOES" and arms go "OUT, IN, UP, DOWN."

• Student uses combined double motions of both hands and feet. Example: Feet go "APART, TOGETHER, TOES, HEELS" and arms go "SNAP, CLAP, OUT, IN."

Once older students are rhythmically competent, they respond very well to the challenge of these LEVEL FIVE activities. They love to create new sequences. Have small groups of older students develop sequences which they present to the class with language. Mastering the more difficult rhythmic coordination of LEVEL FIVE will prepare learners for the more difficult patterns of organized dance.

III.
Teaching Progression Leading to Basic Comfort with Movement

In the preceding chapter, we assumed that children or adults possess a **basic level of rhythmic competency** if and when they can match an underlying beat of music or the beat of a language-based activity. An individual who has reached this **basic level of rhythmic competency** can then organize an arm or leg pattern consisting of two combined double motions executed in two directions (vertical and horizontal): KNEES, SHOULDERS (vertical plane); OUT, IN (horizontal plane).

But rhythmic competency is only one of the two elements needed to achieve successful rhythmic movement. The other element involves movement in space, which culminates in a competency referred to as **basic comfort with movement**. In this chapter, I show teachers how to help their students achieve **basic comfort with movement**. This competency is mastered when a person is able

to move in space with the body free of tension. To achieve this tension-free movement, an individual must *not* be concerned with matching an external beat—instead, each person must be free to move to his or her own beat and tempo.

Basic comfort with movement develops very naturally in the preschool years if children have the opportunity to play. If children do not have play space in which to run, jump, and leap, or if other children are not available to join in simple games, or if children substitute long hours of television watching for physical activity, then they may enter elementary school without having achieved **basic comfort with movement**. Many of these children reach adulthood without achieving this competency. Whether the learner is a child or an adult, however, this competency is a prerequisite to successful rhythmic movement.

As stated in the *Introduction,* older children and adults probably will have more difficulty learning to move comfortably in space because of tension in the body, self-consciousness and fear of failure. Why are older children and adults so threatened by movement activities? After talking with many adolescents and adults over the years about their early childhood experiences in elementary school, it is apparent that, to them, "movement" and "dance" are synonymous—and "dance" was a detested activity in their early school years. Many of the individuals with whom I have conversed *hated* dance because they were required to have a partner. They also remembered being forced to be "creative" or to be an inanimate object, such as a tree or flower—activities which they thought were "dumb." In addition, the respondents had to perform in front of a group which made them feel even more foolish and self-conscious. It appears, then, that negative or positive feelings about movement activities and a corresponding negative or positive self-image are developed, or at the least greatly influenced, by activities occurring in the primary grades. Unfortunately, many children fail and are "turned off" before they really give movement activities an adequate trial period. And, if these children are the class leaders, their attitudes quickly permeate the entire classroom, making it that much more difficult for a teacher to create opportunities for success. No one wishes to fail in front of peers.

Are there strategies teachers can use to help students feel more comfortable with movement activities? Are there sequential activities, as with the rhythmic teaching progression, that can help the students? Are there activities to avoid? I formulated a set of teacher guidelines for movement activities to address these and related concerns.

Basic Strategies for Presenting the Movement Teaching Progression

General Guidelines

1. Do *not* use an external beat with movement activities and initial movement sequences. Allow the students to move comfortably without having to match their movements to an *external* beat. (Matching movement to an external beat is a more complex activity which will be discussed in *Chapter IV*.)

2. Devise ways for students to be as inconspicuous as possible. For example, have older students sit in chairs or stand behind chairs as they begin movement activities. Ask younger children to sit on the floor.

3. Introduce activities that do not require specific use of the right or left side of the body.

4. Present activities that do not require the students to have partners or to move in specific formations, such as a circle.

5. Suggest activities that allow the student to be successful because there is no specific right or wrong way to do the activity or to solve the problem.

6. Begin with simple seated or kneeling activities which parallel the rhythmic activities described in the previous chapter. Through verbal directions, present body awareness activities and help the students understand how the body moves.

7. Suggest stationary movements for your students while they are sitting or standing (movements that require limited space), *before* suggesting locomotor movements that demand moving in a wider area of the room. (The first three elements of the movement teaching progression require only nonlocomotor movements.)

8. Use imagery and activities which are age-appropriate. Don't ask upper elementary students to move as animals—or other inanimate objects.

9. Avoid activities that require the student to be "creative." Guided exploration can lead to creativity.

10. Suggest activities that help students develop visual and aural discrimination.

Other Considerations

The development of **a basic level of rhythmic competency** and **basic comfort with movement** are separate but parallel lines of development. *Therefore, I recommend that teachers move back and forth between the rhythm and movement activities, keeping the two learning sequences separate, but allowing them to unfold at approximately the same time.* In this way, the teacher creates a learning situation which simulates the natural development of these abilities in the preschool child. Thus, if this development does not occur naturally in the preschool years, elementary teachers still have an opportunity to foster development in the areas of rhythm and movement so that elementary children experience success rather than failure. While adults will have a more difficult time, they, too, can be taught to move rhythmically and comfortably.

As with the teaching progression for developing rhythmic competency, the teaching progression leading to **basic comfort with movement** focuses mainly on the elementary-age population. But a section at the end of the chapter suggests modifications of the progression that are more appropriate for the older child and the adult. If the two teaching progressions produce the results desired, children (or adults) will be ready to combine elements of time and space as outlined in *Chapter IV* and to experience success with rhythmic movement activities.

The Movement Teaching Progression

In this section, information is provided on each of the four elements in the teaching progression leading to **basic comfort with movement**: (1) developing body awareness through nonlocomotor problem-solving activities; (2) using imagery with nonlocomotor movement; (3) introducing nonlocomotor activities to enhance the learner's visual and aural discrimination; and (4) introducing locomotor activities with no external beat. While it is better to introduce locomotor activities *after* the students have

experienced the nonlocomotor movements, it is not essential. The order of the teaching progression presented here may be altered to suit the needs of a particular group.

Developing Body Awareness Through Nonlocomotor (In-Place) Problem-Solving Activities

The body is the tool to be used for achieving successful tension-free movement in space. Therefore, it is important for children to understand:

What each part of the body can do.

What body parts can do together.

What the whole body can do.

Preschool and early elementary children can make these discoveries on their own, if they are given opportunities to explore through problem-solving. For example, the teacher only needs to ask a single question, such as, "What can we make our heads do?" and the children will offer many suggestions. The teacher should then ask the class to try out the ideas suggested by several of the children. If a single question does not elicit the desired responses, the teacher poses the question in a different way or asks a different question, such as, "Let's make our heads say 'yes'." Children also should be encouraged to use language to describe their discoveries. The teacher may need to help children with this verbalization. Similar types of exploration may be extended to "arms," "hands," "fingers," "legs," "feet," "shoulders."

This early body awareness exploration may be planned with the children seated, kneeling, lying down, or standing, with each child occupying a large enough space to permit freedom of movement. These first experiences are in-place activities. The activities should be brief each time they are introduced; perhaps exploring only one area of the body. Body awareness exploration should occur at about the same time as the identification of body parts, an activity described in LEVEL ONE of the rhythmic competency teaching progression.

The body awareness developed through movement exploration in the early years may be enlarged upon to enhance understanding of abstract concepts and of contrasting elements. Have your elementary students act out contrasting movement and direction terms:

HIGH and LOW

UP and DOWN

OUT and IN

OVER and UNDER

QUICKLY and SLOWLY

PUSHING and PULLING

BENDING and STRAIGHTENING

Ask students to illustrate these concepts with

"One body part" (one foot).

"Two body parts that are the same" (both hands).

"Two body parts that are different" (one foot and one hand).

"Two body parts performing different actions" (for example, one hand goes "OUT, IN" while the other goes "UP, DOWN").

The following questions can be used by teachers to encourage additional body awareness activities. The teacher does *not* demonstrate.

"How do we lift our arms slowly? How do we put them down quickly?"

"How do we raise one arm and one leg? The same arm and leg? The opposite arm and leg? In front of us? To the side?"

"How do we raise one arm and draw a circle in the air? A square with our leg?"

"How do we draw a circle on the floor with our foot? With one finger? A small circle? A big circle?"

"What parts of the body can bend and straighten?"

"How do we dance with our fingers on the floor?"

"How do we put our arm in front of us? Behind us? To the side of us? Under our leg?"

To answer these and similar questions, children must know what different parts of their body can do, understand concepts like *fast/slow, high/low,* and know the corresponding language. Although the movement activities may be performed while lying down, or in seated, kneeling, or standing positions, students probably will feel more comfortable if they are seated, kneeling, or lying down at first. Once a standing position is assumed, children feel more conspicuous and are more concerned with balance. It is important once again to stress that the suggested activities should not require specific use of "right" or "left," unless the teacher feels that the students can incorporate this additional thought process. The task becomes more complex when the child must think "correct side of the body" as well as be concerned with space, time and language elements of the activity.

Excellent body awareness movement activities include making letters or shapes:

"Put your body in the shape of a letter T, now S, V, C."

"Draw a square with one leg."

"Draw a circle with your head."

"Draw a triangle with one hand—a big one, a little one."

"Put your body in the shape of a quarter note—the shape of a football."

As children become more experienced, two or more may work together on movement problem-solving—making shapes or letters and constructing words or forming the correct number to solve a math problem.

Using Imagery with Nonlocomotor (In-Place) Movement

Along with body awareness activities, teachers can also use imagery as a tool to help students achieve **basic comfort with movement**. The most important principle to remember in using imagery is to create situations in which children are asked *to move like* or *to move as if* versus *to* be *an object:*

"How do you move like a yo-yo?"

"How do you move your arms like those of a puppet in which the strings are pulled slowly (quickly)?" "Now the leg strings make the puppet dance."

"How do you move your arms like branches of a tree in a wind storm?"

"You are driving a jeep on a very bumpy road and the jeep has no shock absorbers. Here we go down this bumpy road. There's a sharp curve. Now a curve the other way. Oops, a stop sign!"

The latter imagery works well with older children and adults, whereas the former examples are more appropriate for younger children. In each case learners can't *be* a yo-yo, a puppet, a tree, or a jeep but they can *move like* them. (The above examples also provide opportunities for aural problem-solving if the teacher does not demonstrate the activities, but only describes them.)

Nonlocomotor (In-Place) Movements that Enhance the Learner's Visual and Aural Discrimination

The third element in the movement teaching progression involves stationary movement experiences that enhance the learner's visual

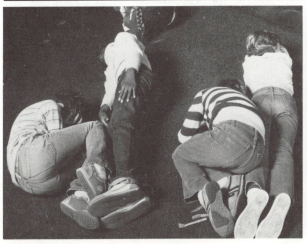

or aural discrimination. Such discrimination is another important skill students need to develop in order to achieve **basic comfort with movement**. The visual and aural experiences are much more directive than the more open-ended, problem-solving and questioning approaches used in the body awareness and imagery activities suggested above and therefore may provide an interesting change of pace for students. For example:

1. A *visual* follow-the-leader game can be very useful when teachers want to provide learners with a variety of movement experiences. Have children sit on the floor with enough space around each child to make large movements possible, then lead them through a silent demonstration of a series of actions, such as raising both arms slowly overhead, wiggling the fingers, shaking the arms and lowering them slowly, resting the hands on the thighs while raising and lowering the shoulders rhythmically, moving the hands to the floor in front of the body and "walking" them rhythmically, returning the hands to the thighs and nodding the head, moving the head in a circle while making a siren-like call, ending the call and flapping the upper arms against the sides of the body. This type of movement sequence can be continued to include all types of movements and sounds; the teacher may have the children move to a standing position during the course of the sequence as they become more comfortable with the activity. Eventually, children can take the leadership role in presenting movements and sounds to the class.

2. A *verbal* follow-the-leader game can be played with the teacher giving verbal directions for actions (such as the ones described above). In this variation, the teacher does *not* demonstrate the actions.

3. The follow-the-leader game may also be played by *using language and movement (SAY AND DO)*. The teacher shakes the wrist and repeats the word "SHAKE" rhythmically as long as the movement sequence continues, or the word "NOD" as the head is nodded, or the word "SWING" as the arms are swung back and forth. The children imitate both the action

and the language. Or ask children to "STRAIGHTEN" as you straighten one or both arms overhead and "BEND" as you bend your arms in. This type of follow-the-leader game gives children an opportunity to use simple action words and movement patterns in many different ways.

4. Another visual game involves "mirroring." Have the children face you and copy your actions. Begin with slow movements. At first allow children to move the body part without concern for "correct" side. Music may be added to set a mood for the activity. Once the children understand the concept of mirroring, they can be placed in small groups with one child acting as the leader, or in pairs (which gives each child the opportunity to be the leader during the same class period). In the early elementary years, the mirror activity seems to work best with the teacher or one child assuming the leadership role. For older and more experienced groups, ask several of the students to be leaders of small groups.

5. In another verbal game the teacher describes, but does *not* demonstrate, movement problems or directions. Children's listening skills (aural discrimination) are strengthened through these activities. For example, the teacher says:

"Cross your legs and stand up quickly."

"Lean over and touch one hand to the floor."

"Lift one leg and sit down, keeping one leg and one hand on the floor."

"Wave your right hand and put your left hand at your waist."

Or the teacher asks the children to follow certain verbal directions:

"Put one hand high in the air."

"Put the other hand on the knee."

"Put the hand high in the air over your mouth."

"Dance your fingers on your knee."

"Nod your head 'yes.' "

The specific use of "right" and "left" may be added, but makes this activity more complex.

Introducing Locomotor Movements with No External (Group) Beat

The previous suggestions for movement activities are *nonlocomotor* or axial; in other words, the learner uses the body without leaving the starting point, responding to verbal or visual cues, such as "BEND," "STRAIGHTEN," "SHAKE," "BOUNCE," "SWAY." *Locomotor* activities, on the other hand, are those in which learners leave the initial starting point and travel to new locations. Locomotor movements range from the very basic—walking, running, jumping, hopping, or leaping—to complex patterns of organized dance.

After children are aware of how their bodies can move while sitting, lying down, kneeling, or standing, after they have mastered many language-to-movement problem-solving activities, and after they have demonstrated that they are relaxed and successful when participating in a variety of nonlocomotor activities, they are ready to begin locomotor movement. Teachers must remember that moving around in the room makes many children feel awkward. This awkwardness may manifest itself in silly or "acting out" behavior, which is more difficult to guide into acceptable behavior because the children are moving about the space rather than remaining in one area. But, once children have

experienced success in a number of different ways in a stationary position, they will be more trusting and more willing to become involved in activities that require basic locomotor movements.

Teachers often mistakenly assume that locomotor movement activities require an external beat—a drum beat, clapping or music. And teachers often feel the need to specify "right" and "left" foot, or to ask children to move in a circle formation with hands joined. These misconceptions set the stage for many children to fail in their first attempts at locomotor movement. There are a number of reasons for this statement:

• First, an external beat may not match a child's natural beat and tempo; if it does not, the child must consciously deny a natural impulse in order to match an external beat.

• Second, as mentioned earlier, the use of commands such as "right" or "left" creates a more complex activity for children, an additional thought layer. Some children may begin the movement naturally with the designated foot, but other children may find the adjustment difficult.

• Third, holding hands in a circle can make children feel very visible and very uncomfortable. In such cases, children begin to feel tense, aware that the persons on either side of

them will witness their successes or failures. And, too, hand-holding itself is an intimate social interaction which many children find distasteful.

The first rule for locomotor movement, then, is to allow children to move freely and successfully to their own beat and tempo. The movement tasks suggested here are designed so that *failure is not possible.* For example, the tasks of walking in a random fashion, walking more quickly, walking more slowly, walking with the body tall *(without an external beat)* allow children to experience immediate success. This success will lead to further successes. (Note: Teachers should consider the management of the class *before* children begin to move about the room, so that constant discipline does not become the lesson presented.) Here are several ideas for locomotor activities using a child's *internal* beat and tempo (no external beat and tempo).

1. **As a necessary first step, ask children to move from one designated spot to another,** such as **across the room.** Use either body awareness terms or imagery to describe the desired movement. The teacher may begin the activity with an open-ended question:

"How can you move across the room?"

Followed by:

"Let's find another way to move across the room!"

The teacher may ask for volunteers to demonstrate a way to move across the room, which the other children will copy. Teachers may structure the activity by suggesting a task such as:

"Let's move across the room with three parts of the body touching the floor."

Followed by:

"Let's change one of the three body parts."

The teacher may also suggest imagery:

"Let's move across the room as an (animal) might move."

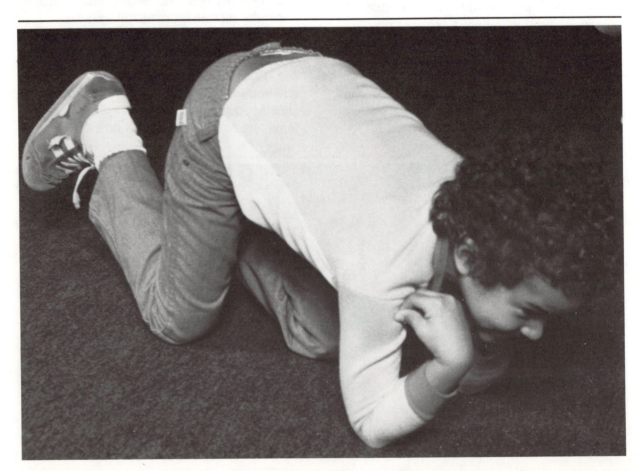

"Let's pretend we are walking a straight (or crooked) line."

"Let's pretend we are pushing (or pulling) a heavy object."

"Let's move as if we have a cast on our leg."

"Let's move as if we are very cold."

Teachers can also ask the children to move across the designated space while giving them specific instructions for placing their hands (such as on the hips), or positioning their bodies (tall, short), or creating a mood (happy, sad, angry).

2. **As a second step, ask the children to walk about freely in a designated space.** The teacher does *not* specify a "correct" foot (right or left) or direction to begin with, and no external beat is used. If you need to exert more control, the word *freeze* may be used before a new direction is given, or to move the children apart from one another.

3. **Vary tempo.** While the children are walking, the teacher may give a new direction:

"Walk more quickly."

"Walk more slowly."

The quick (or slow) command might include imagery:

"Walk as slowly as you think an elephant would walk."

"Walk as slowly as you think a mountain climber would walk up a steep hill."

"Walk as quickly as a person who is walking in a walking race."

4. **Vary direction of movement.** An activity that changes direction is another building block in helping the child achieve **basic comfort with movement.** For example, the teacher asks children to "move forward"; tempo may be added to this activity as illustrated by the following suggestions:

"Walk forward slowly."

"Walk forward quickly."

"Walk the way you walk to school."

The action of moving backward may be introduced now but since moving backward is not a typical movement pattern some children may appear awkward at first. It is often helpful to suggest to the children that they walk backward in a specific manner:

"Walk backward keeping your whole foot on the floor."

"Walk backward skating your feet on the floor."

Backward movement which keeps the whole foot on the floor helps learners master this atypical movement pattern and helps them maintain their balance. Once the basic backward movement has been mastered, variations may be suggested:

"Walk backward slowly."

"Walk backward quickly with tiny steps."

"Walk backward as if the wind were blowing against your back."

The teacher may have the children explore sideward movement by asking:

"How can we move sideward?"

"Walk sideward as if you were going through a narrow doorway."

As each movement activity becomes clear to the learners, the teacher can call out a new direction while the children are moving. The teacher's attention should also center on fostering children's awareness of the space around them. For example, you can suggest that children:

"Walk a tightrope forward (backward) (sideward)."

"Walk around a circle."

"Walk a zig-zag line."

5. **Vary level or position of the body.** A new set of locomotor movement concepts involves asking children to change the level or position of their bodies:

"Walk 'tall' with your body stretched as far into the air as possible."

"Walk 'short' with your body low to the ground."

"Walk 'wide' with your body as big as possible."

"Walk 'narrow' as thin (skinny) as you can."

Different positions of the feet may be used in this activity:

"Walk on your toes (heels) (sides of the feet)."

"Walk with your toes turned in (out)."

"March."

"Walk as if you were on ice."

"Walk as if you were in thick mud."

Once the class has explored the dimensions of tempo and direction, movement tasks that combine level, direction, and/or tempo may be posed by the teacher:

"Walk sideward slowly with the body 'wide'."

"March forward quickly with the body 'stiff'."

"Walk backward quickly as if you were being pushed."

6. **Vary intensity and affect.** Suggest that your students:

"Walk as a person who is very happy (sad) (angry) (tired)."

"Walk as a person who is carrying a heavy load."

"Walk lightly (heavily)."

"Walk noisily (softly)."

"Make the first of each four walking steps a heavy walk."

"As you walk, make your arms happy."

7. **Vary the locomotor movement.** Variations in the basic locomotor movements described earlier include the suggestion to "RUN," "JUMP," "HOP" and "LEAP," "SKIP," "SLIDE," and "GALLOP." (Running should *not* be suggested unless the children are outdoors or in a large space with a nonslippery surface.) The JUMP is much easier than the HOP because of the bilateral nature of the movement and should be introduced first. Many children have difficulty with the HOP

because they have trouble maintaining their balance. Some children will be able to GALLOP, SLIDE, and SKIP quite easily and naturally, whereas other children who lack sufficient movement experiences will find these movements very difficult. A GALLOP (RUN, LEAP) with either foot leading should be the first combination to be mastered by students. Try not to insist on a change of lead foot other than to ask:

"How do you make the other foot be the leader?"

(Beginners who are not rhythmically competent will have difficulty with this request.) In the same way, ask the children:

"How do you make your 'gallop' go sideward?"

By doing this, they are now executing a SLIDE. Because "sideward" is an atypical direction, many children may experience difficulty. The SKIP should not be taught. When students reach a **basic level of rhythmic competency**, they will be able to SKIP by learning this movement as a GALLOP with the lead foot changing constantly:

"The feet can't decide which one should lead—so they take turns!"

In order to practice the five basic locomotor movements (WALK, RUN, JUMP, HOP, LEAP), the teacher suggests activities that combine two or more movements for a specified number of times:

"Do 4 WALKS and 4 HOPS."

"Do 4 HOPS and then 4 JUMPS."

"Do 8 WALKS, 4 HOPS, and 4 JUMPS."

No common group beat is added to the activities and no "right" or "left" foot is specified.

8. **Vary combinations of the above activities.** Once the children are comfortable with specific variations of movement patterns, varying the combinations provides them with a challenging extension of the activity. (These extensions will be difficult for children to perform if the teacher has not allocated

enough practice time for each of the variations.) Examples include the following:

"Walk backward with your toes turned in and your arms to the side."

"Walk quickly with the body tall and your arms overhead."

"Walk slowly sideward on your toes with your arms crossed in front of you."

"Hop 8 times with your hands on your hips."

"Walk sideward shaking your wrists in front of you."

"Tiptoe quickly and make your fingers dance."

"Walk sideward slowly with your body low, as if you were tired."

"March and clap at the same time."

Musical instruments may be used during these activities. For example, when the piano is played in the upper registers, ask the children to "walk tall" and when played in the lower registers, ask them to "walk short." Two or more instruments may be used and a different movement assigned to each instrument as it is heard, or teachers may use their voices by asking children to respond in movement to different sounds or intonations uttered. A drum may be hit in two different ways for two different locomotor movements.

9. **Introducing learners to singing games, action songs, and folk games.** These activities have been part of the early elementary curriculum—music, physical education, and classroom—for many years. The major problems inherent in these songs and games are as follows:

• Children are asked to sing and move at the same time—the most difficult of the rhythmic movement activities.

• "Right" and "left" foot as well as partners often are required or at least necessary to perform the activity "correctly" without modification.

• The teacher's goal often is for children to match an external beat.

• Often the games/songs involve only one or two participants. Even when the teacher begins the activity with a child who often isn't chosen, the more popular children seem to participate more frequently. Thus, children who need practice the most are often excluded.

Modify these games and songs to allow more children to participate and to remove the need for "correctness." Your perspective must change, too, to allow the children to experience these delightful activities in a less restrictive manner. At this point, you can informally and discreetly assess children's ability to match beat and tempo.

Assessing Students' Readiness for Successful Rhythmic Movement

To assess your students' readiness for successful rhythmic movement, I suggest the following strategies which can be implemented in a nonjudgmental and nonthreatening environment.

1. Ask the children to march around the room to different recorded musical selections. By asking, "Can you identify the beat and walk to it?" you can assess their progress. Avoid calling attention to those children who are unsuccessful.

2. Another way to assess student progress, either with each student in turn or with the entire class, is through the use of echo movements. The teacher executes 2-beat or 4-beat sequences and the student echoes the sequence.

3. Suggest rhythmic coordination sequences in the classroom when children have been sitting too long and need activity. You can alleviate their tension while assessing their performance.

4. Music teachers can play a different piece of music each day as the children enter or leave the music room, asking the children to identify the beat and to walk to it. In this way, the teacher can continually assess student progress in matching an external beat.

5. Physical education teachers can plan exercise routines to music (or to a counting cadence) to occur at the beginning of each physical education class and continually assess each student's performance level.

These strategies are especially useful for teachers who do not see the same group of children each day. These types of activities help children become acquainted with diverse selections of music in different tempi and, in a very natural way, introduce them to the process of moving to a steady external beat. Asking different children to lead the class will free you to assess the achievement level of each child.

Suggestions for the Older Child and Adult

The individual who has reached the age of eight or nine without having achieved a **basic level of rhythmic competency** and **basic comfort with movement** is very likely to be threatened or "turned off" by rhythmic movement activities. The most difficult situation for older children and adults seems to be dance classes in which persons enroll without possessing the prerequisite skills of a **basic level of rhythmic competency** and **basic comfort with movement**. Dance classes may reinforce earlier failures for these individuals because the class is not designed, nor should it be designed, to correct these basic deficiencies.

It can be assumed, however, that these older age groups have achieved general body awareness; understand how to move using variations of level, direction, time, and intensity; and probably possess the ability to successfully execute rhythmic activities at LEVELS ONE and TWO of the rhythmic competency teaching progression. Therefore, the teacher should concentrate on helping individuals work on the more complex rhythmic competency skills in which they are deficient (see *Chapter II*) and on helping the participants become more comfortable with the movement activities described in this chapter.

Using Props

Props seem to be one of the best methods for helping individuals of any age feel more secure with movement. The reason older students most often give for their self-consciousness is their supposed visibility in the group: "Everyone is watching me make a mistake." "Everyone is successful except me." I suggest props as a solution to this problem of visibility. This strategy has always worked for me.

Masks. The lack of personal identity achieved by wearing a mask allows some individuals to be less inhibited in movement activities.

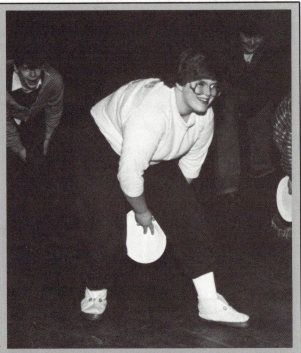

Chairs. Individuals stand behind a chair. The chair allows the individual to "hide" and provides physical support when practicing movements while standing in one place.

Paper plates. Holding one paper plate in each hand makes people less visible because the plates become the focus of attention. The paper plates may be used for exploratory movement sequences, mirroring, and rhythmic sequences, too.

Activity wands and cardboard paper towel tubes, hoops, towels, balls, streamers. These are lightweight props and can be moved about easily.

Chapter IV contains more information about the specific use of props.

Other Strategies for Older Students

Here are a few more suggestions for helping older children and adults become comfortable with movement.

1. Avoid a circle formation in which learners are very visible. Ask the group to walk about the room, then to walk faster, slower, tall, short, and so on. Have them walk backward or sideward, then add a certain number of walks in a specific direction.

2. Develop get-acquainted activities during movement sequences. While individuals are moving about freely, the teacher says:

"Move in front of one other person."
or
"Form small groups of three or four persons, then introduce yourselves."

The teacher returns the group to moving about freely and then asks the individuals to pair up with a different person, or form a new group and repeat the introductions.

3. Instruct people to move next to one other person and copy the other's walking pattern, then to change partners and proceed with a different walking pattern.

4. Ask individuals to move next to another person and create one point of contact (no hands held) and move together (for example, elbow-to-elbow); this activity may be extended using two or more points of contact (for example, elbow-to-elbow and foot-to-foot). Adults have a great deal of fun with this activity which helps them gradually attain comfort with movement. At no time is an external beat introduced.

5. Ask the group to alternate basic locomotor movement with nonlocomotor movement:

"Walk with the 'body tall' and, on a signal, stand still and execute an OUT, IN movement with the arms."

The teacher then has the group proceed with a different walk and a different nonlocomotor movement.

Through the sequence of activities described in this chapter, children and adults gradually become more relaxed as they move. Tension-free movement is a prerequisite to the ability to walk to an external beat, which is discussed in the next chapter.

IV.
Teaching Progression Leading to Successful Rhythmic Movement

Before the basic elements of *rhythmic competency* and *comfort with movement* can be combined to produce successful rhythmic movement, each element must be mastered separately by learners (see *Chapters II* and *III*). As I've mentioned before, students should achieve the desired competency of each element simultaneously, which means both teaching progressions should be presented during the same period of time. The analogy of preparing for a dinner party helps explain this parallel process. The development of *rhythmic competency* may be likened to preparing the dinner: the food must be put in the oven in the correct order to be ready at the designated dinner hour. The development of *comfort with movement* may be likened to getting the house in order and dressing for the party: there is no prescribed order in which these activities must be completed; the important thing is that the house is cleaned on time, the table set, and the host or hostess dressed to greet the guests as they arrive. At the appointed dinner hour, however, all the elements must converge for the party to be a success.

If teachers devote as much thought and preparation to helping their students integrate *rhythmic competency* and *comfort with movement* as they have devoted to each area in the two previous chapters, their learners will succeed with rhythmic movement activities. As illustrated in this chapter, the final link to success is forged when students learn to combine locomotor and nonlocomotor movements comfortably to an external beat.

Learners are successful when:

1. They can identify the steady beat in a musical selection or language-based activity and match that beat at LEVEL FOUR in the rhythmic competency teaching progression (see *Chapter II*).

2. They can move comfortably to their own beat and tempo and have had the opportunity to walk to an *external* beat in a nonjudgmental and nonthreatening environment (see *Chapter III*). Usually, children can achieve such success by the end of the first grade. Sometimes, however, preschool or kindergarten teachers may feel that their youngsters are ready for combined rhythm and movement activities. If so, teachers should assess the students' readiness to begin moving rhythmically, as described in the previous chapter. If the assessment is positive, teachers should proceed with the activities described here.

In this chapter, I present the sequences students should follow as they gradually progress from matching the external steady beat in a seated position, to standing supported by a stationary object and using hand-held props, to moving freely about the room. (Note: Some children, especially those in the early elementary grades, may not need to experience the seated activities and those using props. In such cases, if you feel your class is ready, you may proceed immediately to "Rhythmic Sequences Matching an External Beat, Combining Locomotor and Nonlocomotor Movement.") A separate section at the end of the chapter presents modifications to be used with the adolescent and with adult learners.

Rhythmic Sequences Matching an External Beat—Seated

At this stage, most children will appear secure and ready to combine movement and rhythmic patterns. If, however, moving rhythmically to an external steady beat makes them tense and uneasy, ease their discomfort by asking them to sit in a chair with their feet touching the floor. In this way, students can practice movements in a comfortable, nonweight-bearing position using a minimal amount of space. This procedure will give students (especially upper-elementary students) the confidence to attempt the next stage—rhythmic sequences in a standing position. In a seated position, the class uses SAY for the sequence:

MARCH, 2, 3, 4, 5, 6, 7, 8 (alternating leg movement)

PAT, 2, 3, 4 (both hands patting the thighs)

THUMP, 2, 3, 4 (both fists thumping the chest)

The SAY creates the external beat. The class then proceeds to SAY AND DO. (As explained in *Chapter II*, MARCH is an alternating movement pattern, LEVEL TWO in the rhythmic competency teaching progression; PAT and THUMP are LEVEL ONE patterns.) Another rhythmic sequence in a seated position is:

APART, TOGETHER, APART, TOGETHER (moving legs simultaneously)

HOP, 2, 3, 4 (using one foot)

HOP, 2, 3, 4 (using the other foot)

It is important for students to simulate hopping and jumping movements in a seated position *before* they attempt the more difficult standing position. (The standing position is more difficult because it requires the learner to propel the body off the floor prior to the beat in order to land accurately on the beat.)

With students in a seated position, the teacher has many opportunities to create problem-solving activities that promote aural or visual discrimination. For example:

• Introduce a movement sequence with SAY (no visual demonstration); the children follow with SAY AND DO.

• Demonstrate the movement sequence and ask the children to translate it to SAY.

• Perform a movement sequence and ask the children to "echo" the sequence.

Rhythmic Sequences Matching an External Beat— Standing, Using Stationary Props

At this point in the learning process, the children may fear that "everyone is watching!" Because of this fear, your learners may exhibit "acting-out" behavior when they are asked to stand up. You can avoid this and similar problems by using a chair as a prop for these in-place activities. Chairs provide

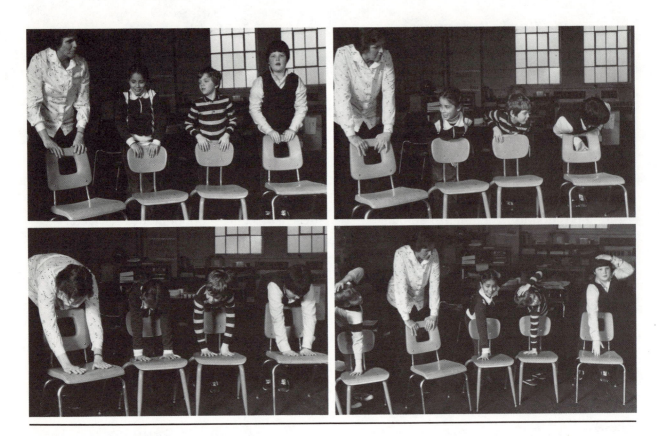

physical support for those children who move awkwardly and psychological support for those children who are self-conscious. The teacher asks children to stand behind the chair and hold the backs of the chairs with one or both hands. Other stationary objects also may be used (a wall, a table). The students then practice leg movements, such as walking in place, jumping, hopping, and arm movements, such as touching the seat of the chair with both hands and then placing the hands on the hips, or raising both arms overhead and then placing the hands on the hips. Students practice first with language and then by matching the words with the movement to create the external steady beat. SAY is followed by SAY AND DO. Then a musical selection is added (it should have a strong beat such as a march) and participants WHISPER AND DO. For a more well-defined beat, use a drum or single chords on the piano first.

At this stage in rhythmic movement development, don't ask your students to accompany movement with their own songs or rhymes. The only language they should use as

they match the external steady beat should be the words describing the motions.

Teachers and students may suggest specific movement sequences to execute in a standing position behind a chair. For example:

"MARCH in place 8 steps (8 beats); OUT, IN, with the arms 4 times (8 beats)."

"MARCH in place 8 steps (8 beats); UP, DOWN with the arms 4 times (8 beats); JUMP 8 times (8 beats); move the arms OUT, IN 4 times (8 beats)."

"HOP on one foot 4 times, then on the other foot 4 times (8 beats); WALK in place 8 steps (8 beats); DOWN, UP with the arms 4 times (8 beats); touch KNEES, SHOULDERS 4 times (8 beats)."

It is important that students use their arms in these sequences because, by doing so, they must remove their hands from the chair, which creates a natural bridge to the next position: standing unsupported. Also, moving the legs and arms in alternating movement sequences is easier for beginners to execute than combining walks, jumps, and hops.

Rhythmic Sequences Matching an External Beat— Standing, Using Hand-Held Props

At this performance level, ask students to assume a standing position without using stationary objects as props; "psychological" support is continued, however, through the use of hand-held props such as paper plates, cardboard paper towel tubes, activity wands, hoops. The teacher must decide on the appropriateness of using hand-held props. Some groups of older children may need this support because of their self-consciousness, whereas younger children may not and may be able to proceed directly to locomotor movement sequences. A great deal depends on the level of competency developed by the children during kindergarten and first grade.

Ask those students who appear to need more practice time with a prop in a stationary position to hold a paper plate in each hand. Executing sequences of arm movements while grasping a paper plate in each hand provides a natural bridge for the learner to walking freely in space because the focus of attention is *not* on the feet. The activity levels of the rhythmic competency teaching progression, presented in *Chapter II,* form the basis for these sequences. You should encourage specific students to suggest motions and lead an activity. Students SAY the sequence, then SAY AND DO and finally WHISPER AND DO and DO as the external beat is added. Motions that might be used to match an external beat include the following, which are presented by level of difficulty.

Single Coordinated Motion (LEVEL ONE)— Both Arms Working Together

HIT the plates on a body part (thighs, hips, shoulders, head).

HIT the plates on the floor.

FAN yourself with the plates—one fanning motion per beat.

HIT the plates together in front of the body.

HIT the plates together overhead.

HIT the plates together behind the back.

HIT the plates together on one side of the body and then on the other (use a *minimum* of 4 beats for each side).

RUB the plates in a circular motion against each other.

(Note: Since students have achieved a **basic level of rhythmic competency**, they should be able to successfully execute the "clapping" motion of the plates.)

Alternating Single Motion (LEVEL TWO)— One Arm Motion Followed by the Other

HIT the plates on a body part (thighs, hips, shoulders, head).

HIT the plates on the floor.

PUNCH with one arm and then the other.

HAMMER with one hand and then the other.

Coordinated Double Motion (LEVEL THREE)—Both Arms Working Together

HIT the plates on a combination of body parts (head, shoulders).

HIT the plates against the thighs and then together in front of the body.

STRETCH the arms to the side (beat 1), HIT them together (beat 2).

STRETCH one arm high and the other low (beat 1), HIT them together (beat 2).

Extend the arms OUT, IN or UP, DOWN.

Combined Double Motions (LEVEL FOUR)—Both Arms Working Together

HIT the plate against the HEAD, SHOULDERS, WAIST, KNEES, or any other combination of body parts.

Extend the arms OUT, IN, UP, DOWN or in other combinations or contrasting motions.

HIT the thighs, HIT the plates together, STRETCH the arms sideward, HIT the plates together.

(Note: Walking in place to an external beat may occur at any age level, as follows:

WALK 8 steps in place, then HIT the plates together 8 times in front of the body.)

Rhythmic Sequences Matching an External Beat— Combining Locomotor and Nonlocomotor Movement

Using paper plate sequences, students can now begin to move freely about the room. Ask students to "WALK 8 steps *around the room*, then stop and HIT the plates together 8 times." You and the students together can plan various combinations of locomotor and nonlocomotor movements and determine the number of times each will be executed. You should ask the younger children for suggestions: "What shall we do first? Second? Third?" "How many times shall we do each movement?" Introduce an external steady beat with SAY AND DO (without props) such as "MARCH, MARCH, MARCH, MARCH" (4 beats) or "MARCH, 2, 3, 4, 5, 6, 7, 8" (8 beats). Proceed to WHISPER AND DO and DO, using a drum or musical selection to mark the beat. Here are some suggested sequences for combining locomotor and nonlocomotor movement:

Eight MARCH steps forward (8 beats), 4 sequences of WAIST, KNEES while standing (8 beats).

Eight JUMPS (8 beats), 8 alternating knee PATS (8 beats).

Keep in mind that the above movement combinations are easier for learners to execute than the following locomotor sequences which are combined with each other:

Eight WALKS with body low, 8 WALKS with body tall.

Eight WALKS forward, 8 WALKS backward.

Here are some additional activities that can occur in specific settings:

1. *Exercise routines* can become rhythmic movement activities in a physical education class or in the classroom. For example:

BEND forward (sideward), STRAIGHTEN 4 times (8 beats).

RUN with high knees (8 beats).

REACH overhead with an alternating sequence (8 beats).

JUMP APART/TOGETHER 4 times (8 beats).

(Note: No arm movements should be required on the JUMP as this would be difficult for beginners to coordinate.)

2. *In music classes* ask students to respond with different movements to two different pitches or two different instruments, or to different measures and phrases.

3. *In the classroom,* ask students to identify geometric shapes with movements. To one sound, ask them to

"WALK in a circle 8 steps"

and to another sound ask them to

"WALK in a square formation 2 steps on each side of the square."

4. Ask the students to answer a *math* problem by executing the correct number of walking steps or arm movements.

5. Ask children to *spell* a word through movement, adding a step for each letter, and then to JUMP as they say the word. For example, "WALK, WALK, WALK, JUMP" becomes "C-A-T, CAT."

After students demonstrate success with basic rhythmic movement sequences, they are ready to attempt the simple dance steps and beginning organized folk dances presented in the next chapter. Figure 3 illustrates the sequential process both the teacher and students have followed to reach this stage of rhythmic movement competency.

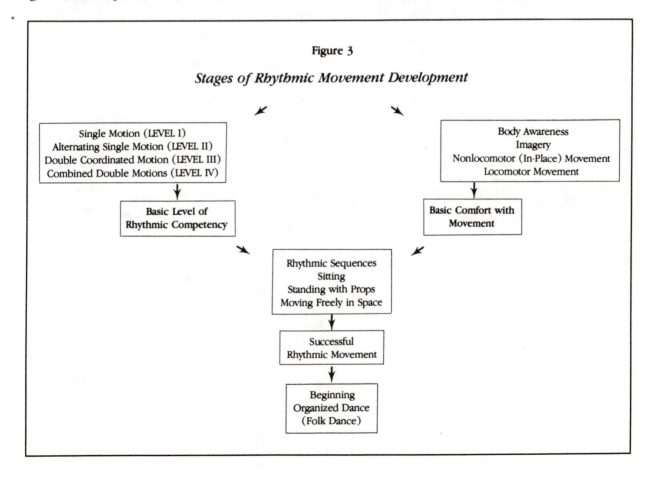

Figure 3

Stages of Rhythmic Movement Development

Suggestions for Adolescents and Adults

Activity sequences involving rhythmic movement to an external steady beat may be very threatening to older children and adults. Many older students will want to be as inconspicuous as possible, to "hide," because they are certain *everyone* will be watching them and noticing their mistakes. A chair provides older children and adults with the necessary psychological and physical support to enable them to identify and move to an external beat in a "safe" environment. As with younger students, you may wish to assess your older students' readiness to move rhythmically to an external beat and then lead them through the preliminary rhythmic sequences in a seated position and then standing behind a chair. After a while, replace the chair with hand-held props for both nonlocomotor and locomotor rhythmic movement activities. Following are some appropriate activities for older learners.

Moving to an External Steady Beat Using Chairs as Stationary Props

1. Ask the older students to stand behind their chairs, holding the backs with one or both hands. Learners execute sequences of movement which include walking, hopping, jumping, bending and straightening the knees, as well as upper body movements (for example, raising and lowering the arms).

2. Suggest that the learner use the chair for a problem-solving activity. For example, ask students to move parts of the body rhythmically while keeping at least one hand on the chair and the chair on the floor.

3. Mirroring: chairs are placed in sets of two around the room and participants face one another, standing behind the chairs. One person leads and suggests activities, the other follows.

4. Suggest that small groups choreograph movement routines using the chairs.

Moving to an External Steady Beat Using Paper Plates as Props

1. Follow the standing routines described in "Rhythmic Sequences Matching an External Beat—Standing, Using Hand-Held Props."

2. Ask individuals to hit the plates against the hips and then to step simultaneously with each hit. This activity begins with individuals organizing the walk/hit to their own beat and tempo. The language of "HIT, HIT . . ." may assist the group. The sounds of the plates hitting against the bodies, or the language added, organizes the beat and tempo for the group and creates a group external beat. The teacher may wish to reinforce this external

beat with a drum. *Individuals have set the external beat through the activity rather than initially responding to an external beat set by the teacher.*

3. Students may identify the external beat in one of the following ways and match the beat with a walking pattern:

HIT the plates together in front of the body.

HIT the plates together overhead.

HIT the plates 4 times in front and 4 times overhead.

HIT the plates 4 times on one side of the body and 4 times on the other.

HIT the plates 4 times in front of the body and 4 times in back.

4. Ask half of the class to provide an external beat by hitting paper plates together, using any of the patterns suggested above, and ask the other half of the class to execute movement sequences to the beat.

5. Ask students to use paper plates to organize walking patterns into various groupings of beat. For example, the plates are hit together on the first of two walking steps, the first of four walking steps, or the first of three walking steps. (The three-step routine is the most difficult because of the alternating footwork involved.)

Moving to an External Steady Beat Using No Props

1. The teacher beats a drum and the older students match the drum beat with walking steps or other locomotor movements.

2. The teacher uses language (SAY) and the students SAY AND DO: such as "WALK, 2, 3, 4"; "JUMP, 2, 3, 4"; "BEND, STRAIGHTEN," "BEND, STRAIGHTEN"; "BEND, STRAIGHTEN," "BEND, STRAIGHTEN."

3. In pairs, one person walks and the partner copies the walking cadence.

4. Working in pairs or small groups, one person initiates some type of walk, such as "toes IN," "WALK on the heels." The partner (or other members of the group) matches the

walk in the same way it was demonstrated and at the same beat and tempo.

5. Working in pairs or small groups, persons walk together with one point of contact between them; then add more points of contact. Elbows may touch for one point of contact. Two points of contact may be shoulders and head.

6. The teacher plays music and asks the group to identify the steady beat and then walk to it. The teacher should encourage the individuals to move freely about the room rather than requiring a circle formation because a circle makes the individual feel very visible.

7. The teacher asks older students to combine locomotor and nonlocomotor movements to music.

Adults and adolescents who successfully complete the above activities now should be visibly comfortable with rhythmic movement and ready to attempt the simple dances and folk dance steps for beginners presented in *Chapter V.*

V.
Introducing Folk Dance to Beginners

Dance is defined as *movement to music.* *Organized dance* is defined as *rhythmic movement sequences combined with music.* Organized dance should be a beautiful "marriage" between music and movement—the more unified, the more aesthetic the experience. There are many types of organized dance but, as noted in the *Introduction,* in this book the focus is on beginning international folk dance. The reason for this decision becomes clear when we compare the different types of organized dance. *Ballroom dancers* must follow difficult rhythmic patterns rather than a step or motion for each beat, must begin with "right" or "left" foot, and must have a partner. *Disco dancers* must master difficult footwork patterns with a great deal of body style added—a feat many beginners will find particularly difficult to achieve. *Square dancers* must have partners and attend to complex movement and directional patterns which beginners cannot handle while they are trying to walk to the beat. *Aerobic* and other fitness-type dancers must follow highly complex and ever-changing movement sequences with arms and legs coordinated in rapid movement. *International folk dancers,* on the other hand, may start off with simple free-space movement and proceed to easy dances in circles and lines which don't require change of direction. In addition, folk dance brings to life both the music and the movement of a specific country, giving teachers the opportunity to introduce the dance culture of the peoples of the world to their students.

In this chapter, I show teachers how to introduce folk dance to students of all ages so that cultural gaps are bridged with music and movement. I recommend that students experience an introductory sequence of organized movements prior to attempting actual folk dances. And, when folk dances are introduced, I recommend that they be presented by level of difficulty. *Chapter VI* contains the actual delivery system for teaching international folk dance to students *after* they have mastered the introductory sequence of activities presented here. I suggest that teachers become familiar with the delivery system described in *Chapter VI* before leading students through the introductory sequence of folk dance presented in this chapter. The information contained in *Chapter VI* will strengthen and deepen your knowledge base—providing a broader perspective on international folk dance. *Part Two* of this book contains a variety of international folk dances that are suitable for beginners who have successfully completed these introductory steps. The dances in *Part Two* are organized by level of difficulty.

Remember, the dances described in this and the following sections of the book should only be attempted by learners who have successfully combined the elements of time and space in rhythmic movement. (Such success is possible for students from second grade to adulthood.) The learners have, therefore, achieved **a basic level of rhythmic competency and a basic comfort with movement.** If your students are lacking in these skill areas, refer to the teaching progressions presented in *Chapters II* through *IV*.

Assuming that a particular group of learners is ready to be introduced to international folk dance, the teacher is faced with three important questions: (1) What are the criteria for selecting introductory organized movement and dance sequences and the corresponding music? (2) How do I plan and introduce the **first organized dance sequences** so that the participants (young or old) succeed? (3) How do I introduce **beginning folk dance?**

Criteria for Introducing Organized Movement and Dance Sequences and Music to Beginners

Music

1. The music should have a strong underlying beat.

2. The music should be instrumental.

3. The phrases of the music should be distinct and occur in groupings of 8 or 16 beats.

4. The music should be organized in either two or three parts which are predictable in their repetition.

5. Only music to which beginners can relate easily should be chosen. Avoid songs sung in a foreign language or played on unfamiliar instruments.

6. Appropriate musical selections might be drawn from marches; American square and round dances; Scottish, Irish and English dances; German quadrilles and schottisches.

Movement and Dance Sequences

1. The beat of the music should first be identified with all students using a leg pat.

2. The sequences should follow the phrases of the music.

3. Each part of the sequence should be simple and highly repetitive.

4. The sequence should involve *basic* locomotor and nonlocomotor movements.

5. The sequence should not require organized formations, such as a circle; students should be able to move about the room in free formation.

6. Complicated directional changes and turns should be avoided.

7. The sequence should not require a specific use of "right" and "left" or "correct" foot.

8. The sequence should not have extra style motions in it, such as CLAP, SNAP, or special use of the arms and body.

9. Hand-holds should not be necessary or required.

10. Partners should not be necessary.

Your First Organized Movement and Dance Sequences

Are there simple folk dances in the literature that satisfy the guidelines mentioned above? There may be a few, but they are very difficult to find. The international folk dance material that is suitable for beginners of any age (from second grade on) often requires learner understanding and competencies well beyond the **basic level of rhythmic competency,** such as sideward patterns, alternating 2-beat sequences, 4-beat movement patterns, and the use of the divided beat. Thus, **before introducing organized folk dance, teachers must provide opportunities for students to practice simple locomotor and nonlocomotor sequences in different combinations and in different directions to a variety of musical selections.**

You may have to choreograph simple dance sequences based on the guidelines presented above in order to bridge the gap from the simple rhythmic activities presented in *Chapter IV* to folk dances. Such introductory dance

sequences should employ the same language-to-movement vocabulary learners have used in the preceding chapters. Students chant an action word to indicate the type of step, after which they chant a counting sequence rather than recite the action word again. Examples of easy sequences in free formation executed to music follow:

1. MARCH, 2, 3, 4, 5, 6, 7, 8 (anywhere around the room); PAT, 2, 3, 4; THUMP, 2, 3, 4 (both hands PAT thighs then THUMP chest).

2. WALK, 2, 3, 4, 5, 6, 7, 8; DOWN UP, DOWN UP, DOWN UP, DOWN UP (BEND and STRAIGHTEN the knees).

3. PUNCH, 2, 3, 4, 5, 6, 7, 8 (alternating thrusting motion of the arms away from the body); JUMP, 2, 3, 4, 5, 6, 7, 8 (in-place JUMP). Note: This is an example of a limited space sequence.

4. MARCH, 2, 3, 4; PAT, 2, 3, 4 (use an alternating leg PAT); HOP, 2, 3, 4 (one foot); HOP, 2, 3, 4 (other foot).

5. JUMP, 2, 3, 4 (in place); APART, TOGETHER, APART, TOGETHER (jump to a position with legs apart sideward then jump to pull them together); KNEES, SHOULDERS, WAIST, HEAD; KNEES, SHOULDERS, WAIST,

HEAD (touch these body parts using both hands).

In addition, I have choreographed two types of simple organized movement and dance sequences for beginners; all age groups have been comfortable with these introductory experiences. The two types of organized sequences are: 1) *Two-Part, Three-Part, and Four-Part* dances which are designed by the teacher or class members and which follow musical phrases; and 2) *Big Circle* dances, which begin to organize locomotor and nonlocomotor movements into a common group formation.

Two-Part Dances

Construct a dance from a musical selection that is grouped into two parts (such as *Blackberry Quadrille, Rakes of Mallow, La Raspa, Circle Follow the Leader, Little Shoemaker*). For a list of recording sources refer to *Two-Part Dance*, page 118. Parts I and II (the A and B sections) each should have 16 to 32 beats to allow for repeated movement; each part should be distinctly different. Use a locomotor pattern for each Part I (A section) and use a nonlocomotor movement for each Part II (B section); for example, in Part I (A)

WALK, in Part II (B) PAT the thighs. Young children may need to repeat the same two parts several times to the music. Older children and adults can repeat Part I and respond to changes in Part II (the nonlocomotor section). "Cue" the new nonlocomotor movement just prior to the change in the music. After a while you may change to a new action in either part by providing the students with a cue before the music changes. For example, for Part I the students WALK tall (short) or MARCH and for Part II they do OUT, IN with their arms or THUMP their chests. For more specific ideas on *Two-Part* dances refer to *Part Two,* page 118. You might also ask different students to suggest new simple movement sequences.

Three-Part Dances

Music that is organized in three parts, such as the German *Zigeunerpolka,* provides a structure teachers can use to create a dance or that students can use to suggest three different sequences to perform to the three parts of music. An example is: Part I, WALK; Part II, TOUCH KNEES, SHOULDERS; Part III, JUMP (in place).

Four-Part Dances

Use the same type of music described in *Two-Part* dances in which the A and B sections repeat, giving four parts of 16 beats, or use music which has four 8-beat phrases, such as *Yankee Doodle,* to choreograph four simple movement sequences. An example is: (1) WALK with toes IN (moving); (2) BEND, STRAIGHTEN the knees (in place); (3) WALK with toes OUT (moving); (4) KICK the legs BACKWARD (in place).

Important points to remember about *Four-Part* dances:

1. Alternate locomotor with nonlocomotor movements at first.

2. Practice each part and link the parts before using music.

3. Ask the learners to recall the sequence: "What do we do first? Second? Third? Fourth?"

4. Don't use a circle formation unless the group will be comfortable with it, or unless you need to exert more control over the group (especially groups of older elementary children and teenagers).

Class-Designed Sequences

Class members may help design sequences for the *Two-Part, Three-Part,* and *Four-Part* dances suggested above. Ask the students: "What shall we do first that will allow us to move around the room?" "What shall we do next that will keep us standing in one place?" The children's answers to these questions should result in a simple movement sequence which may be danced to music such as *Yankee Doodle, Irish Washerwoman, La Raspa, Small World,* and square and contra dance music, all of which are available on records (or you may prefer to play appropriate selections on the piano).

It should be noted that these types of simple movement sequences may be choreographed for limited space in which students convert locomotor patterns to in-place sequences—walking in place using any of the variations. The movement sequences also may be performed by persons who are sitting in chairs.

Big Circle Dances

Learners now switch from randomly walking about a room to moving in an organized circle. Children and adults respond visually or aurally to the leader's changes in the walking *direction* (counterclockwise, clockwise around the circle, walking toward and away from the center) or the *type of walk* (tall, short, wide) or *in-place sequences* (JUMP, HOP, or MARCH in place) or *nonlocomotor movements* (UP, DOWN; PAT, THUMP). Since participants are more visible in *Big Circle* dances, I have designed sequences that are easy to follow and nonthreatening in this type of more "public" activity. Possible patterns include walking right (counterclockwise) 16 beats, walking left (clockwise) 16 beats, walking toward the center 8 beats, walking backward from the center 8 beats; after a while, you can shorten the patterns to 8 beats around the circle and 4 beats IN and OUT. Movements described in the "B" section of *Two-Part Dance* (page 118) may be added.

Important points to remember about *Big Circle* dances:

1. Participants form a circle without joining hands.

2. There are no partners.

3. The teacher uses a "follow-the-leader" format indicating different movements with verbal or visual cues, or choreographs movement sequences that students try out before music is played.

4. This type of dance may be used with all ages.

5. Each pattern is repeated several times.

I feel compelled to interject a note of caution at this point in the learning process. After teachers become familiar with more complex organized dance material, they often tend to disregard these introductory organized movement and dance sequences—ignoring the need for beginners to experience the simple steps and patterns first. An "apple picking" analogy best explains this tendency: teachers reach to different limbs (some higher, some lower) in their search for the apples that are the biggest, reddest, and most free of imperfection. In like manner, dances often are chosen because: (1) the teacher enjoys them;

(2) they *appear* to be simple; (3) the teacher thinks the students will enjoy them; or (4) they serve to demonstrate the teacher's dance ability. Teachers who have climbed the ladder from a **basic level of rhythmic competency** and **basic comfort with movement** to higher levels of rhythmic movement ability must remember to move down to the first rung again when introducing their beginning students to international folk dance.

Introducing Folk Dances and Steps by Level of Difficulty

It is assumed that by this point students have had an opportunity to participate in and help design simple dance sequences, are comfortable moving in different directions with variations, and can comfortably combine and execute locomotor and nonlocomotor movement sequences to music. Therefore, students are now ready to begin learning the dances and steps which are classified as "beginning" folk dance. It is advisable to introduce these steps and dances by level of difficulty, from the simplest to the more complex. Determining which dances to choose for your students depends on several factors:

• The age of the participants.

• The amount of international music to which the students have been exposed.

- How comfortably the students move to the beat with changes of direction and movement.

- How much successful previous dance experience the students have had.

- The amount of space available.

The Levels of Difficulty

The first level of folk dance is designated **Locomotor Movement I** because of the simplicity of the movements; this level is followed by **Locomotor Movement II** and **Locomotor Movement III**. The "locomotor movement" folk dances require *no specific organized folk dance steps*. Dances using **Even Folk Dance Steps** are next in order of difficulty; these steps are referred to as "even" because each movement in the step takes the same amount of time to execute. Dances using **Uneven Folk Dance Steps** are the most difficult for students to master because of the required combinations of beat, divided beat, and held beat. (*Children below the fourth grade should not attempt* Uneven Folk Dance Steps.) I recommend that you start your beginners off at **Locomotor Movement I** and, as they become more skilled, gradually move on through the various levels of difficulty. When students have mastered the special characteristics found in the **Locomotor Movement I** and **II** folk dances, for example, they are ready to proceed either to dances categorized as **Locomotor Movement III** or to dances using **Even Folk Dance Steps**: the CHERKESSIYA followed in order of difficulty by the GRAPEVINE, the STEP HOP and the SCHOTTISCHE. The **Uneven Folk Dance Steps**, in order of difficulty, include the THREE, the TWO-STEP, the YEMENITE, and the POLKA.

To sum up, the beginning folk dances presented here and in *Part Two* of this book are grouped in the following categories: **Locomotor Movement I, Locomotor Movement II, Locomotor Movement III, Even Folk Dance Steps, Uneven Folk Dance Steps.** Figure 4 illustrates this sequence and depicts the relationship of the levels of difficulty to other popular forms of movement and dance.

Please note that the folk dances selected for this book represent primarily circle and line dances or partner and mixer dances in which both persons do the same sequence. I believe that beginning dancers should not be taught couple dances until they are comfortable with dance and then only if couple dances are appropriate for the age and group assembled. For these reasons, dances from many countries will not be found in this book since the dance heritage in those countries is represented by couple dances.

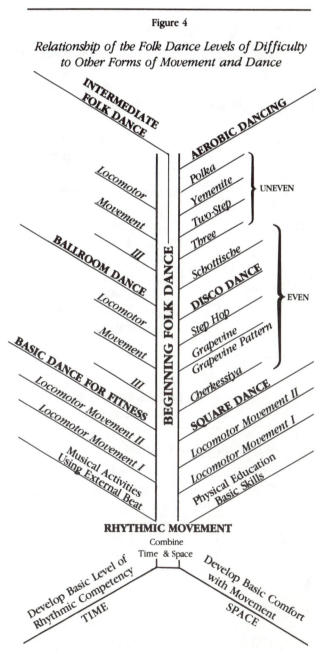

Figure 4

Relationship of the Folk Dance Levels of Difficulty to Other Forms of Movement and Dance

Expanded Use of the Four-Step Language Process

Introducing folk dances and folk dance steps requires the expanded use of the **four-step language process** (see *Chapter I*) as a bridge to movement. Beginners now develop a language-to-dance vocabulary. (Figure 5 presents the introductory language-to-dance vocabulary. The complete language-to-dance vocabulary is defined in the *Glossary.*) Learners SAY and SAY AND DO before music is added, then, with music added, they WHISPER AND DO and DO.

Figure 5

Introductory Language-to-Dance Vocabulary

Words meaning transfer of weight, i.e., STEP/WALK

FORWARD	A step on the designated foot moving in the facing direction (clockwise or counterclockwise) around a circle or one behind the other in a line.
BACKWARD	A step on the designated foot moving away from the facing direction (clockwise or counterclockwise) around a circle or one behind the other in a line.
IN	A step on the designated foot toward the center of a circle or in the facing direction when standing side by side in a line.
OUT	A step on the designated foot away from the center of a circle or away from the facing direction when standing side by side in a line.
SIDE	A step on the designated foot perpendicular to the facing direction. Dancers are facing center in a circle or side by side in a line.
CLOSE	A step on the designated foot to bring it next to the other foot. May occur in any direction.
BACK	A step on the designated foot crossing in back of the other foot.
CROSS	A step on the designated foot crossing in front of the other foot.
TURN	A step on the designated foot which moves the body clockwise or counterclockwise 90° or 180° with a single weight transfer, or the step which begins a multi-step rotation (90°, 180° or 360°).
ACCENT	A forceful step on the designated foot.

Words meaning no transfer of weight

TOUCH	A motion of the designated toes or heel against the floor.
STAMP	A forceful motion of the designated foot against the floor.
KICK	A motion of the designated leg in front, in back or to the side of the body involving a straightening of the knee.
LIFT	A motion of the designated leg in front of the body involving a bent knee. The lower leg is angled in front of the supporting leg.
UP	A motion of the designated leg in front of the body begun by raising the knee.
HEEL	A motion of the designated heel against the floor.

Begin using the language-to-dance vocabulary in movement sequences that employ *direction*:

- FORWARD, 2, 3, 4, 5, 6, 7, 8 (moving in the facing direction); BACKWARD, 2, 3, 4, 5, 6, 7, 8 (moving away from the facing direction)

- FORWARD, 2, 3, 4, 5, 6, 7, 8 (moving around the room); IN, 2, 3, 4; OUT, 2, 3, 4 (toward and away from the center of the room)

Then alter the final movement in a sequence to introduce your students to movements that don't transfer weight (e.g., TOUCH and KICK). These movements occur at the end of 4 or 8 beats:

- FORWARD, 2, 3, 4, 5, 6, 7, TOUCH; BACKWARD, 2, 3, 4, 5, 6, 7, TOUCH

- IN, 2, 3, KICK; OUT, 2, 3, KICK

Then introduce students to sideward patterns:

- SIDE, CLOSE, SIDE, CLOSE

- SIDE, BACK, SIDE, BACK

- SIDE, CROSS, SIDE, CROSS

Introduce alternating 2-beat sequences:

- SIDE, TOUCH, SIDE, TOUCH

- SIDE, LIFT, SIDE, LIFT

Finally, introduce 4-beat sequences:

- SIDE, BACK, SIDE, TOUCH

- IN, KICK, OUT, TOUCH

Introducing Beginners to Locomotor Movement I Dances

The simplest of the folk dances extend the previous movement experiences found in the *Two-Part, Three-Part, Four-Part,* and the *Big Circle* dances to dances with the following characteristics:

1. There is a step or motion for every beat.

2. There is no reference to "right" or "left" foot.

3. There are no hand-holds.

4. The formations can be modified easily for beginners.

5. The music has a strong underlying beat.

Because it is difficult to find ethnic dances that satisfy the beginning criteria listed on page 55, I have modified eight folk dances for teachers to introduce to their beginning students. (The authentic dances are described in *Part Two* of this book.)

1. The Danish dance, *Seven Jumps*, has two parts. **Part I:** STEP HOP 7 times then JUMP. (*Modification:* 14 RUNS or WALKS then JUMP—no "right" or "left" specified and no hands held.) **Part II:** Learners distinguish and respond to chords of longer and shorter duration. (*Modification:* No "right" or "left" specified.)

2. The French-Canadian dance, *Les Saluts,* is suitable for beginners. **Part I:** WALK 16 steps counterclockwise beginning with right foot, then WALK 16 steps clockwise. (*Modification:* No "right" or "left" specified and no hands held.) **Part II:** IN, 2, 3, 4; OUT, 2, 3, 4; IN, 2, 3, BOW (hold until music begins); OUT, 2, 3, 4. (*Modification:* No "right" or "left" foot specified.)

As in *Seven Jumps,* the longer and shorter duration of the bow in *Les Saluts* is fun for participants and requires students to listen carefully. One problem with this dance that teachers should be aware of is the fact that the tempo in Part II is slightly slower than in Part I.

3. Children enjoy the Israeli dance, *Cherkessiya,* but the CHERKESSIYA step used in the Chorus is too difficult for beginners. **Chorus:** 4 CHERKESSIYA steps beginning R foot. (*Modification:* STEP 4 times in place while bending over at the waist with the body and arms down; STEP 4 times in place standing upright with the body and arms up or 8 times down and 8 times up. No "right" and "left" specified.) **Part II:** SKIP. (*Modification:* GALLOP.) **Part IV:** SIDE, BACK. (*Modification:* MARCH). Do the other parts as described or have the students make up the parts.

4. The Israeli dance, *Te Ve Orez,* may also be modified. **Formation:** Groups of three side by side facing counterclockwise. (*Modification:* Alternate circle formation.) **Beats 25-32:** RUN 4 steps then middle person moves to new group.

(*Modification:* JUMP in place—this creates a movement which is different from beats 1-8, RUN.)

5. Beginners enjoy the modified version of *Doudlebska Polka.*   **Part I:** Partners POLKA around the room. (*Modification:* GALLOP without partners around the room.)   **Part II:** WALK into a double circle. (*Modification:* WALK around the room or form a circle.)   **Part III:** Inside partner faces center. Students CLAP their own hands twice as a divided beat and HIT their neighbor's hands on each side (CLAP/CLAP, HIT); outside partners POLKA clockwise around the circle. (*Modification:* PAT legs, CLAP or use CLAP/CLAP, HIT if circle is formed.)

6. The Yugoslavian dance, *Plješkavac Kolo,* may be modified for beginners.   **Part I:** IN, IN, STEP/STEP, STEP; OUT, OUT, STEP/STEP, STEP (diagonally IN and OUT). (*Modification:* IN, 2, 3, 4; OUT, 2, 3, 4.)   **Part II:** IN, IN, ACCENT/ACCENT, ACCENT; OUT, OUT, CLAP/CLAP, CLAP. (*Modification:* ACCENT, ACCENT, ACCENT, ACCENT in place; CLAP,

CLAP, CLAP, CLAP or do as described without "right" and "left" specified.)

7. The Swedish couple dance, *Fjäskern,* may be modified to a circle dance.   **Part I:** 16 STEPS counterclockwise and 16 STEPS clockwise. (*Modification:* No "right" or "left" foot specified.)   **Part II:** 4 SCISSORS KICKS facing partner; change places with partner. (*Modification:* 4 SCISSORS KICKS facing toward center; WALK IN 4 steps; 4 SCISSORS KICKS; WALK OUT 4 steps. Repeat **Part II.**)

8. *Bannielou Lamboal* from Brittany, France may be modified for beginners.   **Part I:** SIDE, CLOSE, SIDE, CLOSE; SIDE, CLOSE, SIDE, TOUCH. (*Modification:* SIDE, CLOSE 4 times.)   **Part II:** TOUCH/TOUCH; TOUCH/STEP, SIDE, TOUCH; TOUCH/TOUCH, TOUCH/STEP, SIDE, CLOSE. (*Modification:* Do only the arm pattern as described in the dance section.)

All the dances described above except *Seven Jumps* are very appropriate for older children and adults. Refer to *Appendix C, Dances by Level of Difficulty* for additional suggestions for **Locomotor Movement I** dances.

Introducing Beginners to Locomotor Movement II Dances

Once students are comfortable with **Locomotor Movement I** dances they are ready to proceed to **Locomotor Movement II**. Third grade is an appropriate time for young students to try these dances. The characteristics of **Locomotor Movement II** dances include the following:

1. There is reference to use of "right" and "left" foot.

2. There is a held beat at the end of an 8-beat or 16-beat phrase.

3. There are 2-beat sequences executed sideward.

4. There are alternating 2-beat sequences.

5. There are 4-beat sequences in place.

6. There is a single divided beat within 4 beats.

Students should learn these skills first with the arms and second with the feet while in a seated position. Once the movements are mastered they may be practiced in the weightbearing position and incorporated into dances.

Use of correct foot. Work with alternating arm patterns and alternating foot patterns (refer to LEVEL II activities in *Chapter II*), adding the correct "right" and "left" designation of arms and legs.

Use of held beat at end of phrases. Practice sequences of 8 beats, substituting the word HOLD for the eighth beat motion. For example:

FORWARD, 2, 3, 4, 5, 6, 7, HOLD;
BACKWARD, 2, 3, 4, 5, 6, 7, HOLD

Practice first using just the arms and then just the legs while in a seated position. Be certain students know that each new sequence begins with the opposite hand or foot.

Two-beat sequences. Practice moving sideward using repetitious patterns of SIDE, CLOSE or SIDE, BACK. Students may use their own beat and tempo first. These skills may be introduced with students in a kneeling

position, using the hands on the floor to simulate the legs. Don't ask older children and adults to kneel. Instead, they should sit in a chair and perform three or four sideward patterns by using small steps and, beginning with their feet to one side, move their feet across in front of the chair.

Alternating 2-beat sequences. Practice an alternating 2-beat pattern with the arms first (refer to LEVEL V activities in *Chapter II*). Students move one hand away from the shoulder in an OUT, IN pattern while holding the other hand still; then they use the other hand to repeat the pattern. If students are unable to perform these arm patterns, they will not be able to attempt similar alternating patterns with the feet (i.e., HEEL, STEP or KICK, STEP). Students should practice the foot patterns first in a seated position and then standing in a weightbearing position. Additional alternating 2-beat sequences include UP, STEP (raise the knee UP then STEP) and TOUCH, STEP (TOUCH the foot sideward or in back, then STEP). All the patterns may be reversed with the STEP occurring first, such as STEP, KICK or STEP, TOUCH.

Four-beat in-place sequences. These 4-beat patterns are practiced with the arms and legs as in LEVEL IV activities in *Chapter II*. At this stage, the students can simulate the patterns of the dances while seated. Examples include: SIDE, BACK, SIDE, TOUCH; SIDE, LIFT, SIDE, STAMP; IN, CLAP, OUT, CLAP; IN, KICK, OUT, TOUCH.

Single divided beat. Patterns of 4 beats with a divided beat such as "1, 2, 3 &, 4" or "1, 2 &, 3, 4" or "1 &, 2, 3, 4" can be practiced by students with both hands patting the thighs, then with hands patting the thighs in an alternating pattern. Note that the repetition begins with the opposite hand. Students can do the same patterns with their feet while they are seated: TOUCH, TOUCH, STEP/STEP, STEP. A list of **Locomotor Movement II** dances can be found in *Appendix C, Dances by Level of Difficulty*. All are appropriate for older children and adults. Try choreographing your own dances with the help of the students. Combine sequences which use sideward 2-beat patterns and alternating 2-beat and 4-beat patterns with the locomotor movements. Here are examples using two-part music:

1. **Part I:** SIDE, CLOSE, SIDE, TOUCH; SIDE, CLOSE, SIDE, TOUCH; IN, 2, 3, KICK; OUT, 2, 3, TOUCH. Repeat if music repeats. **Part II:** FORWARD, 2, 3, 4; 5, 6, 7, 8; IN, TOUCH, OUT, TOUCH; IN, TOUCH, OUT, TOUCH. Repeat if music repeats.

2. **Part I:** FORWARD, 2, 3, 4; BACKWARD, 2, 3, 4; FORWARD, KICK, FORWARD, KICK; FORWARD, KICK, FORWARD, KICK. Repeat if music repeats. **Part II:** IN, 2, 3, 4; OUT, 2, 3, 4; SIDE, LIFT, SIDE, STAMP; SIDE, LIFT, SIDE, STAMP. Repeat if music repeats.

3. **Part I:** IN, KICK, OUT, TOUCH; IN, KICK, OUT, TOUCH; FORWARD, 2, 3, 4; 5, 6, STEP/STEP, STEP (beat 7 is the divided beat followed by a single beat 8). Repeat Part I using music which repeats. **Part II:** SIDE, BACK, SIDE, KICK; SIDE, BACK, SIDE, KICK. (Note that the word SIDE brings the dancers into a position facing center.) IN, 2, 3, KICK; OUT, 2, 3, TOUCH. Repeat Part II.

The teacher now has a choice of proceeding to dances which are categorized as Locomotor Movement III or of introducing dances requiring Even Folk Dance Steps. I often intersperse the Locomotor Movement III dances with dances using Even Folk Dance Steps in order to give students some variety. For the purpose of grouping similar experiences, however, the dances are presented separately in this book.

Introducing Beginners to Locomotor Movement III Dances

These dances are more difficult than the preceding dances for the following reasons:

1. Quicker footwork may be demanded because the beat of music is faster.

2. There may be several parts to the dance.

3. There are groupings of beats other than in twos or fours. Movement sequences grouped in threes or fives are introduced.

4. The dances may require complex changes of direction.

5. The music may have a more ethnic sound with a less easily defined beat.

Dances classified as **Locomotor Movement III** are found in *Appendix C, Dances by Level of Difficulty*.

Introducing Beginners to Even Folk Dance Steps

After students have mastered combinations of locomotor steps and sideward patterns plus 2- and 4-beat sequences, such as those found in **Locomotor Movement II**, they are ready to proceed to **Even Folk Dance Steps**. The most basic of these steps are the CHERKESSIYA, the GRAPEVINE, the STEP HOP, and the SCHOTTISCHE. As noted earlier, these steps are referred to as "even" because each movement in the sequence takes the same amount of time to execute. Each of these steps is described below with suggestions for practicing and linking them into dances. The CHERKESSIYA step and the GRAPEVINE step should be mastered first because they are extensions of a basic walking pattern which now is executed in a specific manner.

The CHERKESSIYA Step

The CHERKESSIYA (sometimes spelled TCHERKESSIYA) dance step is found most often in Israeli dance. It originated with the Cherkessians, one of the ethnic groups of Israel.

CHERKESSIYA
4/4 Meter

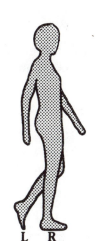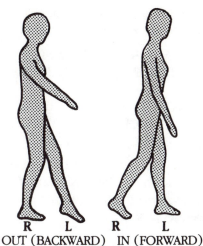

LR	L R	L R	R L	R L
START	IN (FORWARD)	OUT (BACKWARD)	OUT (BACKWARD)	IN (FORWARD)

Important Characteristics

1. The CHERKESSIYA step consists of a sequence of four movements executed in a forward and backward (IN and OUT) rocking motion.

2. This step is a combination of the 2-beat sequences IN, OUT and OUT, IN or FORWARD, BACKWARD and BACKWARD, FORWARD.

3. The four movements use alternate feet.

4. Each movement uses an equal time duration.

5. The CHERKESSIYA step generally is executed in 4/4 or 2/4 meter:

4/4 Meter CHERKESSIYA R foot

Beat 1	Step R foot in	"IN"
2	Step L foot out	"OUT"
3	Step R foot out	"OUT"
4	Step L foot in	"IN"

2/4 Meter L foot CHERKESSIYA

Beat 1	Step L foot in	"IN"
&	Step R foot out	"OUT"
2	Step L foot out	"OUT"
&	Step R foot in	"IN"

6. Dancers may be facing any direction.

7. The CHERKESSIYA step is recurring because it repeats each time on the same foot, in contrast to an alternating dance step.

8. Style may be added to fit the character of the dance and music or the wishes of the choreographer. For example, "leap forward on the first beat while raising the opposite leg behind with the knee bent" is a stylistic addition.

CHERKESSIYA Step Teaching Progression

1. SAY	"IN, OUT" or "FORWARD, BACKWARD"
SAY AND DO	Add the first two motions to the language
WHISPER AND DO	Retain the language with the motions
DO	Think the language and do the motions
2. SAY	"OUT, IN," or "BACK-WARD, FORWARD"
SAY AND DO	Add the second two motions to the language
WHISPER AND DO	Retain the language with the motions
DO	Think the language and do the motions
3. SAY	"IN, OUT, OUT, IN"; or "FORWARD, BACKWARD, BACKWARD, FORWARD"
SAY AND DO	Do the entire step with the language.
WHISPER AND DO	Retain the language with the motions
DO	Think the language and do the motions

4. Provide individual practice time, if needed, with persons using their own beat and tempo, followed by practice to the common group beat. Be certain that the students practice beginning with each foot.

5. Play a selection of music and have students identify the steady beat. Add the WHISPER AND DO and DO steps to the music.

6. Combine the CHERKESSIYA with other locomotor patterns. For example:

IN, 2, 3, 4; CHERKESSIYA;
OUT, 2, 3, 4; CHERKESSIYA
or
CHERKESSIYA; CHERKESSIYA;
SIDE, CLOSE, SIDE, TOUCH;
SIDE, CLOSE, SIDE, TOUCH

7. Teach dances that use the CHERKESSIYA step, such as *Cherkessiya,* or *Mechol Hagat,* or *Ciocarlanul,* or choreograph your own sequences.

The GRAPEVINE Step

The GRAPEVINE step (referred to as a MAYIM step in Israeli dance) is common in dances from many countries. As a result, there are variations to the GRAPEVINE (which are still called GRAPEVINE) in many dance descriptions; this creates confusion for dancers and teachers. GRAPEVINE, as it is used in this book, always refers to the same sequencing of steps and the terms "GRAPEVINE PATTERN" and "REVERSE GRAPEVINE" (described below) refer to the variations.

Important Characteristics

1. The GRAPEVINE step consists of a sequence of four movements executed in a sideward direction. It may be perceived as a CHERKESSIYA step moving sideward.

2. It is a combination of the 2-beat sequences CROSS, SIDE and BACK, SIDE.

3. The four movements alternate feet.

4. Each movement takes the same duration of time to execute.

5. The GRAPEVINE step generally is executed in 4/4 or 2/4 meter:

4/4 Meter GRAPEVINE moving left

Beat		
1	Step R foot, crossing in front of L foot	"CROSS"
2	Step L foot sideward left	"SIDE"
3	Step R foot, crossing in back of L foot	"BACK"
4	Step L foot sideward left	"SIDE"

2/4 Meter GRAPEVINE moving right

Beat		
1	Step L foot, crossing in front of R foot	"CROSS"
&	Step R foot sideward right	"SIDE"
2	Step L foot, crossing in back of R foot	"BACK"
&	Step R foot sideward right	"SIDE"

6. Dancers may be facing any direction, but it is most common to execute the GRAPEVINE step facing center in order to travel sideward around the circle.

7. The GRAPEVINE step is recurring because it repeats on the same foot, in contrast to an alternating dance step. Holding the fourth beat in sequence or hopping on the fourth beat are the most common alterations to allow the GRAPEVINE to travel in the opposite direction.

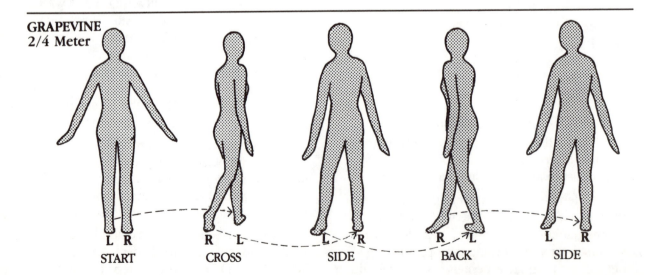

GRAPEVINE
2/4 Meter

L R	R L	L R	R L	L R
START	CROSS	SIDE	BACK	SIDE

8. The GRAPEVINE step begins with the foot opposite to the travelling direction.

9. Style is added to fit the dance. In many Israeli dances, the first beat is accented and the fourth beat becomes a sideward leap. The dancer's hips generally rotate to make the front and back crossing steps easier to execute.

GRAPEVINE Step Teaching Progression

1. SAY — "CROSS, SIDE"

SAY AND DO — Do the motions and repeat the language

WHISPER AND DO — Retain the language with the motions

DO — Think the language and do the motions

2. SAY — "BACK, SIDE"

SAY AND DO — Do the motions and repeat the language

WHISPER AND DO — Retain the language with the motions

DO — Think the language and do the motions

3. SAY — "CROSS, SIDE, BACK, SIDE"

SAY AND DO — Do the motions and repeat the language

WHISPER AND DO — Retain the language with the motions

DO — Think the language and do the motions

(Note: Be certain students face center as it is easy to turn the beginning of this step into a walking pattern which makes the final two motions very difficult to execute.)

4. Allow individuals time enough to practice using their own beat and tempo, followed by practice to the common group beat. Practice both directions. It takes time to make the difficult crossing on the first beat automatic. Encourage learners to begin with one CHERKESSIYA and to take small steps.

5. Play a musical selection and have students identify the steady beat. Add the WHISPER AND DO followed by DO to the music.

6. Combine the GRAPEVINE step with other locomotor patterns and with the CHERKESSIYA:

> CHERKESSIYA; CHERKESSIYA;
> GRAPEVINE; GRAPEVINE
> > or
> IN, 2, 3, 4; OUT, 2, 3, 4;
> GRAPEVINE; GRAPEVINE

7. Teach dances that use the GRAPEVINE step, such as *Mayim, Hora Medura, Corrido, Romanian Hora*, or choreograph your own.

The GRAPEVINE PATTERN Step

The GRAPEVINE PATTERN step, sometimes referred to as the CARIOCA, is found in many dances. The sequence of steps is executed in one of two ways, either SIDE, CROSS, SIDE, BACK or SIDE, BACK, SIDE, CROSS. For clarity, it is recommended that the GRAPEVINE PATTERN step be taught separately from the GRAPEVINE step.

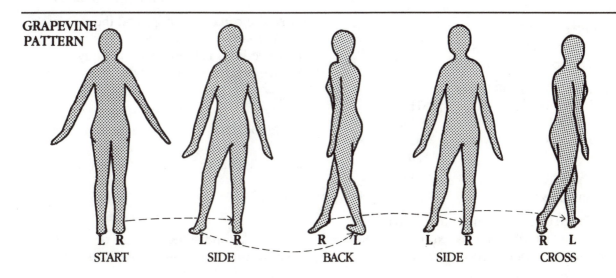

GRAPEVINE PATTERN

| L R | L R | R L | L R | R L |
| START | SIDE | BACK | SIDE | CROSS |

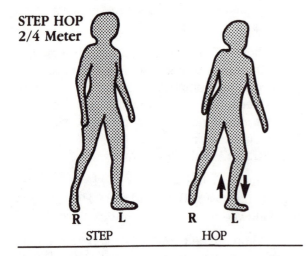

STEP HOP
2/4 Meter

R   L
STEP

R   L
HOP

The STEP HOP

The STEP HOP is found in dances from many countries around the world. It was often combined with the SCHOTTISCHE step in the ballrooms of western Europe and the United States toward the end of the nineteenth century.

Important Characteristics

1. The STEP HOP has two motions: a STEP followed by a HOP.

2. The STEP and the HOP use the same amount of time and the same foot. (The same two motions executed with unequal time duration become a SKIP.)

3. The STEP HOP generally is executed in 2/4 meter, but may occur in 4/4 meter as two STEP HOPS, or one STEP HOP executed very slowly:

2/4 Meter STEP HOP L foot

| Beat 1 | Step on the L foot | "STEP" |
| 2 | Hop on the L foot | "HOP" |

4/4 Meter STEP HOP R foot

Beat 1	Step on the R foot	"STEP"
2	Hold	"HOLD"
3	Hop on the R foot	"HOP"
4	Hold	"HOLD"

4. The STEP HOP may be danced in place, or in any direction.

5. The STEP HOP is an alternating dance step; if the first STEP HOP is executed on the R foot, the next one occurs on the L foot.

6. The STEP HOP as a dance step may be executed several times in sequence, or in combination with other dance steps, or as a transition from one direction to another, or as a transition in a recurring step (CHERKESSIYA or GRAPEVINE) to the opposite foot.

7. The STEP HOP is more difficult to learn than the CHERKESSIYA or the GRAPEVINE steps because two motions are executed on the same foot; the hop following the step demands timing and balance. The dancer's body actually leaves the floor before the beat in order to land on the beat. If the dancer's body is not in good alignment on the first step, the second step will occur too soon.

8. Style usually is added to include movements of the free leg during the step and hop. For example, dancers can lift their free leg backward while stepping, and swing it forward on the hopping motion. The hop is frequently used to change direction: 1/4 or 1/2 turns.

STEP HOP Teaching Progression

1. Practice hopping on one foot and then the other.

2. SAY	"STEP, HOP, HOP, HOP"
SAY AND DO	Do the motions and repeat the language
WHISPER AND DO	Retain the language with the motions
DO	Think the language and do the motions

(Note: Be certain the hops and the step each take the same amount of time. The reason for the three hops is to prepare the body for the balance needed when only one hop is used.)

3. SAY	"STEP, HOP, STEP, HOP"
SAY AND DO	Do the motions and repeat the language
WHISPER AND DO	Retain the language with the motions
DO	Think the language and do the motions

4. Provide individual practice time with persons using their own tempo, followed by

SCHOTTISCHE
4/4 Meter

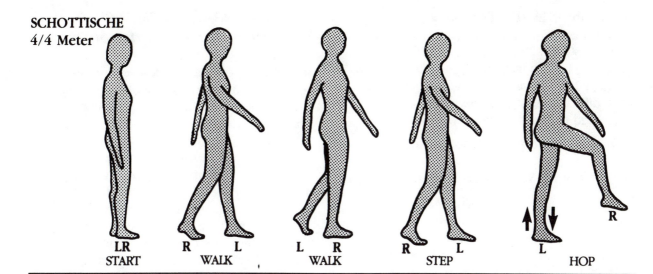

LR	R	L	L	R	R	L	L	R
START	WALK		WALK		STEP		HOP	

practice to the common group beat. Ask your students to practice the STEP HOP more quickly (slowly). Ask students to try out different motions with the free leg.

5. Play a musical selection and identify the steady beat. Add the WHISPER AND DO, followed by DO to the music.

6. Combine the STEP HOP with the GRAPEVINE step, the CHERKESSIYA step, and other locomotor sequences. Give the students movement problems which they practice first to their own beat and tempo, such as

> STEP HOP 4 times
> WALK 8 steps
> CHERKESSIYA twice

7. Teach dances that use the STEP HOP, such as *Debka Kurdit, Hasapikos, Hora*.

The SCHOTTISCHE Step

The SCHOTTISCHE step originated with peasants in Germany. It was danced in ballrooms in Europe, the Scandinavian countries, and the British Isles during the nineteenth century. It also appeared in social dances in the United States, and in the twentieth century became a basic step of the *Jitterbug* and of the *Big Apple*.

Important Characteristics

1. The SCHOTTISCHE step pattern consists of a sequence of four motions: three steps followed by a hop.

2. It is a combination of two walking (running) steps plus a STEP HOP, and therefore logically follows the learning of the STEP HOP.

3. Each motion takes the same amount of time to execute.

4. The SCHOTTISCHE step generally is executed in 4/4 or 2/4 meter:

4/4 Meter SCHOTTISCHE L foot

Beat 1	Step on the L foot	"WALK"
2	Step on the R foot	"WALK"
3	Step on the L foot	"STEP"
4	Hop on the L foot	"HOP"

2/4 Meter SCHOTTISCHE R foot

Beat 1	Step on the R foot	"RUN"
&	Step on the L foot	"RUN"
2	Step on the R foot	"STEP"
&	Hop on the R foot	"HOP"

5. The SCHOTTISCHE step may be danced in place or in any direction.

6. It is an alternating dance step; beat 1 is executed with the opposite foot on each repetition.

7. The SCHOTTISCHE step can be used by itself in a dance or can be combined with other dance steps or locomotor patterns.

8. The greatest difficulty beginners encounter when learning this dance step seems to be with the hop. Some learners turn the hop into a leap to the other foot. Because of this tendency, I recommend that you

present the STEP HOP first and use it in the SCHOTTISCHE step (i.e., explain to students that the SCHOTTISCHE step is a STEP HOP preceded by two walking steps—WALK, WALK, STEP, HOP). I have found that learners have little difficulty mastering the movement if it is presented to them in this way.

9. Add style to fit the dance and music.

SCHOTTISCHE Step Teaching Progression

1. SAY	"WALK, WALK, STEP, HOP"
SAY AND DO	Do the motions and repeat the language
WHISPER AND DO	Retain the language and do the motions
DO	Think the language and do the motions

(Note: The language may be converted to the usual "STEP, STEP, STEP, HOP" as soon as learners are comfortable with the sequence.)

2. Allow individual practice time during which beginners use their own beat and tempo, followed by practice to the common group beat.

3. Play a musical selection and have students identify the underlying beat. Add the WHISPER AND DO followed by the DO to the music.

4. Combine the SCHOTTISCHE step with the STEP HOP, GRAPEVINE and CHERKESSIYA steps and with locomotor sequences. Give the students movement problems:

> SCHOTTISCHE IN
> SCHOTTISCHE OUT
> CHERKESSIYA twice

5. Practice the SCHOTTISCHE step in different directions: forward, backward, sideward, turning. A sideward SCHOTTISCHE generally is executed as SIDE, BACK, SIDE, HOP.

6. Teach dances that use the SCHOTTISCHE, such as *Kuma Echa, Salty Dog Rag, Road to the Isles, Korobushka.*

Introducing Beginners to Uneven Folk Dance Steps

It is much more difficult for beginning students to organize sequences of movements that use held beats or movements that combine divided beats with single beats. These types of patterns in dance are referred to as **Uneven Folk Dance Steps** or "uneven rhythmic movement sequences." Elementary-age children should have reached the fourth grade before attempting uneven patterns and uneven movement sequences with the feet, if those patterns are longer than one single measure. Although some third graders may be capable of executing these uneven patterns, it is best to wait until most of the class can be successful. Older children and adults who have not had appropriate dance experience will also need to master material that is "even" before they can be successful with "uneven" rhythmic movement. The lead-up activity for this step uses hand/arm patterns: PAT, PAT, PAT, HOLD, or three alternating PATS followed by a HOLD.

The four beginning folk dance steps using "uneven rhythmic movement" are the THREE, the TWO-STEP, the YEMENITE, and the POLKA. These steps are described below; they bridge the gap to intermediate folk dance.

The THREE

The THREE ("BALKAN THREE") dance step originated in eastern Europe; the same sequence is also called "PAS DE BAS" and "BALANCE" in dances from other parts of the world.

Important Characteristics

1. The THREE consists of three steps, executed either in place or while the dancer is moving. It is a SCHOTTISCHE step without a HOP.

2. The first two steps take equal amounts of time to execute and the third step takes the same amount of time as the combination of the other two steps.

3. The THREE may be executed in 2/4 or 4/4 meter:

2/4 Meter THREE L foot

Beat 1	Run L foot (slight leap)	"LEAP"
&	Run R foot	"RUN"
2	Run L foot	"RUN"

4/4 Meter THREE R foot

Beat 1	Step on R foot	"WALK"
2	Step on L foot	"WALK"
3	Step on R foot	"WALK"
4	Hold	"HOLD"

4. The THREE is an alternating dance step; the first beat is executed with the opposite foot each time.

5. The greatest difficulty for beginners is in the held beat (the step of longest duration). Learners of any age should not be expected to master this step until they have experienced the steps mentioned earlier; remember, most children below the fourth grade are not developmentally ready for this uneven movement sequence.

6. Add style to fit the dance and music.

THREE Teaching Progression

| 1. SAY 4/4 | "WALK, WALK, WALK, HOLD" (the word "HOLD" is whispered) |
| SAY 2/4 | "LEAP, RUN, RUN" (this occurs too quickly to add the word "HOLD") |

SAY AND DO	Do the motions and repeat the language
WHISPER and DO	Retain the language with the motions
DO	Think the language and do the motions

2. Practice the slower sequence before adding the faster one. Lead up from the SCHOTTISCHE, eliminating the HOP and replacing it with a CLAP. Then eliminate the CLAP.

3. Allow individual practice time during which the students use their own beat and tempo, followed by practice to the common group beat.

4. Play a musical selection and have the students identify the underlying beat. Add the WHISPER AND DO followed by the DO to the music.

5. Practice the THREE in different directions and in place.

6. Combine the THREE with other dance steps and with locomotor sequences. Ask the students to execute:

4 THREES moving counterclockwise
1 SCHOTTISCHE IN
1 SCHOTTISCHE OUT

7. Teach dances that use the THREE such as *Hora Pe Gheaţa, Hora Bialik.*

THREE
4/4 Meter

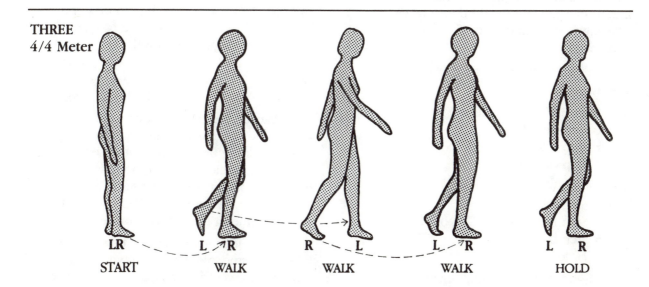

| LR | L ⁄R | R L | L ⁄R | L R |
| START | WALK | WALK | WALK | HOLD |

TWO-STEP
4/4 Meter

LR   L   R   L   R   L   R   L   R
START   STEP   CLOSE   STEP   HOLD

The TWO-STEP

The TWO-STEP is believed to be of Hungarian origin; it was danced in ballrooms toward the end of the 1800s. The TWO-STEP is related to the FOXTROT and may be danced as a form of the FOXTROT. The movement sequence in 2/4 meter is identical to one form of the POLKA found in a number of countries (i.e., Mexico and Russia). The TWO-STEP is a lead-up to a POLKA step as often danced in the United States.

Important Characteristics

1. The TWO-STEP consists of three steps executed in any direction or in place. It is a THREE with a closing step as the second movement.

2. The first two steps take equal amounts of time to execute and the third step takes the same amount of time as the first two steps combined.

3. The TWO-STEP may be executed in 2/4 or 4/4 meter:

2/4 Meter TWO-STEP L foot

Beat 1	Step on L foot	"STEP"
&	Step R foot next to L foot	"CLOSE"
2	Step on L foot	"STEP"

4/4 Meter TWO-STEP R foot

Beat 1	Step on R foot	"STEP"
2	Step L foot next to R foot	"CLOSE"
3	Step on R foot	"STEP"
4	Hold	"HOLD"

4. The TWO-STEP is an alternating step; each repetition begins with the opposite foot.

5. The greatest problem beginners encounter in executing this step occurs with the CLOSE. A change in weight on that movement must occur; if the weight is shifted to both feet, one may not remember which foot to use next. As with the THREE, participants in the TWO-STEP should have prior dance experience, and children below the fourth grade should not be taught the step.

TWO-STEP Teaching Progression

1. SAY	"STEP, CLOSE, STEP, HOLD" or "RIGHT, CLOSE, RIGHT, HOLD" or "LEFT, CLOSE, LEFT, HOLD" or leave out the word "HOLD" in the 2/4 meter ("HOLD" should be whispered)
SAY AND DO	Do the motions and repeat the language
WHISPER AND DO	Retain the language and do the motions
DO	Think the language and do the motions

2. Practice the slower sequence before adding the faster one. Lead up from the THREE, adding the CLOSE on the second step. Watch for potential uneven motions in the first two steps, particularly in the faster form; the students may revert to a GALLOP, which has unequal time in the first two movements.

3. Allow individual practice time during which the students use their own beat and tempo, followed by practice to a group beat using a drum or other external beat.

4. Play a musical selection and add WHISPER AND DO, followed by DO.

5. Practice the TWO-STEP in different directions and in place.

6. Combine the TWO-STEP with other dance steps and locomotor sequences, for example:

2 TWO-STEPS IN
2 TWO-STEPS OUT
SCHOTTISCHE SIDEWARD
SCHOTTISCHE SIDEWARD

7. Teach dances that incorporate the TWO-STEP, such as *Misirlou* and *Nebesko Kolo*.

The YEMENITE Step

The YEMENITE is a dance step found in many Israeli dances. It originated with the YEMENITE people who came from Yemen and settled in Israel and is a characteristic step in the dances of these people. It has the same rhythmic format as the THREE and the TWO-STEP.

Important Characteristics

1. The YEMENITE step consists of three steps executed in a side-to-side pattern.

2. The third step takes the same amount of time as the combination of the other two steps. The first two steps are of equal duration.

3. The YEMENITE step may be executed in 4/4 or 2/4 meter, but it more frequently is found in the slower form:

4/4 Meter YEMENITE L foot
Beat 1   Step L foot sideward left   "SIDE"

2   Step R foot sideward right "SIDE"
3   Step L foot crossing in
front of R foot   "CROSS"
4   Hold   "HOLD"

2/4 Meter YEMENITE R foot
Beat 1   Step R foot sideward right "SIDE"
&   Step L foot sideward left   "SIDE"
2   Step R foot crossing in
front of L foot   "CROSS"

4. The YEMENITE step is an alternating step; each repetition begins in the opposite direction.

5. The greatest difficulty for the dancer seems to be in putting weight on the crossing step. There is a tendency to TOUCH rather than CROSS with weight. The *uncross* to begin a second YEMENITE also poses a problem. I have successfully used the words "FAKE, SIDE, CROSS" to teach this dance step.

6. The YEMENITE step is very fluid; there is a great deal of bending and straightening of the knees. The step has a low-to-high-to-low movement pattern.

YEMENITE Step Teaching Progression

1. SAY	HOLD" ("HOLD" should be whispered) whispered
SAY AND DO	Do the motions and repeat the language
WHISPER AND DO	Retain the language and do the motions
DO	Think the language and do the motions

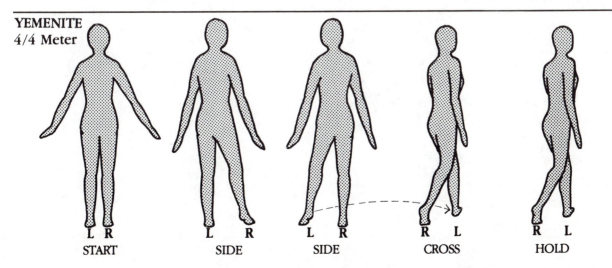

YEMENITE 4/4 Meter

L R	L R	L R	R L	R L
START	SIDE	SIDE	CROSS	HOLD

2. Practice a series of front crossing steps with a held beat after each step (CROSS, HOLD, CROSS, HOLD and so on). Do the first two steps in place followed by the CROSS (STEP, STEP, CROSS, HOLD); watch for students who TOUCH instead of CROSS).

3. Allow individual practice time during which students use their own beat and tempo, followed by practice to the common group beat.

4. Play a musical selection and add WHISPER AND DO, then DO.

5. Practice the YEMENITE in combination with the TWO-STEP. Combine it with other dance steps and provide movement problems:

2 YEMENITES beginning R foot
1 SCHOTTISCHE IN
1 SCHOTTISCHE OUT
2 TWO-STEPS moving counterclockwise

6. Teach dances using the YEMENITE, such as *Ma Na' Vu, Leor Chiyuchech, Hineh Ma Tov.*

The POLKA Step

The POLKA step originated in central Europe in the 1800s. It spread rapidly throughout the world both as a dance by itself and as a step incorporated into other dances and retains its popularity today. The style of the POLKA step will vary from country to country, but its liveliness is a characteristic wherever it is danced.

Important Characteristics

1. The POLKA step, as it is most commonly danced in the United States, consists of four motions. It may be thought of as a TWO-STEP preceded by a HOP (or a "hiccup") into a TWO-STEP.

2. The HOP of the POLKA step is an upbeat into the TWO-STEP. The time that the HOP uses is borrowed from the step of longest duration in the TWO-STEP.

3. The POLKA step generally is executed in 2/4 meter:

2/4 Meter POLKA

Ah	Hop L foot	"HOP"
Beat 1	Step on R foot	"STEP"
&	Step on L foot next to R foot	"CLOSE"
2	Step on R foot	"STEP"

4. The POLKA is an alternating step; a R foot POLKA step is followed by a L foot POLKA step.

5. Two problems exist for students learning the POLKA step. First, there is a tendency, as with the fast TWO-STEP, for them to execute the STEP, CLOSE portion of the step in an uneven fashion as a GALLOP. Second, students often turn the HOP into a LEAP (in error), or they leave out the HOP, turning the step into a TWO-STEP.

POLKA
2/4 Meter

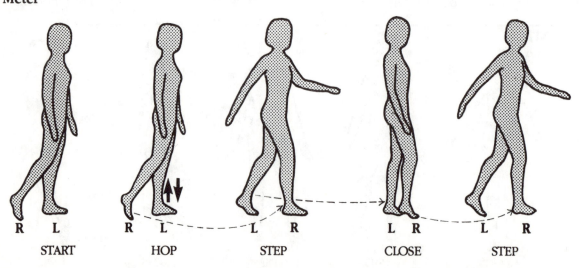

R L	R L	L R	L R	L R
START	HOP	STEP	CLOSE	STEP

POLKA Step Teaching Progression

1. Begin with the TWO-STEP and have the students sneak in a HOP just prior to each TWO-STEP.

SAY	"HOP, STEP, CLOSE, STEP"
SAY AND DO	Do the motions and repeat the language
WHISPER AND DO	Retain the language and do the motions
DO	Think the language and do the motions

2. Allow students to practice to their own beat and tempo, followed by practice to the common group beat.

3. If students have difficulty, return to a GALLOP POLKA: GALLOP twice on one foot; GALLOP twice on the other foot. Then demonstrate the difference between the GALLOP POLKA and the POLKA step that follows a TWO-STEP rhythm.

4. Play a musical selection and add the WHISPER AND DO followed by DO.

5. Practice the POLKA step in combination with other dance steps in 2/4 meter and other locomotor movements.

6. Teach dances using the POLKA step, such as *Jessie Polka* and *Doudlebska Polka*.

VI.

Folk Dance— The Delivery System

When students have mastered the basic rhythmic movement competencies described in *Chapters II-IV,* as well as the introductory steps and beginning dance sequences presented in *Chapter V,* they are ready for full-fledged instruction in international folk dance. The teacher's guidance has been necessary throughout this nurturing process; this special guidance continues to be of utmost importance and is at the heart of a successful delivery system. While teachers may be very knowledgeable about folk dance and folk dance style, unless they can convert this knowledge into teaching methods that produce successful experiences for the learner, the teaching/learning cycle will be incomplete and ineffective. Effective teachers provide their students with experiences that help them achieve an in-depth understanding of the material presented. I believe one proof of effective teaching is found in the learner's desire to pursue folk dance and other dance experiences when not in a teacher's presence. The delivery system I outline in this chapter is designed to help teachers achieve such success.

Chapter VI is a transition chapter—it marks both the end of *Part One* of this book and the beginning of *Part Two.* The delivery system described here is a culmination of the teaching progressions presented throughout *Part One,* providing teachers with additional guidelines and suggestions for introducing the international folk dances described in *Part Two.* I reiterate and expand upon certain guidelines and techniques because the teaching/learning cycle I have designed is a multiplicity of interrelated processes—one step leads to another and steps converge to build a more solid foundation for successful rhythmic movement and beginning folk dance.

In this chapter, I show you how to use space and equipment, provide special recommendations for teaching the first few dances, and suggest general teaching techniques to use that will lead to success for the learner and feelings of accomplishment for you, the teacher. I also provide specific teaching techniques for you to follow when presenting a dance, and some ways to vary your teaching. In addition, I offer some more ideas for simplifying and modifying selected dances for beginners (extending the ideas presented in *Chapter V*) and discuss how to use *chair dancing.*

I have directed this chapter toward the teacher who is presenting a folk dance class or a unit in folk dance to children in the upper elementary grades, or to adolescents and adults (including special populations and senior citizens). But teachers who are presenting other types of organized movement and dance activities to persons in these age groups will also find the teaching suggestions useful.

Space and Equipment

You may not be able to choose the room you must work within or the equipment you must use; consequently, you may encounter space and equipment problems which create a less than adequate or desirable teaching

environment. To counter such problems, most of the dances presented in this book may be modified for limited space by converting sequences that "travel" to steps in place. You may also use *chair dancing* in a confined space. The *chair dancing* suggestions may be easily converted to in-place standing sequences. (*Chair dancing* is described later in this chapter and suggestions for *chair dancing* are presented with each dance in *Part Two*). If you have poor equipment, discuss your needs with your administrators, helping them understand how important good sound reproduction is to the success of your classes. The following discussions concerning space and equipment will help you make the best of whatever situation you are faced with.

Space

What type of room will you be using? A physical education teacher probably will have access to a gymnasium or activity room of adequate size in which all the students can move comfortably. Music and elementary classroom teachers may or may not have access to a large-sized room and may have to use classroom space for the dance activities. (The physical education teacher will often work cooperatively with classroom and special

teachers to permit use of the gymnasium or activity room if plans are made in advance.) You should choose dances that are appropriate for the space you must use, or modify dances for limited space.

Since dance demands movement around a room, a room's floor covering is of special concern. A wood floor is ideal, particularly if it has been constructed with air space under it—the floating floor. But, remember, wooden floors can be very slippery if students move about in socks. Tile over concrete, a very common floor covering, is very hard on the legs and back if long periods of jumping and hopping are planned. This type of surface may also be slippery for students who are moving about in socks. Carpeting, while providing some cushioning, may make it difficult for students to move about smoothly. Carpet also must be vacuumed frequently, as the dust raised from the carpeting may create problems for those students who have allergies.

A room's lighting, acoustics, and ventilation also are important considerations. You should consider all these factors if you have any input into choosing the room within which you will be conducting your class, as well as when planning the activities you will be presenting to your class.

Equipment

Can the record or tape be heard throughout the room without the volume being raised to levels of distortion? If using a record player, is the base of the turntable adequately sprung to prevent the needle from jumping as students move about? Is your equipment on a sturdy table to prevent unnecessary jarring and bouncing? Cassette tapes or reel-to-reel tapes are well suited for movement and dance activities and are more durable than records, but they require adequate playback equipment. A small portable tape recorder is not suitable for use in a classroom or activity room unless it can be "jacked" into a sound system or auxiliary speakers. If this modification can be made, cassette tapes (ten minutes in length) can be purchased in specialty shops and tapes can be made of appropriate records, thus preserving the records. One dance should be recorded on each side of a short tape. Try to avoid recording several dances on one side of a longer tape. You will find the longer tapes are less convenient, requiring you to spend time locating the portion of the tape desired.

First Steps

Get to Know Your Group or Class

Before attempting to develop goals and objectives for a dance class, you should answer several preliminary questions about your students:

- What are their ages?
- How large is the class?
- How many males and how many females are participating?
- What are the capabilities of the learners? What previous experience has the group had with dance or with other rhythmic movement activities?
- What is the probable receptivity of the group to dance?
- Will the participants be capable of vigorous activity, or is their level of fitness low?

- Are there special populations within the group, such as the physically or mentally impaired?
- Are there students whose parents, grandparents, or other relatives come from foreign countries?
- What activities precede and follow the dance class?
- Will the dance session be part of a music, physical education, or classroom experience, or will it be a separate class?
- How long will the session last?

By answering these questions first, the teacher will be able to choose the most appropriate material and methods for teaching folk dance to a particular group.

Know Your Material

A dance has two important components—the music and the rhythmic sequence of movements. Teachers must become thoroughly familiar with each of these components and must concentrate on both throughout the duration of the dance.

The music. Listen to the music several times in order to understand and be comfortable with it, and then answer the following questions:

- What is the dancer's beat—the steady pulse of the music—the base for the dance steps? Is it slow? Is it fast? Is it easily perceived?
- What is the meter? Is the music organized in twos or threes?
- Is there an introduction? If so, when does the dance begin with respect to the introduction? If not, can the dance begin with the second part, omitting the first part the first time through the dance?
- What is the musical form—how is the music organized? Is it organized into two parts? Is it verse/chorus (rondo)?
- How long are the phrases? How often do they repeat?

The rhythmic movement sequence. The teacher must clearly understand the steps and motions in a dance's rhythmic movement sequence. To achieve this understanding, you must:

• Visualize the sequence from start to finish, and dance it mentally. Use an identifying word for each step or motion—a language-to-dance vocabulary.

• Know the directions the body faces throughout the dance. Is the "road map" for the dance clear?

• Recognize the transitions from one part of the dance to the next, and from the end of the dance back to the beginning.

Once the overall dance pattern is clear, you can concentrate on specific sections as needed. Teachers may find it useful to write out a dance, using single-word descriptions of steps and directions to identify the dance sequence (refer to *Glossary*). In order to fully understand a dance and to know the language needed to teach it, a teacher must be able to describe a dance either mentally or in writing. For example, *Twelfth St. Rag* may be described as follows:

FORWARD, 2, 3, 4, TOUCH, TOUCH, STEP/STEP, STEP; Repeat; OUT, 2, 3, 4; IN, 2, 3, 4; IN, KICK, OUT, TOUCH; IN, KICK, OUT, TOUCH.

Thus, from the language-to-dance vocabulary, the teacher knows that on the first 16 beats the dancers will travel around the circle, on the next 8 beats they will move away from the center of the circle and then toward the center, and on the final 8 beats they will face the center of the circle.

Combining music and movement. When combining music and movement, teachers should ask themselves:

• How do the movements fit the music? Do the different parts of the dance follow the musical phrases and the musical form?

• How does the rhythmic structure of the dance fit the steady beat of the music?

• How many repetitions of the dance will be executed to the piece of music?

• Does the end of the dance coincide with the end of the recording?

Music and movement must converge. If teachers "feel" this unity, they will present dance as a musical experience and not as a sequence of movements with music in the background.

"Warm Up" Your Class

At the beginning of a class, teachers need to "warm up" the group, dispelling any lethargy or fear that might be present in the students and providing for immediate learner success. You can't expect most groups to be "ready" if you don't provide warm-up activities. For example, you might involve everyone in a very simple movement, such as running, or jumping in place, or simple stretching exercises to music. Or you might have music playing when the group arrives and immediately lead them around in a circle in a follow-the-leader experience. Or you might begin the session with a dance the group knows well and enjoys—a dance that doesn't need review. It is unwise, however, to begin the class in the same way each day because the desired effect of "turning on" the group could become a "turn off" if the warm-up pattern becomes routine.

Plan Each Class

When planning a dance class, teachers should ask themselves:

- What shall I do first?

- How shall I end the class?

- What new (and old) material shall I use?

- When in the lesson shall I present new material?

- How will the class be paced?

- Shall I honor requests to perform dances the class has learned before?

- Have I prepared enough material and a sufficient variety of material to respond to the needs of the group each day?

The major activities for a specific class need to be planned carefully. Dances from the previous class should be reviewed during the body of the lesson. The material should be paced (i.e., alternate faster and slower sequences, vary familiar and unfamiliar music). Until students develop a very accepting attitude about ethnic music and dance, teachers need to plan carefully the music and dances that precede and follow the ethnic sound, and to determine what preparations for the unfamiliar sound would be the most useful. For example, if the Yugoslavian dance, *Djurdjevka Kolo,* is going to be taught, it might follow *Alley Cat* which uses the same "TOUCH, TOUCH, TOUCH, STEP" sequence. You might play a little of the ethnic music first and provide information about the different sounds created by the combination of ethnic stringed instruments. Exhibiting a picture of one or more of the instruments or a map of the country of origin would help your students bridge the cultural gap. The next dance you present to the class should have more familiar sounding music, such as *Count 32.*

New movement patterns may be reinforced by planning a few dances in sequence that require the new pattern. For example, the beat structure "1, 2, 3 &, 4" can be reinforced through a review of *Limbo Rock, Plješkavac Kolo,* and *Dučec.* The alternating 2-beat pattern of "STEP, LIFT" can be practiced in *Ugros,*

Hasapikos, and *Dimna Juda.* The 6-beat sequence found in dances from four countries can be compared and contrasted: *Hasapikos* (Greece), *Hora* (Israel), *Körtanc* (Hungary), and *Pravo Horo* (Bulgaria). (Remember, all of the dances mentioned in this chapter are described in *Part Two* of this book.)

Don't forget to make a plan for the last few minutes of a class. A successful ending promotes a feeling of group unity; the class closes on a high note with students wanting to dance more and looking forward to the next dance experience. Teachers can create good feelings by choosing an ending dance that students will enjoy immediately, or by repeating a favorite, or by introducing part of a new dance that students will look forward to finishing during the next class period.

Plan a Series of Classes

The goals and objectives for the entire course or unit must be considered as teachers plan a series of classes. What aspects of the basic teaching progressions (*Chapters II-V*) should be presented? What countries should be represented in dance? Are there resource people from the community who could bring costumes, art objects, or pictures to class in order to enrich the cultural experience for the students? How many classes will be offered? A suggested lesson sequence for such a series is presented in *Appendix D.*

Special Recommendations for Teaching the First Few Folk Dances

Some of the special recommendations I present here have been mentioned before in this book. They are presented again to assure learner success at this skill level. In another section of this chapter, I discuss simplifying and modifying folk dances for special populations as well as for beginners; these special recommendations form the basis for that discussion, too. You won't have to use all the techniques all the time; your group will dictate their necessity. These are the "break-in tips" for older elementary students, adolescents, and adult beginners who are in classes where it is not possible to spend sufficient time on the progressions outlined in *Chapters II* through *V*. If your group experiences difficulty, however, you should refer to the sequencing of the beginning dance experiences presented in *Chapter V*.

No hands held. As mentioned throughout this book, it is much easier for students to learn to move rhythmically and to dance when teachers do not ask them to hold hands. Students are already self-conscious about learning unfamiliar material; if they hold hands, their palms may perspire from the tension, increasing their discomfort and embarrassment. Therefore, students (both beginners and advanced) who start off learning dances without holding hands feel more comfortable during the entire learning process.

No right or left foot specified. Starting off with folk dances that allow beginners to use their preferred foot, be it "right" or "left," will create less tension and more success for beginners. Beginners have enough trouble mastering new material without the added burden of using the "correct" foot. The dances classified as **Locomotor Movement I** (see *Appendix C, Dances by Level of Difficulty*) all have as one characteristic no right or left foot specified. Dances classified as **Locomotor Movement II** which do not require a "correct" foot are designated with an asterisk in

Appendix C. Once beginners have sufficient experiences with dances in which no right or left foot is specified, they can move on to more difficult dances which require the use of "correct" foot.

No partners. If dancing with a partner causes self-consciousness for many of your beginning folk dancers (those who feel partners will witness their mistakes), don't require partners. Beginners should feel comfortable with a dance before working with someone else. Elementary-age children, particularly boys, may be especially uncomfortable with partner dances. Many junior and senior high school students I have talked to have been quick to point out that they disliked dance in elementary school because of the required partner formations.

Repetition. Most learners cannot master a dance pattern instantly. Dances in which short sequences have several repetitions usually produce a level of success that makes beginners feel good about the activity. The *Two-Part Dance*, which is predictable once it begins, is a satisfying experience for many beginning folk dancers.

Step or motion for every beat. The first folk dances taught should have a step or motion for every beat. It is much more difficult for the beginner to stop for held beats and to divide beats than to keep going in an even sequence.

Strong steady beat of music. A strong, well-defined beat of music helps the beginning folk dancer who must attend to the steady beat while representing that beat with a movement. Instrumental music should be used first because vocal selections often create a distraction for beginning folk dancers if they attempt to identify the words of the song.

Dance sequences following the musical phrase. Movement sequences that change as the music changes create a natural bridge between music and movement. When movement sequences do not follow the musical phrase, learners are apt to be distracted. Many may "tune out" the music because the music doesn't "fit."

Simplifying and Modifying Folk Dances

Certain elements of a folk dance may be too difficult or may be impossible for beginners or for specific populations such as older adults or the mentally and physically handicapped. In such cases, teachers may simplify or modify the dance for that particular group. Simplifying or modifying dance steps also provides more material for teachers, and makes it possible for you to introduce many more ethnic dances to beginning students. You must examine a difficult dance to see what elements could be modified or simplified: tempo, dance steps added to simple sequences, turns, right or left foot designations, the rhythmic structure, style, changes of sequence (parts), partners.

But simplifying a dance is not a license for the teacher to be "creative" with another country's ethnic dance; American music should be used for creative endeavors. Simplifications or modifications of dances should closely follow the authentic dance movements, thus making it possible for students to perform the actual dance (when and if they are ready) without having to "unlearn" incorrect patterns. One question a teacher should keep in mind when modifying dances is, Have I produced a simplified dance or an altered dance which is just as difficult as the original?

It is very important for teachers to understand the difference between simplifying or modifying a dance and destroying or "watering down" cultural material from another country.

Many line and circle dances from around the world are "easy" folk dances and are suitable for beginners, while other dances could be suitable for beginners if a difficult section could be altered. The important thing for you to remember when simplifying or modifying a dance is to retain the character and authenticity of the material, while making just enough alteration to create an appropriate movement sequence for your beginning class or special group. Remember, you should replace the simplified dance with the authentic dance if and when the group is ready for the more difficult movements.

I have used the following dance modifications successfully with many special populations as well as with beginning folk dancers. (Refer back to "Introducing Beginners to Locomotor Movement I Dances" on page 61 for additional modifications.)

1. No right or left foot specified: *Alley Cat, Cherkessiya, Count 32, Djurdjevka Kolo, Haya Ze Basadeh.* Additional examples appear in *Appendix C, Dances by Level of Difficulty* and are marked with an asterisk.

2. Partner dances modified so the students learn only one part as a circle dance: *Doudlebska Polka* (the male part), *Haya Ze Basadeh* (the male part), *Good Old Days* (the male part), *Mexican Mixer* (the female part), and *Corrido* (the female part).

3. Sections of divided beats modified to WALKS or single motions, using the underlying beat: *Limbo Rock, Twelfth St. Rag,* and *Good Old Days.*

4. Four-part dances simplified to two-part dances, with each part repeated once if the musical form permits this alteration: *Popcorn, Alley Cat.*

5. BUZZ TURNS modified to TURNS using WALKS: *Ve David, Niguno Shel Yossi, Tant' Hessie.*

6. FULL TURN modified to four STEPS IN PLACE: *Erev Shel Shoshanim, Bele Kawe.*

7. A GRAPEVINE simplified to WALKS in the specified direction: *Hora Medura, Mayim.*

8. A STEP HOP modified to a STEP HOLD, leaving out the HOP: any dance which uses the STEP HOP.

9. WALK patterns that include held beats modified to include STEPS on each beat: *Hora Pe Gheața, Hora Bialik.*

10. A SCHOTTISCHE modified to four WALKS; a POLKA modified to a GALLOP or GALLOP POLKA; a YEMENITE to three STEPS IN PLACE: see the dances which use these dance steps.

General Techniques for Teaching All Dances

Teachers should keep these general teaching techniques in mind for all their presentations.

Instructor Enthusiasm

An enthusiastic teacher who fosters enthusiasm in beginning students and attempts to assure immediate success for individual dancers will find students more willing to take a chance and will find teaching much more rewarding. When learners experience success, they tend to be more cooperative.

Sensitivity to the Learner

As with enthusiasm, the instructor who is sensitive to the beginner's needs and is a caring person will be more likely to create a positive learning environment which, in turn, will more likely result in a successful experience for the beginner. Such a teacher will not "wear blinders" while teaching, but will be aware of the progress made by each learner and the degree of learner tension that is present.

Using the Four-Step Language Process

You should use the **four-step language process** (see *Chapter 1*) when teaching organized folk dance. SAY may be omitted if the sequence is short and easily understood by your students; use SAY AND DO instead as the dance is presented. Follow up with WHISPER AND DO and DO when the music is played. The single descriptive words used in the **four-step language process** are the organizing force for the learner's conceptual understanding of the rhythmic movement sequences. The words must be simple, have meaning for the learner, and be used consistently in all folk dances. As each word is introduced, make sure your beginning folk dancers understand completely the movement you are describing. This language-to-dance approach will help most learners master a dance more rapidly because they will be actively involved in the learning process. There is no magic in watching a teacher's feet move unless the learner can convert the visual image into successful action.

The *Glossary* contains the language-to-dance vocabulary used to describe the dances found in this book.

Adding a Visual Model

There will be times when you may want to demonstrate visually a movement sequence or use SAY AND DO to help your students master a movement. Two things should be kept in mind:

(1) Avoid small, indistinguishable movements and steps. Make each step or motion distinct, without distracting arm and body movements.

(2) Change your location with respect to the formation the students are using. If you are demonstrating a dance while moving inside a circle formation, for example, you should continually position yourself in front of different sections of the group, eventually covering the entire circle, because many of your students may be experiencing mirroring and reversal problems. (I wear a garter on my right ankle to help students keep track of the foot I am using.) Remember, "Watch me and do as I do" is effective only for beginners who are rhythmically competent, and only should be used with the language-to-dance vocabulary of the **four-step language process**.

Teaching from the Known to the Unknown

Dances are combinations of sequences which are learned over time. Very often you can use a dance step or movement sequence the group already has mastered and "precede" or "add on" new sequences. (See "Adding On" and "Combining Familiar Dance Steps into New Patterns and Dances" in the next section of this chapter for more information.) Realizing that the learners may already "know" parts of a new dance, you will find it easier to teach the dance if you make use of this information.

Teaching Quickly

It is important to teach dances quickly—no more than five minutes should be allotted for teaching a beginning folk dance. Almost all of the students in the class will be able to dance to the music with a minimum of movement errors within this five-minute time limit. If the teaching process takes longer than five minutes, the teacher should consider these questions:

- Is the dance too difficult for the students? Are they "ready" for it?

- Have I prepared the material carefully enough to permit a logical learning sequence? Am I organized?

When the whole dance is put together quickly it is easier to remember. A dance that is taught slowly, with each section practiced many times, does not provide the learner with a sense of the whole. No matter what specific teaching technique is used to present the dance (see "Specific Techniques for Teaching Each Dance"), it is important to complete the practice within five minutes. Otherwise students lose track of what precedes and follows each part of the dance. *Once the sense of the whole is created, however, the parts can be practiced to perfection.* Remember, *teaching* and *learning* a dance are different from *perfecting* the dance steps. As used in this book, *teaching/learning* refers to the process of presenting the movement sequences of the dance, practicing them briefly, then dancing

them to music. No special formations or hand-holds are added to the movements. Don't ask your students to incorporate "style" until they feel comfortable with the movement sequence. A later section of this chapter, "Adding Style," provides further clarification of this point.

Teaching Rhythmically

Time is an integral part of any movement sequence. *Rhythmic language* is an important bridge to *rhythmic movement.* Therefore, teachers should SAY the dance pattern rhythmically, then ask the students to SAY AND DO the pattern rhythmically, thus creating the critical link between rhythm and movement. If the dance sequence is too difficult for your students at the tempo presented, practice the SAY AND DO a little more slowly (see the following section), but be certain to retain the accuracy of rhythmic grouping. For example, a stepping pattern of "TOUCH, TOUCH, STEP/STEP, STEP" which occurs in a beat structure of "1, 2, 3 &, 4" cannot be taught or executed as 5 beats then changed to the divided third beat. As your students practice sequences to their own beat and tempo, stress the need for them to retain rhythmic accuracy, regardless of the tempo they use.

Teaching Close to Tempo

If the students are able to perform the desired sequence at the appropriate tempo they should do so; it is much more difficult for students to begin a sequence considerably under tempo and then have to increase that tempo. If, however, you see that your students are having problems with the learning tempo, you can reduce the tempo gradually—until you reach a point that permits student success. But remember, sequences that are practiced too slowly become isolated bits of single-beat movements rather than the integrated whole of longer patterns of movement. An appropriate analogy may make this point clearer: reading slowly word by word does not often result in learner comprehension of the material. Therefore, when you work on a movement sequence at a slower tempo, the reduced tempo should be used *after* the actual sequence has been presented to the students at tempo and *after* they have tried it. A slower tempo is useful for clarifying a complex sequence, perhaps correcting a portion of the dance that has been perceived incorrectly, or making clearer the style of a particular movement pattern.

Practicing the Sequence at Tempo Before Adding Music

The movement sequence of the dance should be practiced at the actual tempo of the music *before* adding the music. If you have been practicing at a slower tempo, use SAY AND DO to bring the sequence up to tempo when your group is ready. Ask your students to SAY the sequence a little faster and they will naturally quicken their movements. This technique is preferable to asking students to "move more quickly." If a dance sequence is not up to tempo when the music is added, learners may have difficulty making the transition from the practiced tempo to the musical tempo. Another useful technique to counter this problem is for you to play a little of the music for your students before teaching the dance, and then ask them to identify the underlying beat. This technique will give the students a sense of the tempo and will help you recall the accurate tempo before beginning to teach or review the dance.

Specific Techniques for Teaching Each Dance

These teaching techniques are designed to help teachers become familiar with a dance's unique combination of movement sequences. Some dances are constructed very logically from beginning to end and thus can be taught easily in sequential order. Other dances, however, are taught more successfully if the teacher begins with the most difficult movements, even if they occur at the middle or end of a dance. The following questions can guide you as you decide how to present a specific dance to your students:

• Is it logical to begin at the beginning and teach in sequence? Or are there more difficult sequences that should precede easier ones?

• Is it possible to begin with 4 beats and "add on" an additional 2 beats with each practiced repetition?

• Is it possible to integrate dance steps that the learners already know and have practiced by putting them together in different combinations to learn a new dance?

• How are the parts of the dance "glued" together, and how can I assure that the transition from the end of the dance to the beginning is executed smoothly?

● Are there sections of the dance which may be particularly troublesome?

● How will I ask the learners to practice sections of the dance?

● When should I add style?

Each of these questions is discussed in turn in the sections that follow.

Presenting the Most Difficult Sequences First

My experience tells me that students will master the more difficult sections of a dance more quickly if they are presented to them first. An example of teaching the most difficult sequence of the dance first and then teaching the simpler movements that come before it is found in *Twelfth St. Rag.* Begin the teaching sequence with the slightly more difficult movements of "TOUCH, TOUCH, STEP/STEP, STEP" in a rhythm of "1, 2, 3 &, 4." After your students have executed this sequence successfully, present the simpler sequence that immediately precedes it: "FORWARD, 2, 3, 4." Then combine the sequences "FORWARD, 2, 3, 4; TOUCH, TOUCH, STEP/STEP, STEP." Another good example is found in the dance *Armenian Misirlou.* Teach the last four motions of "CROSS/SIDE, BACK/SIDE" first, then teach the sequence that immediately precedes it: "CROSS, CROSS." Finally, teach the first and easiest movement sequence to the dance: "TOUCH, TOUCH, TOUCH, TOUCH." Then combine the sequences "TOUCH, TOUCH; TOUCH, TOUCH; CROSS, CROSS; CROSS/SIDE, BACK/SIDE." (Note the "/" between CROSS and SIDE denotes a divided beat. In this dance example, beats 7 and 8 are divided.)

Adding On

The dance, *Áis Giórgis,* provides an example of the "add-on" teaching technique, in which students do a short sequence and then learn the sequences that follow by "adding on" two more movements (2 beats) at a time, linking these to the preceding sequences. For example, the first 4 beats of *Áis Giórgis* are "WALK, WALK, SIDE, TOUCH." Ask your

students to execute these steps with the SAY AND DO method. At the completion of these 4 beats, immediately ask the students to "add on" the next 2-beat sequence, "SIDE, HEEL" then "SIDE, HEEL" again (another 2-beat sequence). Finally, ask them to "add on" the last 2-beat sequence of the dance, "SIDE, BRUSH." Another good dance with which to use the "add on" process is *Popcorn*: students first learn the alternating 2-beat sequences of "HEEL, STEP, HEEL, STEP" then "KICK, STEP, KICK, STEP" then "SIDE, BOUNCE, SIDE, BOUNCE" followed by "RUN, 2, 3, 4."

Combining Familiar Dance Steps into New Patterns and Dances

Another way to guide your students smoothly from the known to the unknown is to create situations that integrate dance steps they have already mastered into new combinations and dances. This process helps learners fully integrate a particular step into their dance repertoire. Once a dance step is mastered, the students should know how that dance step begins and ends, its directional movements, the steps needed to create a change of direction, and how to combine it with other familiar movement sequences. For example, learners will know that the GRAPEVINE step begins with a CROSS and ends with a SIDE; the dancer moves sideward with four even steps and cannot move in the opposite direction sideward without altering one sequence. (See the sections of *Chapter V* on Even and Uneven Dance Steps for information on specific dance steps and linking dance steps.)

By combining dance steps with each other (SCHOTTISCHES and STEP HOPS or SCHOTTISCHES and GRAPEVINES), or with 2-beat sequences (SCHOTTISCHES and SIDE CLOSES), or with locomotor movements (HOPS and WALKS), students will learn to be flexible in their approach to dance. This technique enables students to practice the basic steps of international folk dance in a variety of contexts. By using this integrated approach, you show students that many new dances are really just different combinations of already familiar movements. A student's dance ability improves dramatically when this integrated problem-solving technique is used and students combine familiar sequences into new patterns. For example, they learn that the first half of the dance, *Kuma Echa*, is a combination of two SCHOTTISCHE steps and two GRAPEVINE steps, while *Salty Dog Rag* combines two SCHOTTISCHE steps and four STEP HOPS.

Transitions

Why is it difficult for students to make the transition from one major part of a dance to the next, and from the end back to the beginning? Because often dances are presented by teaching one part at a time. Students practice each part over and over again, creating mental stopping points between parts. Dancers will have great difficulty with transitions unless the teacher consciously builds a bridge to link the sequences of a dance together, thus preparing the learner to go from one part to the next, or from the end to the beginning. These transitions must be practiced in the same manner as sequences within a part are practiced. If a dance has only one part, ask the students to practice the sequence by starting and ending at different places so a "mental block" is not created. If a dance has more than one part, ask the students to practice moving from the end of one part through the beginning of the next, as well as from the last several beats of the dance back to the beginning sequence. Remember, the suggestions for handling transitions should only be considered *after* the part has been

presented using the "add on" technique, or the technique of presenting the most difficult sequences first, or the technique of combining familiar dance steps in new ways. Working with transitions should occur during the *practice* phase of learning a dance.

Anticipating Trouble Spots

By analyzing dance material carefully, teachers generally can predict which sections of a dance may be particularly troublesome for their group or for certain individuals. Starting off with the more difficult sections and then presenting the easier material has already been suggested as one way for teachers to avoid trouble spots. Occasionally, a trouble spot may occur when students misunderstand a particular language-to-dance term; in such cases, the teacher must clarify its meaning for the students. Rhythmic groupings are often difficult for students to understand and extra help from you will be needed. Transitions, as discussed previously, may prove troublesome for learners and teachers must remember to work on them, too.

Group Drill Versus Individual Practice

The basic difficulty with group drill is the fact that a movement sequence usually is practiced at a constant tempo and the problems an individual may be experiencing are often ignored. If any of your students are having trouble learning a dance or sections of a dance, a group drill usually will produce neither success nor improvement. If, however, all of your students understand the material and are successfully executing the movements, repetitions (group drill) may prove useful in making them completely comfortable with the dance before the music is played. In such cases individual practice time is not necessary. But individual practice time for those learners who do not understand the movement sequences they are practicing is a must. Remember, once your students can SAY the sequence, they can practice it to their own tempo. In such situations, you are then free to move about the group and provide assistance to those students who need help, without creating an embarrassing situation for them by putting them in the spotlight. By individual practice time I mean one to two minutes for persons to work alone, for small groups to practice with one student put in charge of each group, or for two or three students to work together informally.

Reviewing a Dance

Students should not be expected to master a dance in a single session. If you are teaching a large group of students, you may not notice everyone's errors during the first session in which a dance is introduced; incorrect movements are very difficult to change once the learner has integrated them into a routine through repeated practice. Therefore, since learners often are not aware of their incorrect movements during the first teaching session, by reviewing the dance during the next class, both the learners and the teacher can catch and correct mistakes before a great deal of change in the movement patterns is necessary. Your review of a beginning dance should take no more than one or two minutes.

Adding Style

When should you add style to a dance, including hand-holds? Style, the movement of the arms and body, is a very visible part of a dance and students will want to "do it right." Consequently, if style is presented too early, students will center their attention on the stylistic elements to the exclusion of the movement sequences. Teachers should wait to add style until footwork becomes "automatic" and students are able to combine the movement sequences with music, which usually is not before the first or second review of the dance in subsequent class periods. Learners become very frustrated when a dance seems to "fall apart" because they are concentrating on style before they are adept enough at performing the movement sequences. Teachers must guard against creating such learner frustration.

Certain stylistic additions, however, may be incorporated almost immediately into some

dances. In Israeli circle dances, for example, the arms are often *raised* and *lowered* as the dancer moves IN and OUT of the circle. These movements are a logical and natural outgrowth of the sequence and thus can be integrated easily by beginners. An in-place movement, such as a "SWAY, CLAP" which has a CLAP on the held beat after the SWAY, is another example of a stylistic addition that can be added immediately in most learning situations. The kicking motion of "FORWARD, 2, 3, KICK," a special use of the leg on the beat, may also be added as the sequence is taught. The key question you must keep in mind is whether or not the style of a dance is a very natural part of the dance sequence. If you decide the style might be difficult or more complicated for beginners, wait to introduce it until students are very comfortable with the movement sequence; likewise, hand-holds should be avoided until the students are comfortable with the dance.

Don't add extra language when students are practicing style. For example, in *Bannielou Lamboal,* students say "SIDE, CLOSE" as they execute the foot movements and, at the same time, move their arms in an *around* and *back* motion. They cannot say "around and back" at the same time because two sets of language—one for the leg movements and one for the arm movements—would be impossible. Thus, to avoid confusion, first demonstrate the arm motions (without the foot patterns) with *no* language and ask the students to copy the motions. Second, do the arm movements while SAYING the foot pattern, *without moving the feet* (say "SIDE, CLOSE" as the arms are moving). Third, demonstrate the complete movement—the stylistic arm motions with the SAY AND DO foot movements. Have the students then follow your lead. In the second part of *Bannielou Lambaol* follow the same procedure. First, practice the pushing and pulling of the arms *away from* and *toward* the body twice, followed by one *around* and *back* motion without language, then add the language of the foot pattern "TOUCH/TOUCH, TOUCH/STEP; SIDE, TOUCH," and finally SAY AND DO the entire sequence, with arm style added. Adding the stylistic arm movements to the sequence of leg movements is much more successful than attempting both arm and leg movements at once.

One last point about style—most folk dance style is understated rather than overstated. If you are uncertain about the style of a particular dance, it is wise to use a regular hand-hold and omit any special stylistic features. Teachers should use general rather than specific style unless certain of authenticity so that misrepresentation does not occur.

Strategies for Varying Your Presentations

Teachers can present dances in a variety of ways. By varying your presentations, you heighten the interest and curiosity of your students. Following are ten different methods you can use, with appropriate dances as examples.

1. **Present the language-to-dance words (the SAY). Ask the students to move to the language without prior demonstration.** Ask the students to listen to the music and identify the underlying beat and the phrases. This translation of language into dance movement may be accomplished by students individually, or in pairs, or in small groups; then the music is played and the dance executed. The group then discusses any variations in interpretation. This method should be employed only with material that is completely clear. *Zemer Atik* or *Djurdjevka Kolo* are good dances for this method.

2. **Verbally describe a segment of a dance (SAY) to the students and ask them to respond with SAY in a "verbal echo."** Then demonstrate the dance segment with SAY AND DO, asking the students to respond with a SAY AND DO echo. This method and the one described above foster learner independence because learners must rely on their own thought processes to execute the movements. *Bele Kawe* or *Alunelul* could be taught this way.

3. **Present a dance through "echo moving"; you execute a movement sequence without using any language and your students copy your movements.** Then ask the students to add the appropriate language to the movement pattern. This is a good way to help students achieve a more complete understanding of a dance. This method enables you to test your students' comprehension of the language-to-dance patterns. *Bannielou Lambaol* or *Áis Giórgis* are suggested for this method.

4. **As suggested in an earlier section of this chapter, after the students have mastered particular dance steps, present a sequence that combines the familiar dance steps into a new dance.** For example, you could ask the class to face counterclockwise in a circle and do a "SCHOTTISCHE sideward right (OUT)," a "SCHOTTISCHE sideward left (IN)," and four "STEP HOPS FORWARD" around a circle. In this way, you have presented the first part of

Salty Dog Rag without mentioning to the class that they are actually learning a new dance. The working language-to-dance vocabulary is used in a very natural way. Relying on movements the students have already learned, you can then present another new dance, *Nebesko Kolo*: "four TWO-STEPS counter-clockwise (beginning right foot), four TWO-STEPS clockwise, two CHERKESSIYA steps facing center, four THREES in place, and a STAMP with the right foot." Once they have mastered the basic dance steps, students will respond enthusiastically to this teaching method and will want to learn a number of dances or parts of dances in the same manner. The popularity of this method seems to be that each dance becomes a different sequence of "known" pieces.

5. **Demonstrate an entire dance with the music.** This teaching technique, if used carefully and with appropriate dances, is a great motivational tool. Following the demonstration, present the parts of the dance to the students in sequence from beginning to end using SAY AND DO without music. Then lead students through the dance sequence with music. *Işte Hendek* or *Dučec* are appropriate dances for this method.

6. **Present several parts of a dance "one at a time."** You may wish to add the music after each segment is mastered or may not add music until after several parts have been mastered. A good dance for this technique is *Cumberland Square*. Your group could learn the first figure, or the first two figures and then dance these two sequences to the music before they learn the rest. The same technique could be used with *Debka Kurdit*; students could dance the first three figures with the music before going on to the rest. If this strategy is used, however, be certain to practice the transitions at the points where the dance is broken apart.

7. **If a dance is very short, or each section is repeated often, you might choose to put on the music and encourage students to join you as you dance.** *Hasapikos* is a short and easy

dance with a 6-beat sequence that could be taught in this way; the dance, *Ugros*, a multipart dance with high repetition of each part also could be taught in this way. Keep in mind, however, that presenting a dance in this manner may be frustrating for some students who have trouble learning movement sequences by visual imitation. Therefore, it is important to cue your students just prior to a change in sequence and to retain a WHISPER AND DO for the first few repetitions. Watch for signs of frustration and failure, and change the teaching method if students are unable to follow your lead immediately.

8. **Teach a dance to several students outside of class and have each of them be responsible for teaching the dance to small groups of students during the next class period.** This technique gives those students who learn very quickly and proficiently an opportunity to extend their knowledge. These students also will realize that *dancing* a dance and *teaching* a dance require different competencies. Teachers who use this technique are helping students develop new areas of expertise. *Close Encounters* or *Debka Daluna* are suggested for this method.

9. **Write the language-to-dance sequence on a chalkboard and have the students recite with SAY and then SAY AND DO.** This strategy may help learners who are very visually oriented. The learner now *sees* as well as *hears* the language-to-dance words. A variation of this strategy would be to give each student a written description of a dance to be learned. Ask the students to execute the dance from the description—working alone, in pairs, or in small groups. This is an excellent way for you to help students understand the language-to-dance vocabulary more fully. *Alunelul* or *Twelfth St. Rag* may be used with this method.

10. **Teach students a dance while they are sitting in a chair (I call this *chair dancing*).** This technique is described in more detail at right and is especially appropriate for senior citizens and special populations. *Dučec* and *Pata Pata* work well with this method.

Chair Dancing: A Mainstreaming and Modification Technique

Chair dancing (a term I coined) gives many beginning dancers and special populations the opportunity to "dance" while sitting in a chair. Many folk dances need only slight alterations or modifications to become *chair dances*. Movement sequences to music can be modified for senior citizens who are sitting in a chair, as well as for persons who can use their legs while seated, but who cannot function in a standing position with the rest of the group. Persons who do not have the use of their legs but have the use of both arms can simulate the leg movements with their arms and participate with the group in a seated position. Teachers will find that *chair dances* are useful for *all* beginning folk dancers; in this nonweightbearing position, many students can learn footwork more comfortably than in a standing position. Almost any dance can be *chair danced* and suggestions for this form of modification are given with each dance presented in *Part Two* of this book. You will note that arm patterns occasionally replace foot patterns in part of a dance to make the sequence more interesting for the *chair dancer*.

The general rules for *chair dancing* follow:

(1) WALKS and other locomotor patterns are modified to in-place STEP sequences.

(2) Sideward 2-beat sequences such as SIDE, CLOSE or SIDE, BACK are modified to alternating 2-beat sequences (SIDE, TOUCH, SIDE, TOUCH) or are executed as described with very small steps.

(3) IN and OUT foot patterns are executed by moving away from and toward the chair.

(4) Partner sequences are modified to use only one of the parts.

(5) All foot/leg patterns can be converted to hand/arm patterns.

(6) Many dances are converted to wheelchair dances by using one push on the wheels for each 2 or 4 beats and by making other alterations, such as a DO-SA-DO modified to moving toward a partner (4 beats) and back to place (4 beats).

Where Do We Go From Here?

Once you have guided your students through the beginning folk dance experiences presented in this book and your students can comfortably integrate **Even** and **Uneven Dance Steps** in the beginning dances presented in *Part Two,* they are ready for intermediate folk dance. Intermediate folk dance involves longer sequences, integration of more complicated movement patterns, new dance steps, unusual meters (such as sevens and nines), and more creative choreography than beginning folk dance. I recommend that you, the teacher, move on to the intermediate level of folk dance as soon as *you* are ready, in order to gain a broader perspective—a greater sense for the whole. Then, when the students you have guided successfully through beginning folk dance are ready for intermediate folk dance (if you are dealing with children they should be ready by grades five or six), you will be able to meet their needs.

To enlarge your dance repertoire, you should try to attend some of the numerous folk dance workshops that are presented in this country.* If there is a recreational folk dance group in your area, the leaders of the group generally know about special workshops that are being conducted nearby. Folk dance "camps" are often scheduled on weekends, at holiday times, and during the summer for teachers' convenience. The folk dance magazine, *Viltis* (see *Bibliography* for address), lists many of these workshops.

---

*The author conducts rhythmic movement and folk dance workshops and conference sessions upon request. To contact her, write to the High/Scope Foundation, 600 North River Street, Ypsilanti, MI 48197, or call (313) 485-2000 to obtain more information about scheduling the sessions.

Part Two

Beginning Folk Dances

Introduction to Part Two

Every attempt has been made to represent each dance as accurately as possible. The descriptions are drawn from choreographers' guides and from workshops led by teachers who have researched their dances in the countries of origin. The dances are organized as follows: Locomotor Movement I, Locomotor Movement II, Locomotor Movement III, Even Folk Dance Steps, Uneven Folk Dance Steps.

How to Follow the Dance Descriptions in Part Two

Each dance description is organized into the following categories: Record, Introduction, Formation, Part (Beat), Rhythmic Notation, Lead-Up Activities, Teaching Suggestions, Chair Dancing. Explanations on how to use each of these categories are provided here. When necessary, the dance *Twelfth St. Rag,* page 180, is used for illustration.

RECORD: Each dance description contains information on the record to use when teaching that particular dance. Sources for obtaining the records are listed in *Appendix E.*

INTRODUCTION: This section tells you that you must adjust your beat and tempo to conform to a certain number of beats. Identify the steady beat of the music and match that beat with the number of beats listed in the introduction. For example, *Twelfth St. Rag* has an 8-beat introduction. If you identify a slow or quick tempo beat, you will count either 4

beats or 16 beats for the introduction and will have to adjust your beat and tempo to 8 beats.

FORMATION: Check the formation for the dance. If you don't understand the terminology, refer to the *Glossary* in the back of the book.

RHYTHMIC NOTATION: Match the rhythmic pattern shown in the rhythmic notation boxes to the steady beat. (See "The Visual Representation of Beat" on the following page for clarification of the notation system.) Use a patting motion of the hands on the thighs to identify the rhythmic sequence, first without music and then with music. *Do not* try to follow the correct foot designated under each box at this stage.

PART (Beat): After you are comfortable with the rhythmic sequence, SAY the language-to-dance words (those in capital letters directly opposite each PART) as you pat the rhythmic pattern without music, then WHISPER the words to the music. (Note that in *Twelfth St. Rag* the divided beat in box 7 of PART I is represented with "/" between the words "STEP/STEP.") For the next step, I find it helpful to sit in a chair and SAY the capital letter words while using the "correct foot" shown under each box. If you are familiar with the language-to-dance vocabulary, you might try to SAY AND DO the dance at this point. If, however, you do not understand the language-to-dance vocabulary (capital letter words), refer to the *Glossary* in the back of the book for definitions.

Read the descriptions directly opposite the numbered beat(s). These descriptions clarify the capital letter words for each dance. All the words in the description are important: the *movement* is given (STEP, KICK, TOUCH); the *foot to be used* for that movement; and the *direction* of the movement (counterclockwise, in, out). Check for NOTE or TO SIMPLIFY to see if there are any special directions. (I often present the simplified version of a dance first.) SAY AND DO the dance and then add music.

LEAD-UP ACTIVITIES: These activities are presented to provide experiences for your students which will make it easier for them to learn the dance.

TEACHING SUGGESTIONS: A specific sequence for teaching the dance is offered in this section. These suggestions have been tried in classes with many age groups.

CHAIR DANCING: *Chair dancing* suggestions may be used to create a nonweightbearing position for students who are practicing a dance or may be adapted for special populations of older adults and the handicapped who cannot perform the dance in a standing and moving position.

The Visual Representation of Beat (Rhythmic Notation)

In organized dance, the movement sequences are executed against a steady beat of music, creating a rhythmic structure for the dance. I have designed a system to visually represent this rhythmic structure—the sequence of movements in folk dance. Many students do not understand the time relationships of beat and divided beat. They don't understand symbolic representations such as " | " and " ⊓ " or " ♩ " and " ♫ " and that " ⊓ " or " ♫ " is " | " or " ♩ " divided into two parts of equal duration. But when a "box" ☐ representing the beat is drawn around the abstract symbols |✛| and |♫| or |♩| and |♫| the time relationships are clarified for students in a concrete manner. Thus, your students can respond to representations that show one or more divided beats in a 4-beat sequence, such as |✛|✛|♫|✛| and |✛|♫|♫|✛|

The rhythmic structure of each of the dances is represented visually in a series of boxes. Each box is equivalent to one steady beat of music. For example, four beats of music = ⬜⬜⬜⬜.

When "X" is placed in the box, it indicates a step or motion (TOUCH, KICK, STAMP) for that beat. Four steps or motions to the underlying beat of music = ☒☒☒☒.

Two "X's" in one box ⧄ refer to two steps or motions of equal duration, 1/2 beat each, the total equal to the single beat.

Thus, ☒☒⧄☒ is translated to one step (motion) on beat 1, one step (motion) on beat 2, two equal steps (motions) which divide beat 3, and one step (motion) on beat 4.

A box with no "X" in it signals a "hold" (there is no movement for this beat.) Thus, ☒☒☒⬜ means one step (motion) on beats 1, 2, 3 and no step (motion) on beat 4.

The beats in the description of a dance correspond to the squares in the notation as follows:

 One step or motion for each steady beat

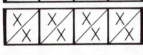 Two steps or motions for each steady beat

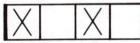 One step or motion followed by a hold for each 2 beats

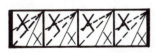 One step or motion for 3/4 of the beat and one for 1/4 of the beat

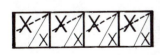 One step or motion for 2/3 of the beat and one for 1/3 of the beat

 One step or motion for each 1/3 of the beat moving in "triplets"

The following abbreviations are used with rhythmic notations:

B	A weight transfer to both feet
(L)	Use of the left foot in a motion without weight transfer
L foot (leg, hand)	Left foot
(R)	Use of the right foot in a motion without weight transfer
R foot (leg hand)	Right foot

Therefore, R, (R), L, (L), B under each box designate the "correct" foot to be used for that beat:

 four weight transfers moving right, left, right, left foot

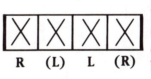 five weight transfers moving right, left on beats 1, 2; right/left on the divided beat 3; right on beat 4

one weight transfer to the right foot on beat 1; one motion (no weight transfer) of the left foot on beat 2; left foot weight transfer on beat 3; one motion (no weight transfer) of the right foot on beat 4

Locomotor Movement I

Characteristics:
1. There is a step or motion for every beat.
2. There is no reference to "right" or "left" foot.
3. There are no hand-holds.
4. The formations can be modified easily for beginners.
5. The music has a strong underlying beat.

Big Circle Dance*
Movement Sequence
U.S.A.

RECORD	Music in AB form with a strong underlying beat (see *Two-Part Dance* for suggestions)
FORMATION	Circle, no hands held
	Leader improvises walking sequences using a counter-clockwise or clockwise direction, using IN and OUT of the circle with 4 or 8 beats, using in-place movements, or moving sideward around the circle. Be certain to change direction or movement sequences at ends of phrases. Add a hand-hold if the group is comfortable. Try doing the whole sequence without verbal directions.
NOTE	This type of sequence is an excellent warm-up for any class and can be made more difficult with dance steps added.
CHAIR DANCING	Many follow-the-leader sequences may be executed while seated.

*Choreographed by Phyllis Weikart.

Count 32*
Novelty Dance
U.S.A.

RECORD	Any music in A or AB form which has sections of 32 beats (see *Two-Part Dance*)
INTRODUCTION	Dependent on music selected
FORMATION	Circle, no hands joined
PART I	WALK
Beat 1-8	Walk 8 steps counterclockwise turning 180° on beat 8
9-16	Walk 8 steps backward counterclockwise
VARIATION	WALK different ways
	WALK 16 steps without TURN
	WALK clockwise, beats 9-16
	Use other locomotor movement
PART II	STEP, KICK, STEP, KICK; STEP, KICK, STEP, KICK; IN, 2, 3, 4; OUT, 2, 3, 4
Beat 1	Step in place
2	Kick opposite foot toward center
3-4	Repeat beats 1-2 using opposite footwork
5-8	Repeat Part II, beats 1-4
9-12	Walk 4 steps in
13-16	Walk 4 steps out
VARIATION	Omit WALKS IN and OUT and repeat beats 1-8. Change STEP, KICK to STEP, TOUCH or use other 2-beat sequences.
TO SIMPLIFY	Move IN, OUT twice; omit the STEP, KICK.

RHYTHMIC NOTATION

PART I

X	X	X	X	X	X	X	X	**REPEAT**
R	L	R	L	R	L	R	L	

PART II

X	X	X	X	X	X	X	X
R	(L)	L	(R)	R	(L)	L	(R)

X	X	X	X	X	X	X	X
R	L	R	L	R	L	R	L

*Choreographed by Phyllis Weikart.

Count 32 *(continued)*

LEAD-UP ACTIVITIES	Practice walking with different variations (individual's tempo); teacher calls out variations.
	Practice walking forward and then turning and walking backward (individual's tempo).
	Practice an alternating 2-beat sequence with the arms— one arm goes OUT, IN (straightening, bending) and then the other arm repeats the arm movement. Success with this sequence is necessary for success with alternating 2-beat foot patterns.
	Practice STEP, KICK, STEP, KICK (individual's tempo).
TEACHING SUGGESTIONS	Have group WALK forward 8 steps counting the steps as they WALK (SAY AND DO). Repeat and substitute the word TURN on the 8th beat and execute a 180° turn.
	Young children should not TURN and should use Part II simplification.
	WALK backward 8 steps counting the steps (SAY AND DO).
	Practice STEP, KICK 4 times (SAY AND DO).
	"Add on" IN, 2, 3, 4; OUT, 2, 3, 4.
	Do the dance, SAY AND DO; then add music.
CHAIR DANCING	Substitute steps in place or construct a two-part dance which uses arm movements.

Djurdjevka Kolo
Yugoslavia

RECORD	RCA EPA 4130 or *The World of Folk Dances* 1620
INTRODUCTION	None or 32 beats
FORMATION	Broken circle, hands joined in "V" position
PART I	FORWARD, 2, 3, 4; 5, 6, STEP/STEP, STEP
Beat 1-6	Walk 6 steps counterclockwise beginning R foot
7 &	Step R foot, L foot in place
8	Step R foot and turn to face clockwise
9-16	Repeat beats 1-8 in opposite direction beginning L foot
TO SIMPLIFY	WALK 8 steps counterclockwise and 8 steps clockwise with no R foot or L foot specified.
PART II	TOUCH, TOUCH, TOUCH, STEP
Beat 1	Touch R foot in front of L foot
2	Touch R foot sideward right
3	Touch R foot in front of L foot
4	Step R foot in place
5-8	Repeat beats 1-4 beginning L foot
9-16	Repeat Part II, beats 1-8
NOTE	No R foot or L foot is necessary.

RHYTHMIC NOTATION

PART I

X	X	X	X	X	X	X⁄x	X	**REPEAT W/OPP. FTWK.**
R	L	R	L	R	L	RL	R	

PART II

X	X	X	X	X	X	X	X	**REPEAT**
(R)	(R)	(R)	R	(L)	(L)	(L)	L	

LEAD-UP ACTIVITIES

Practice standing on one foot for 3 beats and changing feet on the 4th beat (individual's tempo).

Practice touching one foot for 3 beats and then stepping on the touching foot on the 4th beat. Alternate feet (individual's tempo).

TEACHING SUGGESTIONS

Practice walking to the music (the walking beat is rather slow).

Practice TOUCH, TOUCH, TOUCH, STEP with SAY AND DO.

Do the dance with SAY AND DO and add the music.

CHAIR DANCING   Substitute in-place steps for walking steps. Do Part II as described.

Fjäskern
Hurry Scurry
Sweden

RECORD	Viking Records V200
INTRODUCTION	8 beats
FORMATION	Partners in a double circle facing counterclockwise
ALTERNATE FORMATION	Single circle, no partners

PART I	FORWARD (15 WALKS), TURN; FORWARD (16 WALKS)
Beat 1-15	Walk 15 steps forward counterclockwise
16	Step forward counterclockwise and turn 180°
17-32	Walk 16 steps forward clockwise and end facing partner
PART II	KICK, 2, 3, 4; CHANGE, 2, 3, 4
Beat 1-4	Kick 4 times touching heels to the floor in front of the body
5-8	Step 4 times changing places with partner
	Pass R shoulders, clap with first step
9-32	Repeat Part II, beats 1-8, three times
TO SIMPLIFY	Use Alternate Formation.
PART I	Do as described above.
PART II	KICK, 2, 3, 4; IN, 2, 3, 4; KICK, 2, 3, 4; OUT, 2, 3, 4

RHYTHMIC NOTATION	PART I

PART I

X	X	X	X	X	X	X	X	**REPEAT 3X**
R	L	R	L	R	L	R	L	

PART II

X	X	X	X	X	X	X	X	**REPEAT 3X**
R	L	R	L	R	L	R	L	

LEAD-UP ACTIVITIES	WALK counterclockwise then clockwise in a continuous movement sequence (individual's tempo).
	KICK 4 times then WALK forward 4 steps (individual's tempo then partner beat).
TEACHING SUGGESTIONS	Learn simplified version first.
	Change Part II to partner version. Practice using partner beat then group SAY AND DO. Add music.
CHAIR DANCING	Use simplified version. Part I, WALK in place. Part II, WALK feet away from the chair then toward the chair.

Haya Ze Basadeh
Once in the Field
Israel

RECORD	Hed-Arzi MN 581
INTRODUCTION	8 beats
FORMATION	Double circle counterclockwise; directions given for left-hand person—boy if co-ed group—person on right, opposite footwork
ALTERNATE FORMATION	Single circle
PART I	FORWARD, 2, 3, 4; TURN, 2, 3, 4; FORWARD, 2, 3, 4; IN, 2, 3, 4; OUT, 2, 3, 4; CHANGE, 2, 3, 4
Beat 1-4	Step R, L, R, L foot forward counterclockwise
5-8	Turn toward partner R, L, R, L foot (end facing clockwise)
9-12	Step R, L, R, L foot forward clockwise (end facing partner with both arms joined in upper arm hold)
13-16	Step R, L, R, L foot toward center of circle (inside person backing up)
17-20	Step R, L, R, L foot away from center; clap on beat 20
21-24	Step R, L, R, L foot in place (outside person advances 4 steps counterclockwise to new partner)
NOTE	No R foot or L foot is necessary.
CIRCLE DANCE	Use Alternate Formation.
	Dance as outside person and substitute 4 accented steps in place for beats 21-24.

RHYTHMIC NOTATION

REPEAT 2X

LEAD-UP ACTIVITIES

Practice walking 4 steps in one direction, turning 180° in place using 4 steps, and then walking the opposite direction with 4 steps (individual's tempo).

Practice walking IN 4 steps, OUT 4 steps, adding a CLAP with the 4th step OUT.

Haya Ze Basadeh (continued)

TEACHING SUGGESTIONS	Practice the first 12 beats (FORWARD, 2, 3, 4; TURN, 2, 3, 4; FORWARD, 2, 3, 4) with SAY AND DO.
	"Add on" IN, 2, 3, 4; OUT, 2, 3, 4.
	Practice the final 4 beats with partners mixing or as a circle dance accenting 4 steps in place.
	Do the dance with SAY AND DO; then add the music.

CHAIR DANCING

Beat 1-4	Step in place
5-8	Thigh pat
9-12	Step in place
13-20	Move feet away from and toward the chair
21-24	Accent in place

Irish Stew *
Two-Part Dance
U.S.A.

RECORD	RCA EPA 4131 *Join the World and Folk Dance*
INTRODUCTION	8 beats
FORMATION	Circle, no hands joined
PART I	WALK
Beat 1-16	Locomotor movement counterclockwise (walk or use variations)
17-32	Repeat locomotor movement clockwise
PART II	JUMP, JUMP, CLAP, CLAP
Beat 1-2	Jump 2 times (in place, out-in, or scissors fashion)
3-4	Clap hands 2 times
5-16	Repeat Part II, beats 1-4, three times
17-32	Change jump
NOTE	Make up your own easy motions executed in place.

RHYTHMIC NOTATION

PART I

PART II

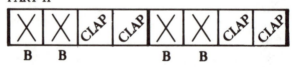

LEAD-UP ACTIVITIES	Practice different locomotor and nonlocomotor sequences.
TEACHING SUGGESTIONS	This type of two-part music gives students the opportunity to practice many sequences to music, alternating locomotor and nonlocomotor movements.
CHAIR DANCING	Use feet/legs for Part I and hands/arms for Part II.

*Choreographed by Phyllis Weikart.

La Raspa
The Rasp (Mexican Shuffle)
Mexico

RECORD	Folkraft 1119
INTRODUCTION	4 beats
FORMATION	Partners facing each other, both hands joined
ALTERNATE FORMATION	Single circle, no partners
PART I	LEAP, LEAP, LEAP, HOLD (Bleking step)
Beat 1	LEAP on R foot extending L foot forward, heel touching floor
2	Change feet, extending R foot
3	Repeat beat 1
4	Hold (2 quick claps may be added)
5-8	Repeat beats 1-4 with opposite footwork beginning leap L foot
9-32	Repeat Part I, beats 1-8, three times
NOTE	Using partner formation, thrust arm forward corresponding to the foot which is extended forward.
PART II	ELBOW SWINGS
Beat 1-8	R elbow swing, L hand high; release elbows and clap on beat 8
9-16	Repeat, using L elbow (R hand high)
17-32	Repeat R and L elbow
NOTE	Part II may be used as a mixer, changing partners with each 8 beats or after 16 beats; boys advance counterclockwise, girls clockwise.
ALTERNATE FORMATION PART II	RUN
Beat 1-16	Run right (or use any other locomotor step)
17-32	Run left

RHYTHMIC NOTATION

PART I

X	X	X		X	X	X	
R	L	R		L	R	L	

REPEAT 3X

PART II

X	X	X	X
R	L	R	L

REPEAT 7X

(continued)

La Raspa (continued)

LEAD-UP ACTIVITIES	Practice the LEAP, LEAP, LEAP, HOLD (Bleking Step) (individual's tempo).
	Practice 8-beat ELBOW SWINGS with partner (partner beat).
	Practice locomotor movements to the music (RUN and HOP) if using Alternate Formation Circle Dance.
TEACHING SUGGESTIONS	Practice Part I with SAY AND DO.
	If teaching the partner dance, work on Parts I and II with SAY AND DO before adding the music.
CHAIR DANCING	Do steps in place.
	May be adapted for wheelchairs.

Les Saluts
French-Canadian

RECORD	Laridaine ML 7902 *La Bastringue*
INTRODUCTION	None
FORMATION	Circle with or without hands joined
PART I	WALK
Beat 1-16	Walk 16 steps counterclockwise
17-32	Walk 16 steps clockwise
NOTE	To give students additional experiences, vary the WALK or use other locomotor movements; no R foot or L foot specified.
PART II	IN, 2, 3, 4; OUT, 2, 3, 4; IN, 2, 3, BOW; OUT, 2, 3, 4
Beat 1-4	Walk 4 steps in
5-8	Walk 4 steps out
9-12	Walk 3 steps in and bow; hold bow until music begins again
13-16	Walk 4 steps out

RHYTHMIC NOTATION

PART I

X	X	X	X	X	X	X	X	**REPEAT 3X**
R	L	R	L	R	L	R	L	

PART II

X	X	X	X	X	X	X	X	**REPEAT**
R	L	R	L	R	L	R	L	

LEAD-UP ACTIVITIES	Experiment with locomotor movements.
	Experience walking to the steady beat of music.
	Experience walking FORWARD 4 steps then BACKWARD 4 steps.
TEACHING SUGGESTIONS	Practice Part II with SAY AND DO, then add music. Practice Part I with the music.
CHAIR DANCING	Do sequences in place.

Little Shoemaker
U.S.A.

RECORD	Windsor 7141
INTRODUCTION	Pickup plus 8 beats
FORMATION	Double circle, partners facing each other
ALTERNATE FORMATION	Circle, no partners
PART I	MARCH
Beat 1-16	Inside circle march clockwise (16 steps); Outside circle march counterclockwise (16 steps)
17-32	Turn and march 16 steps opposite direction and turn to face partner
NOTE	Other locomotor steps may be substituted for the MARCH.
PART II	CLAP, R (hand), CLAP, L (hand); CLAP/CLAP, CLAP/CLAP, CLAP, HOLD; ELBOW TURN
Beat 1-2	Clap own hands, clap R hands together
3-4	Clap own hands, clap L hands together
5-8	Clap own hands 5 times (beats 5/&, 6/&, 7, hold 8)
9-16	Hook R elbows and turn 8 running steps
17-32	Repeat clapping sequence and hook L elbows
NOTE	This dance may be used as a mixer. At the end of Part I move ahead one person each time.
CIRCLE DANCE	Use Alternate Formation
PART I	MARCH
Beat 1-16	March 16 steps counterclockwise
17-32	March 16 steps clockwise
PART II	CLAP, PAT, CLAP, PAT; CLAP/CLAP, CLAP/CLAP, CLAP, HOLD; RUN
Beat 1-2	Clap own hands, pat thighs
3-4	Repeat beats 1-2
5-8	Clap own hands 5 times as above
9-16	Run in place with knees high or substitute scissors kicks, jumps or other in-place motions

Little Shoemaker (continued)

RHYTHMIC NOTATION

PART I

X	X	X	X	X	X	X	X
R	L	R	L	R	L	R	L

REPEAT 3X

PART II

CLAP	R HAND	CLAP	L HAND	CLAP CLAP	CLAP CLAP	CLAP	

X	X	X	X	X	X	X	X
R	L	R	L	R	L	R	L

REPEAT

LEAD-UP ACTIVITIES

Practice different locomotor movements to the music.

Practice "hand-jive" with a partner including a pattern as described.

TEACHING SUGGESTIONS

Do the Circle Dance as described before teaching the partner dance.

Do Part I of the partner dance as described—practice with a new partner if the mixer is to be used.

Practice Part II with partner (use partner beat then SAY AND DO).

CHAIR DANCING

CLAP, PAT thighs, CLAP, PAT thighs, CLAP 5 times as in the Circle Dance, then move feet APART, TOGETHER 4 times.

The dance may be adapted for wheelchairs.

Seven Jumps
Denmark

RECORD	Gateway GSLB 3528, *International Folk Dance Mixer* LPM 1623 *The World of Folk Dances*
INTRODUCTION	3 chords plus 1-note pickup
FORMATION	Open circle, hands may be joined for STEP HOPS
CHORUS	STEP HOP (repeat 6 times); JUMP
Beat 1-2	Step Hop forward clockwise beginning L foot
3-14	Repeat beats 1-2 six times alternating feet
15-16	Jump and turn to face counterclockwise
17-32	Repeat Part I, beats 1-16, forward counterclockwise, beginning R foot
TO SIMPLIFY	RUN 14 steps or WALK 7 steps then JUMP. Do not specify R foot or L foot.
PART I	
1st Chord	Raise R leg
2nd Chord	Lower R leg
3rd Chord	Prepare to repeat Chorus
CHORUS	Repeat Chorus, beats 1-32
PART II	
1st Chord	Raise R leg
2nd Chord	Lower R leg
3rd Chord	Raise L leg
4th Chord	Lower L leg
5th Chord	Prepare to repeat Chorus
CHORUS	Repeat Chorus, beats 1-32
PART III	Add: R knee almost touching floor, R knee touching floor
PART IV	L knee almost touching floor, L knee touching floor
PART V	R elbow almost touching floor, R elbow touching floor
PART VI	L elbow almost touching floor, L elbow touching floor
PART VII	Head almost touching floor, head touching floor
CHORUS	End with Chorus, beats 1-32

Seven Jumps (continued)

RHYTHMIC NOTATION

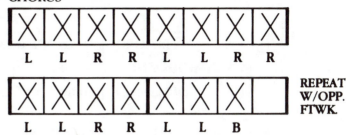

CHORUS

X	X	X	X	X	X	X
L	L	R	R	L	L	R	R

X	X	X	X	X	X	
L	L	R	R	L	L	B	

REPEAT W/OPP. FTWK.

LEAD-UP ACTIVITIES

Practice balancing on one foot then the other foot for different lengths of time.

Practice STEP HOP if authentic sequence in Part I is to be taught (individual's tempo).

TEACHING SUGGESTIONS

Teach the dance first with WALKS and RUNS and later substitute STEP HOP (individual's tempo then with SAY AND DO).

Practice the sequences in the parts of the dance.

Do the dance with the music.

CHAIR DANCING

Do Chorus in place.

PART I-VII

Substitute raising knee and lowering leg.
Substitute heel held off the floor and then lowered for KNEE TOUCH. Substitute elbow to thighs and head to thighs.

Sneaky Snake*
Novelty Dance
U.S.A.

RECORD	*Songs of Fox Hollow* by Tom T. Hall
INTRODUCTION	16 beats
FORMATION	Individuals facing one direction
PART I	CLAP, CLAP, PAT, PAT; BEND, STRAIGHTEN, BEND, STRAIGHTEN; KICK, STEP, KICK, STEP; TURN, 2, 3, 4
Beat 1-2	Clap hands 2 times
3-4	Pat thighs 2 times
5-6	Bend knees, Straighten knees
7-8	Repeat beats 5-6
9-10	Kick, Step
11-12	Kick other foot, Step
13-16	Step in place 4 steps turning 1/4 right; begin again facing new direction
NOTE	After the dance has been done 8 times, wait 4 beats before beginning again.
TO SIMPLIFY **Beat 5-8**	Repeat beats 1-4
13-16	Repeat beats 9-12

RHYTHMIC **NOTATION**	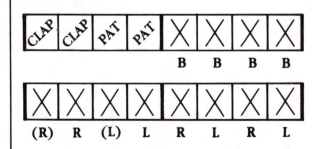
LEAD-UP **ACTIVITIES**	Practice KICK, STEP (individual's tempo). Practice BEND, STRAIGHTEN, BEND, STRAIGHTEN.
TEACHING **SUGGESTIONS**	Do the simplified version first and then make it more complicated. Practice the sequences with SAY AND DO before adding the music.
CHAIR DANCING	Beats 5-8—Substitute raising and lowering both heels.

*Choreographed by Phyllis Weikart.

Te Ve Orez
Tea and Rice
Israel

RECORD	Hed-Arzi MN 581
INTRODUCTION	8 beats
FORMATION	Three persons side by side facing counterclockwise
ALTERNATE FORMATION	Single circle
PART I	RUN (repeat 7 times); SLIDE (IN & OUT); WALK & CLAP (IN & OUT); RUN & CHANGE
Beat 1-8	Run 8 steps forward counterclockwise beginning L foot
9-12	Slide sideward left 4 times toward center of circle beginning L foot
13-16	Repeat beats 9-12 sideward right beginning R foot; turn to face center of circle (one behind the other)
17-20	Step L, R, L, R foot in (clap hands with steps)
21-24	Step L, R, L, R foot out (clap hands)
25-28	Run L, R, L, R foot forward counterclockwise
29-32	Middle person runs forward 4 steps to new group, outside persons run in place
CIRCLE DANCE	This dance may be done in a single circle without hands joined. Use a RUN on beats 1-8 and then SKIP on beats 25-32. May be taught without reference to R foot and L foot.

RHYTHMIC NOTATION

BEAT 1-8, 17-24, 25-32

X	X	X	X	X	X	X	X
L	R	L	R	L	R	L	R

BEAT 9-16

X	X	X	X	X	X	X	X
LR	LR	LR	LL	RL	RL	RL	RR

LEAD-UP ACTIVITIES	Practice combinations of running and sliding (individual's tempo).
	Practice sliding IN and OUT then walking IN and OUT (individual's tempo).

(continued)

Te Ve Orez (continued)

TEACHING SUGGESTIONS	Practice beats 1-16, the RUN followed by the SLIDE, with SAY AND DO.
	"Add on" the WALK IN and OUT and then the final 8 beats.
	Do the entire dance with SAY AND DO and add the music.
CHAIR DANCING	
Beat 1-8	Run in place
9-16	Side, close, side, touch left and right
17-24	Move feet away from the chair and toward the chair
25-32	Kick, step 4 times

Troika
Russia

RECORD	Folk Dancer MH 1059
INTRODUCTION	8 beats
FORMATION	Sets of 3 dancers side by side facing counterclockwise, inside hands held
PART I	RUN
Beat 1-16	Run 16 steps forward counterclockwise (light, long steps)
PART II	ARCHES
Beat 1-8	Dancer on right runs 8 steps under arch formed by the other 2 dancers and returns to place; center dancer follows through the arch
9-16	Repeat with dancer on left going through the arch formed by the other 2 dancers; center dancer follows
PART III	CIRCLE; ACCENT, ACCENT, ACCENT, HOLD Join hands in circle of 3 dancers
Beat 1-12	Run to left with 12 steps (3 Grapevine steps may be substituted for the runs)
13-16	Accent 3 steps and hold beat 16
17-32	Repeat Part III, beats 1-16, running to the right; open out to original side-by-side formation on final 3 accents

Troika (continued)

RHYTHMIC NOTATION

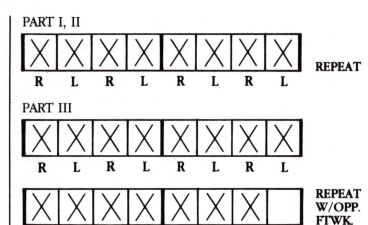

PART I, II

X	X	X	X	X	X	X	X	**REPEAT**
R	L	R	L	R	L	R	L	

PART III

X	X	X	X	X	X	X	X
R	L	R	L	R	L	R	L

X	X	X	X	X	X		**REPEAT W/OPP. FTWK.**
R	L	R	L	R	L		

LEAD-UP ACTIVITIES

Practice running in groups of 3; synchronize the running steps.

Practice running clockwise and counterclockwise in a circle of 3 dancers; synchronize the running steps.

TEACHING SUGGESTIONS

RUN 16 steps forward with SAY AND DO.

Practice the arch sequence first with a beat common to the 3 dancers and then a group SAY AND DO.

Practice circling left 12 steps plus 3 accents then right 12 steps plus 3 accents (SAY AND DO).

Do the entire dance with SAY AND DO and add the music.

CHAIR DANCING

May be adapted for wheelchairs.

Two-Part Dance*
U.S.A.

RECORD	"Blackberry Quadrille" RCA LPM 1620 *The World of Folk Dances;* "Rakes of Mallow" RCA LPM 1620 *The World of Folk Dances;* "Irish Washerwoman" RCA LPM 1622 *The World of Folk Dances;* Folkraft 1119 *La Raspa;* Windsor 7141 *Little Shoemaker;* "Circle Follow the Leader" Educational Activities AR 55 *Rhythm Stick Activities*
INTRODUCTION	Depends on music chosen
FORMATION	Persons moving around in free space
PART I	WALK
Beat 1-32	Walk 32 steps forward
PART II	PAT
Beat 1-32	Pat thighs 32 times
NOTE	Part I consists of locomotor movement. Part II consists of movement standing in one place.
VARIATION	
PART I	WALK tall, WALK short, WALK wide, WALK pidgeon-toed, WALK with feet turned out, WALK on toes, WALK on heels, HOP—change feet each 4 beats.
VARIATION	
PART II	PAT alternating hands; extend arms forward (out), bring arms back to shoulders (in); extend arms overhead (up), bring arms back to shoulders (down); with arms in running position alternate moving them forward; PAT, CLAP, SNAP, CLAP, BEND knees, STRAIGHTEN knees.

RHYTHMIC NOTATION

PART I & II

REPEAT 7X

LEAD-UP ACTIVITIES	Practice rhythmic coordination patterns. Practice walking to different pieces of music.
TEACHING SUGGESTIONS	Identify the walking beat and PAT the thighs, WALK to the music.
CHAIR DANCING	Do movements in place.

*Choreographed by Phyllis Weikart.

*Yankee Doodle**
U.S.A.

RECORD	Folkraft 1080X45
INTRODUCTION	8 beats
FORMATION	Free formation or open circle facing counterclockwise, no hands held
PART I	JUMP (repeat 7 times); WALK (repeat 7 times); BEND, STRAIGHTEN (repeat 3 times); IN, 2, 3, 4; OUT, 2, 3, 4
Beat 1-8	Jump 8 times
9-16	Walk 8 steps counterclockwise
17-24	Bend, straighten 4 times
25-28	Walk 4 steps in
29-32	Walk 4 steps out
VARIATION	Change locomotor movements to fit the age and interest of the group. Use only 2 different movement patterns (16 beats each). Have the group create the movement pattern.

RHYTHMIC NOTATION

BEAT 1-8, 17-24

BEAT 9-16

BEAT 25-32

LEAD-UP ACTIVITIES	Combine the locomotor and nonlocomotor movements to be used. Have the students suggest sequences.
TEACHING SUGGESTIONS	Practice the sequence the correct number of times with SAY AND DO.
CHAIR DANCING	Do any desired sequences while seated.

*Choreographed by Phyllis Weikart.

Zigeunerpolka*
Germany

RECORD	Folkraft 1486X45
INTRODUCTION	8 beats
FORMATION	Individuals in free formation
PART I	DOWN, 2, 3, 4; UP, 2, 3, 4
Beat 1-4	Step in place 4 times, body low
5-8	Step in place 4 times, body high
9-16	Repeat beats 1-8
VARIATION	BEND body 4 times each direction (sideward, sideward, forward, backward)
PART II	CLAP, CLAP, CLAP, CLAP; ACCENT, ACCENT, ACCENT, ACCENT
Beat 1-4	4 claps
5-8	4 accented steps
9-16	Repeat beats 1-8
PART III	JUMP, 2, 3, 4; 5, 6, 7, 8; KICK, 2, 3, 4; 5, 6, 7, 8
Beat 1-8	Jump in place 8 times
9-16	Kick legs backward 8 times

RHYTHMIC NOTATION

PART I

REPEAT

PART II

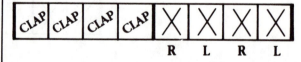

REPEAT

PART III

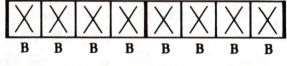

*Choreographed by Phyllis Weikart.

Zigeunerpolka (continued)

LEAD-UP ACTIVITIES	Practice stepping with body low then with body tall (individual's tempo) or BEND 4 times in each direction.
	Practice 4 CLAPS plus 4 ACCENTED STEPS (individual's tempo).
	JUMP 8 times then KICK legs backward 8 times (individual's tempo).
TEACHING SUGGESTIONS	Practice the parts of the dance with SAY AND DO.
	Ask the students "What comes first? Second? Third?"
	PAT thighs to the beat of the music.
	Do the dance with the music.
CHAIR DANCING PART I AND II	Do sequences as described.
PART III Beat 9-16	Do apart/together with feet.

Locomotor Movement II

Characteristics:

1. There is reference to "right" and "left" foot.

2. There is a held beat at the end of an 8-beat or 16-beat phrase.

3. There are 2-beat sequences executed sideward.

4. There are alternating 2-beat sequences.

5. There are 4-beat sequences in place.

6. There is a single divided beat within 4 beats.

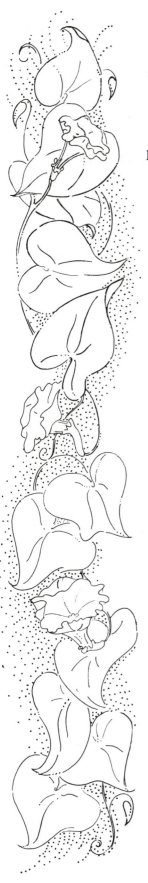

Áis Giórgis
St. George
Greece

RECORD	Folkraft 1466
INTRODUCTION	4 beats
FORMATION	Front basket (open circle in "W" position may be substituted)
PART I	WALK, WALK; SIDE, TOUCH; SIDE, HEEL; SIDE, HEEL; STEP, BRUSH
Beat 1-2	Step R foot, L foot forward counterclockwise and turn to face center
3	Step R foot sideward right
4	Touch L foot behind R foot
5	Step L foot sideward left
6	Extend R heel diagonally forward right
7	Step R foot sideward right
8	Extend L heel diagonally forward left
9	Step L foot next to R foot
10	Brush R foot in and toward the right

RHYTHMIC NOTATION

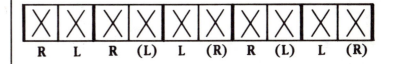

R   L   R   (L)   L   (R)   R   (L)   L   (R)

LEAD-UP ACTIVITIES

WALK to the music.

Practice the 2-beat sequences as alternating foot patterns using individual's tempo:
SIDE, HEEL, SIDE, HEEL
SIDE, TOUCH, SIDE, TOUCH
SIDE, BRUSH, SIDE, BRUSH.

(continued)

Áis Giórgis (continued)

TEACHING SUGGESTIONS

Practice SIDE, HEEL, SIDE, HEEL beginning L foot (SAY AND DO).

Practice SIDE, TOUCH, SIDE, HEEL beginning R foot (SAY AND DO).

Practice SIDE, HEEL, SIDE, BRUSH beginning R foot (SAY AND DO).

Practice SIDE, TOUCH, SIDE, HEEL;
SIDE, HEEL, SIDE, BRUSH beginning R foot (SAY AND DO).

Practice WALK, WALK, SIDE, TOUCH beginning R foot.

Do the entire sequence with language (SAY AND DO) then add music.

CHAIR DANCING

WALK, WALK — step R foot, L foot in place.
SIDE, TOUCH — step R foot, touch L foot behind R foot.
SIDE, HEEL — step L foot, extend R heel forward.

Ajde Noga Za Nogama
Let's Go Foot Behind Feet
Yugoslavia (Croatia)

RECORD	AMAN Vol. 6
INTRODUCTION	12 beats
FORMATION	Broken circle, escort hold (R hand on hip, L hand holding elbow of person to left)
PART I	FORWARD, 2, 3, 4; SIDE, TOUCH, OUT, TOUCH
Beat 1	Step L foot forward clockwise
2	Step R foot forward clockwise
3	Step L foot forward clockwise
4	Step R foot forward clockwise and turn to face center
5	Step L foot sideward left
6	Touch R foot next to L foot
7	Step R foot out (facing center)
8	Touch L foot next to R foot

RHYTHMIC NOTATION

L R L R L (R) R (L)

LEAD-UP ACTIVITIES	WALK to the music.
	Do SIDE, TOUCH, SIDE, TOUCH without the music (individual's tempo).
	Do OUT, TOUCH, IN, TOUCH without the music—begin R foot OUT (individual's tempo).
TEACHING SUGGESTIONS	Practice SIDE, TOUCH, OUT, TOUCH beginning with L foot (SAY AND DO).
	Practice 4 slow walking steps to the left beginning with L foot and add the SIDE, TOUCH.
	Practice the whole sequence "adding on" the OUT, TOUCH.
	SAY AND DO the dance; then add music.
CHAIR DANCING	
Beat 1-4	Step L, R, L, R foot in place
5	Step L foot sideward left
6	Touch R foot next to L foot
7	Step diagonally backward right
8	Touch L foot next to R foot

Alley Cat
U.S.A.

RECORD	Atco 45-6226
INTRODUCTION	3-note pickup
FORMATION	Individual dance, dancers in free space
PART I	TOUCH, TOUCH, TOUCH, STEP
Beat 1	Touch R foot sideward right
2	Touch R foot next to L foot
3	Touch R foot sideward right
4	Step R foot next to L foot
5-8	Repeat beats 1-4 using L foot
	TOUCH, TOUCH, TOUCH, STEP
9	Touch R foot backward
10	Touch R foot next to L foot
11	Touch R foot backward
12	Step R foot next to L foot
13-16	Repeat beats 9-12 using L foot
	UP, TOUCH, UP, STEP
17	Raise R knee up in front of body
18	Touch R foot next to L foot
19	Raise R knee up in front of body
20	Step R foot next to L foot
21-24	Repeat beats 17-20 using L foot
	UP, STEP, UP, STEP; JUMP, HOLD, CLAP, HOLD
25	Raise R knee up in front of body
26	Step R foot next to L foot
27	Raise L knee up in front of body
28	Step L foot next to R foot
29-30	Jump turning 1/4 right or pat thighs without turn
31-32	Clap once and hold beat 32
	Repeat dance facing new direction (if turn has been executed)
NOTE	No R foot or L foot is necessary. For more complexity add arm movements from the rhythmic competency teaching progression (see *Chapter II*) to the dance.
RHYTHMIC NOTATION	BEAT 1-24

X	X	X	X	X	X	X	X	REPEAT 2X
(R)	(R)	(R)	R	(L)	(L)	(L)	L	

Alley Cat (continued)

BEAT 25-32

(R) R (L) L B

LEAD-UP ACTIVITIES

PAT the thighs and CLAP the hands to each 2 beats of music (PAT, CLAP).

PAT the thighs 3 times and CLAP the hands on the last beat of each 4 beats of music (PAT, PAT, PAT, CLAP).

Balance on one leg for 3 beats and change feet on the 4th beat.

Practice touching the foot not bearing weight 3 times before changing feet. Encourage touching at different angles—sideward, forward, backward—individual's tempo.

Practice raising and lowering each leg, touching the foot as the leg is lowered (individual's tempo).

TEACHING SUGGESTIONS

Practice the TOUCH, TOUCH, TOUCH, STEP with each foot using the sideward touching patterns and then the backward touching patterns.

Practice 1 sideward pattern to each side followed by 1 backward pattern to each side. (Do not specify R foot or L foot.) SAY AND DO.

Practice UP, TOUCH, UP, STEP with each foot.

Practice UP, STEP with each foot.

Combine 2 patterns of UP, TOUCH, UP, STEP (1 with each foot) with 2 patterns of UP, STEP (1 with each foot) SAY AND DO.

Combine the sideward, backward, raising and lowering patterns and add the thigh PAT, CLAP or the JUMP, CLAP.

SAY AND DO entire dance; then add music.

CHAIR DANCING
Beat 9-16
29-30

Extend touching foot diagonally backward
Use the thigh pat

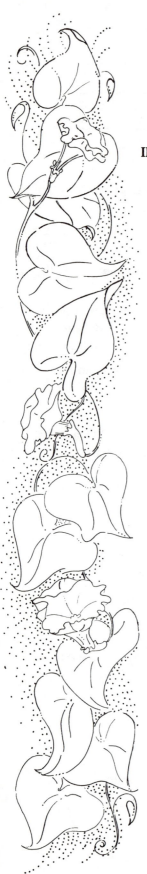

Amos Moses
Novelty
U.S.A.

RECORD	RCA Gold Standard 447-0896
INTRODUCTION	12 beats
FORMATION	Individual free formation

PART I	HEEL, STEP; HEEL, STEP; IN, BACK; TURN, CLOSE
Beat 1	Extend R heel in
2	Step R foot next to L foot
3	Extend L heel in
4	Step L foot next to R foot
5	Step R foot in with 1/4 turn left
6	Step L foot crossing in back of R foot
7	Step R foot sideward and turn 1/2 clockwise
8	Step L foot next to R foot
TO SIMPLIFY	Don't indicate a specific foot for HEEL, STEP. Do 4 steps in place while turning 1/4 right.

RHYTHMIC NOTATION

(R)   R   (L)   L   R   L   R   L

LEAD-UP ACTIVITIES

Practice OUT, IN with one arm and then the other, extending the arm forward from the shoulder (the arm not used should remain still with the hand touching the shoulder).

Practice HEEL, STEP with each foot (individual's tempo).

Practice executing 1/4 TURNS using 4 steps in place.

Practice 1/2 TURNS on 1 foot followed by a CLOSE to the other foot.

Amos Moses (continued)

TEACHING SUGGESTIONS	Practice simplified dance as described without reference to R or L foot.
	Practice simplified dance beginning R foot (SAY AND DO).
	Practice beats 5-8 to incorporate the appropriate TURNS of the body. Note for the group which way they face for beats 5-6 and beats 7-8.
	Practice the transition from 1/2 TURN, CLOSE to HEEL, STEP.
	Do the dance with SAY AND DO; then add music.
CHAIR DANCING **Beat 5-8**	Step in place

Apat-Apat
Four by Four
Philippines

RECORD	Folk Dancer MH 2022
INTRODUCTION	Pickup plus 16 beats
FORMATION	Partners, double circle facing counterclockwise, inside hands joined
PART I	FORWARD, 2, 3, TURN; FORWARD, 2, 3, TURN; AWAY, 2, 3, 4; TOWARD, 2, 3, 4; FORWARD, 2, 3, 4; BACKWARD, 2, 3, 4; AROUND, 2, 3, 4; CHANGE, 2, 3, 4
Beat 1-4	Step R, L, R, L foot forward counterclockwise (on beat 4 release hands and execute 1/2 turn right to face clockwise)
5-8	Step R, L, R, L foot forward clockwise, end facing partner
9-12	Back up away from each other—R, L, R, L foot
13-16	Walk toward each other—R, L, R, L foot, end with 1/4 turn right (men face clockwise, women counterclockwise)
17-20	Walk forward 4 steps (inside circle clockwise, outside counterclockwise)
21-24	Walk backward 4 steps to meet partner (turn to face partner)
24-28	Turn with partner 4 steps clockwise (R forearms together)
29-32	Outside person turn again in 4 steps while inside person walks R, L, R, L foot forward counterclockwise to new partner
NOTE	Keep steps small and the movements continuous. This should not be a march. No R foot or L foot is necessary.

RHYTHMIC NOTATION

PART I

REPEAT 3X

Apat-Apat *(continued)*

LEAD-UP ACTIVITIES	Practice walking 4 steps turning 1/4 then moving in the new direction either FORWARD or BACKWARD until persons are comfortable with directional changes (individual's tempo).
	Practice walking 4 steps executing a 1/2 TURN on the 4th step; then WALK 4 steps in the other direction.
	Practice backing up 4 steps followed by walking FORWARD 4 steps.
TEACHING SUGGESTIONS	Practice each combination of 8 beats with a partner (partner beat).
	Practice the transitions after each set of 8 beats.
	Practice the 4-step TURN with a partner (partner beat).
	Combine the parts of the dance (SAY AND DO).
CHAIR DANCING	May be adapted for wheelchairs.

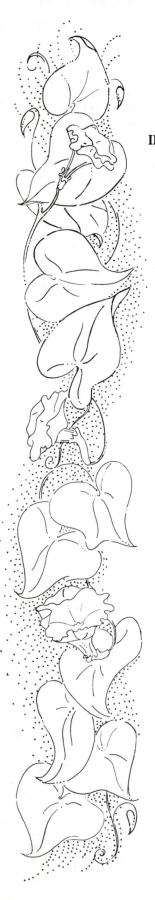

Bannielou Lambaol
France (Brittany)

RECORD	Worldtone WT 10014
INTRODUCTION	One-chord
FORMATION	Circle or broken circle facing center, little fingers joined
PART I	SIDE, CLOSE; SIDE, CLOSE; SIDE, CLOSE; SIDE, TOUCH
Beat 1	Step L foot sideward left on ball of foot
2	Step R foot next to L foot
3-6	Repeat beats 1-2 two times
7	Step L foot sideward left
8	Touch R foot next to L foot
NOTE:	Arms make a forward circle with each 2 beats.
	TOUCH/TOUCH, TOUCH/STEP; SIDE, TOUCH; TOUCH/TOUCH, TOUCH/STEP; SIDE, CLOSE
9	Touch R foot in, push arms in
&	Touch R foot next to L foot, pull arms out
10	Touch R foot in, push arms in
&	Step R foot next to L foot, pull arms out
11-12	Repeat beats 7-8, circling arms
13-14	Repeat beats 9-10
15-16	Repeat beats 1-2 (side, close)
NOTE	Music stops momentarily so wait to begin dance each time.

RHYTHMIC NOTATION

BEAT 1-8

L   R   L   R   L   R   L   (R)

BEAT 9-16

(R)(R)(R)R   L   (R) (R)(R)(R)R   L   R

Bannielou Lambaol (continued)

LEAD-UP ACTIVITIES	Practice walking sideward different ways including the SIDE, CLOSE (individual's tempo).
	Practice the TOUCH, TOUCH, TOUCH, STEP sequence in different ways (individual's tempo).
	Practice SIDE, TOUCH bringing the touching foot next to the stepping foot (individual's tempo).
	Practice moving both arms in a forward circle.
	Practice pushing both arms forward away and pulling them toward the body in 2-beat patterns.
TEACHING SUGGESTIONS	Practice moving sideward left with 3 SIDE, CLOSE steps followed by a SIDE, TOUCH (SAY AND DO).
	Practice TOUCH/TOUCH, TOUCH/STEP beginning R foot "adding on" first SIDE, TOUCH (sideward left) and then the next time "add on" SIDE, CLOSE (SAY AND DO).
	Combine the SIDE, CLOSE pattern (first 8 beats) with the second 8-beat pattern (SAY AND DO).
	Learn the arm pattern after the foot pattern is secure— use no language with the arms.
	SAY the foot pattern while executing the arm pattern— use no movement of the feet in this learning stage.
	Add the arm pattern to the foot pattern with SAY AND DO and then with music.
CHAIR DANCING	Change sideward steps to steps in place, or do the arm movements alone.

Bele Kawe
Creole-African (Caribbean Island of Carriacou)

RECORD	AR36 *African Heritage Dances*
INTRODUCTION	8 beats
FORMATION	Free formation or circle, no hands joined
PART I	IN/OUT, CLOSE
Beat 1	Step R foot in with bent knees (men with backs of hands on hip pockets, ladies hold long skirts)
&	Step L foot out
2	Step R foot next to L foot
3-4	Repeat beats 1-2 with opposite footwork
5-16	Repeat Part I, beats 1-4, three times
TO SIMPLIFY	IN, TOUCH, OUT, TOUCH (the TOUCH is next to the other foot).
PART II	HEEL, OUT, HEEL, OUT; HEEL, OUT, HEEL, OUT; HEEL, IN, HEEL, IN; HEEL, IN, HEEL, IN
Beat 1	Touch R heel diagonally sideward right (arms extended sideward, elbows slightly bent)
2	Step R foot slightly out
3	Touch L heel diagonally sideward left
4	Step L foot slightly out
5-8	Repeat beats 1-4
9-16	Repeat Part II, beats 1-8, moving in
TO SIMPLIFY	8 steps OUT, 8 steps IN.
PART III	TURN, 2, 3, JUMP
Beat 1-3	Step R, L, R foot turning right a full wide turn (arms sideward, bend body forward slightly)
4	Jump with feet apart (the jump is the men's part; women hold beat 4 and may shake shoulders)
5-8	Repeat beats 1-4 turning left beginning L foot
9-16	Repeat Part III, beats 1-8
TO SIMPLIFY	Step in place without TURN.
NOTE	No R foot or L foot is necessary.
RHYTHMIC NOTATION	PART I

PART I

X X	X	X X	X
RL	R	LR	L

REPEAT 3X

PART II

X	X	X	X
(R)	R	(L)	L

REPEAT 3X

Bele Kawe (continued)

PART III

R   L   R   B

REPEAT 3X
W/OPP.
FTWK.

LEAD-UP ACTIVITIES	Practice a rocking motion of IN, HOLD, OUT, HOLD then IN, TOUCH, OUT, TOUCH (individual's tempo).
	Practice walking FORWARD and BACKWARD in a 2-beat sequence using a TOUCH before the STEP. TOUCH on beat 1 and STEP on beat 2 (individual's tempo).
	Practice turning right and left in 3 steps with a JUMP on the 4th beat (individual's tempo).
TEACHING SUGGESTIONS	Part I — Use the simplification IN, TOUCH, OUT, TOUCH until dancers are able to do the IN/OUT, CLOSE successfully.
	Practice 4 HEEL, OUT steps followed by 4 HEEL, IN steps. HEEL, OUT is much more difficult because the foot is moved farther following the TOUCH of the heel (SAY AND DO).
	Practice the transition of the IN, TOUCH, OUT, TOUCH to the HEEL, OUT (the TOUCH to the HEEL is difficult).
	Combine Parts I and II, SAY AND DO.
	Practice the 3-step TURN followed by the JUMP moving right then left (SAY AND DO).
	Practice the transition from the final HEEL, IN to the TURN right.
	Do Parts II and III, SAY AND DO.
	Practice the transition from the final JUMP to the IN, TOUCH at the beginning.
	SAY AND DO entire dance, then add music.
CHAIR DANCING PART I	Do as described.
PART II	Do the HEEL, OUT and HEEL, IN in place or begin with the feet away from the chair in order to move them toward and away from the chair.
PART III	Do 3 steps in place and add a JUMP motion of both feet.

Chiotikos
Syrto from Chios
Greece

RECORD	Tikva T-131 *Greek Dance Party*
INTRODUCTION	16 beats
FORMATION	Circle or broken circle, hands joined in "W" position
PART I	WALK, WALK; SIDE, LIFT; SIDE, LIFT
Beat 1	Step R foot forward counterclockwise
2	Step L foot forward counterclockwise, and turn to face center
3	Step R foot sideward right
4	Lift L foot in front of R leg
5	Step L foot sideward left
6	Lift R foot in front of L leg
7-24	Repeat Part I, beats 1-6, three times
PART II	TURN, TURN; SIDE, LIFT; SIDE, LIFT
Beat 1-2	Step R foot, L foot turning full turn counterclockwise; clap on beat 1
3-6	Repeat Part I, beats 3-6
7-24	Repeat Part II, beats 1-6, three times
PART III	SIDE/BACK, SIDE/BACK; SIDE, LIFT; SIDE, LIFT
Beat 1	Step R foot sideward right
&	Step L foot crossing in back of R foot
2 &	Repeat beat 1 &
3-6	Repeat Part I, beats 3-6
7-12	Repeat Part III, beats 1-6
13-14	Repeat Part III, beats 1-2
15-16	Step R foot, L foot in place

RHYTHMIC NOTATION

PART I & II

X	X	X	X	X	X	**REPEAT 3X**
R	L	R	(L)	L	(R)	

PART III

X/X	X/X	X	X	X	X	**REPEAT**
RL	RL	R	(L)	L	(R)	

PART III   BEAT 13-16

X/X	X/X	X	X
RL	RL	R	L

Chiotikos (continued)

LEAD-UP ACTIVITIES	Review the basic step of the *Hasapikos* (individual's tempo). Practice a 3-step TURN followed by a LIFT on the 4th beat (individual's tempo). Practice SIDE/BACK in a divided beat rhythm (individual's tempo).
TEACHING SUGGESTIONS	Do Part I, SAY AND DO, then add music. Help the students understand the change of the first 2 WALKS in Part I to the full TURN in Part II to 2 SIDE/BACK steps in Part III. Do the sequence of Part III that ends with 2 steps in place and practice the transition to Part I; SAY AND DO. Do the dance, SAY AND DO, then add music.
CHAIR DANCING	Change the WALK and TURN to steps in place and the SIDE/BACK to SIDE/CLOSE.

Close Encounters*
Novelty
U.S.A.

RECORD	PSR 45, 073 *California Strut*
INTRODUCTION	32 beats or begin with no introduction
FORMATION	Partners side by side facing counterclockwise
PART I	FORWARD, 2, 3, KICK; BACKWARD, 2, 3, TOUCH
Beat 1	Step R foot forward counterclockwise
2	Step L foot forward counterclockwise
3	Step R foot forward counterclockwise
4	Kick L foot forward counterclockwise
5-8	Repeat Part I, beats 1-4, backward beginning L foot (moving clockwise)—touch beat 8
9-16	Repeat Part I, beats 1-8, and turn to face partner (inside person has back to center of circle)
NOTE	To increase complexity, move sideward right and left, beats 1-8.
PART II	AROUND, 2, 3, 4; 5, 6, 7, 8; HIT, HIT, BUMP, BUMP; CHANGE, 2, 3, 4
Beat 1-8	Do-sa-do 8 steps (partners move forward passing R shoulders; move back to back; then step backward to place passing L shoulders)
9-10	Partners hit hands 2 times
11-12	Partners bump hips 2 times
13-16	Inside person: walk 4 steps forward counterclockwise to new partner Outside person: turn clockwise 4 steps in place or hold 4 beats
NOTE	No R foot or L foot is necessary.

*Choreographed by Phyllis Weikart.

Close Encounters (continued)

RHYTHMIC NOTATION

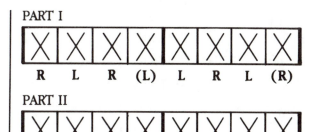

PART I

X	X	X	X	X	X	X	X	**REPEAT**
R	L	R	(L)	L	R	L	(R)	

PART II

X	X	X	X	X	X	X	X
R	L	R	L	R	L	R	L

HIT	HIT	BUMP	BUMP	X	X	X	X
				R	L	R	L

LEAD-UP ACTIVITIES

Move forward 3 steps and CLAP and backward 3 steps and CLAP (individual's tempo), then change to FORWARD, 2, 3, KICK and BACKWARD, 2, 3, TOUCH (individual's tempo).

Review or learn a DO-SA-DO.

TEACHING SUGGESTIONS

Partners practice Part I with language, SAY AND DO.

Partners practice transition from Part I to the DO-SA-DO.

Partners do the sequence HIT, HIT, BUMP, BUMP, then SAY AND DO.

Partners SAY AND DO Part II, adding the change of partners.

CHAIR DANCING

Move feet away and toward the chair for the FORWARD and BACKWARD.

Step in place for the DO-SA-DO or away and toward the chair.

Substitute PAT, PAT, CLAP, CLAP for the HIT, HIT BUMP, BUMP.

Cumberland Square
England

RECORD	Folkraft 1241
INTRODUCTION	4 beats
FORMATION	Square sets
PART I	SLIDE
Beat 1-8	Head couples 8 slides across the set, men passing back to back
9-16	Head couples 8 slides back again, women passing back to back
17-32	Repeat beats 1-16 (side couples)
PART II	STAR
Beat 1-8	Head couples walk 8 steps clockwise with R hands joined in star formation (skipping steps may be substituted)
9-16	Head couples walk 8 steps counterclockwise with L hands joined in star formation
17-32	Repeat beats 1-16 (side couples)
PART III	BASKET
Beat 1-16	Head couples form a back basket and buzz turn clockwise
17-32	Repeat beats 1-16 (side couples)
PART IV	CIRCLE; PROMENADE
Beat 1-16	All join hands and walk (or skip) 16 steps clockwise
17-32	Promenade 16 steps counterclockwise with partner (end in original position)

RHYTHMIC NOTATION

PART I MEN

LR LR LR LR LR LR LR LL

REPEAT W/OPP. FTWK.

PART II

R L R L R L R L

REPEAT

Cumberland Square (continued)

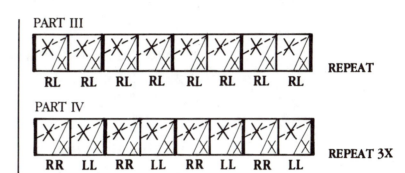

PART III

RL RL RL RL RL RL RL RL **REPEAT**

PART IV

RR LL RR LL RR LL RR LL **REPEAT 3X**

LEAD-UP ACTIVITIES	Practice SLIDE and SKIP and GALLOP (individual's tempo).
	Practice SLIDE and SKIP with a partner (partner beat).
	Practice SLIDE and SKIP using a circle formation (group beat).
	Practice the STAR formation.
	Practice PROMENADE with a partner moving around the room (partner beat).
TEACHING SUGGESTIONS	Form square sets and practice the SLIDE (SAY AND DO); add the music.
	Practice the STAR figure.
	Practice the BUZZ TURN for the BASKET with partners holding both hands then add BASKET formation.
	Practice the 4th figure (SKIP left and PROMENADE right).
	Do the entire dance with music.
CHAIR DANCING	May be modified for wheelchairs.

Debka Daluna
Israel (Arab)

RECORD	Tikva T-100 *Debka*
INTRODUCTION	8 beats
FORMATION	Short lines in the shoulder hold, "T" position

PART I	SIDE, BACK; SIDE, STAMP; SIDE, STAMP
Beat 1	Step R foot sideward right
2	Step L foot crossing in back of R foot
3	Step R foot sideward right
4	Stamp L foot sideward left
5	Step L foot sideward left
6	Stamp R foot sideward right
7-24	Repeat Part I, beats 1-6, three times
NOTE	Part I is done with knees slightly bent, backs straight.
PART II	IN, HOP; SQUAT, STRAIGHTEN; OUT, STEP/STEP; OUT, STEP/STEP
Beat 1	Step R foot in
2	Hop R foot and extend L heel in
3	Jump into squat position with R foot slightly ahead of L foot
4	Rise up extending R heel
5	Step R foot out
6 &	Step L foot, R foot
7	Step L foot out
8 &	Step R foot, L foot
9-16	Repeat Part II, beats 1-8
TO SIMPLIFY	Substitute JUMP, JUMP; BEND, STRAIGHTEN for beats 1-4 and OUT, 2; 3, 4 for beats 5-8.

RHYTHMIC NOTATION

PART I

R   L   R   (L)   L   (R)   **REPEAT 5X**

PART II

R   R   B   L   R   LR   L   RL   **REPEAT**

Debka Daluna *(continued)*

LEAD-UP ACTIVITIES	Practice SIDE, BACK (individual's tempo). Practice SIDE, STAMP (individual's tempo). Practice 4 JUMPS in sequence, squatting on the third JUMP (individual's tempo). Practice 4 JUMPS followed by 4 BACKWARD steps (individual's tempo).
TEACHING SUGGESTIONS	Practice SIDE, STAMP; SIDE, STAMP beginning R foot (SAY AND DO). Have students "precede" SIDE, STAMP; SIDE, STAMP with SIDE, BACK beginning R foot. Do Part I several times with SAY AND DO. Do JUMP, JUMP; JUMP, JUMP; OUT, 2; 3, 4 then substitute JUMP, JUMP; SQUAT, STRAIGHTEN; OUT, 2; 3, 4. Do Part II several times (SAY AND DO). Practice the transition from Part II to Part I. Practice the dance with SAY AND DO; then add music.
CHAIR DANCING **PART I** **PART II**	 Substitute SIDE, CLOSE for SIDE, BACK. JUMPS—Bounce both feet to the floor 4 times. OUT, 2; 3, 4—Step in place.

Dimna Juda
Macedonia

RECORD	Festival 4001 "Kopacka"—1st half
INTRODUCTION	4 beats
FORMATION	Broken circle, leader at right; hands joined in "W" position

PART I	WALK, WALK; SIDE, TOUCH; SIDE, TOUCH
Beat 1	Step R foot forward counterclockwise
2	Step L foot forward counterclockwise
3	Step R foot sideward right
4	Touch L foot diagonally left
5	Step L foot sideward left
6	Touch R foot diagonally right
7-30	Repeat beats 1-6 four times
31-32	Step R foot sideward, touch L foot
33-38	Repeat beats 1-6 forward clockwise beginning L foot
39-40	Step L foot sideward left touch R foot

RHYTHMIC NOTATION

PART I BEAT 1-30

R   L   R   (L)   L   (R)   **REPEAT 4X**

BEAT 31-32

R   (L)

BEAT 33-40

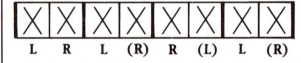

L   R   L   (R)   R   (L)   L   (R)

LEAD-UP ACTIVITIES

Practice SIDE, TOUCH; SIDE, TOUCH (individual's tempo).

Practice walking in one direction followed by 3 SIDE, TOUCH patterns then walking in the other direction beginning with the opposite foot (individual's tempo).

Dimna Juda (continued)

TEACHING SUGGESTIONS	Practice SIDE, TOUCH; SIDE, TOUCH beginning R foot (SAY AND DO).
	"Precede" the SIDE, TOUCH; SIDE, TOUCH with WALK, WALK beginning R foot (SAY AND DO).
	Practice 3 SIDE, TOUCH patterns beginning R foot then reverse the WALK, WALK and do 3 SIDE, TOUCH patterns beginning L foot.
	Do the entire sequence with SAY AND DO, then add the music.
CHAIR DANCING	Substitute steps in place for WALK.

Dučec
Yugoslavia

RECORD	Folkraft 1491X45
INTRODUCTION	None
FORMATION	Free formation
PART I	JUMP, JUMP; JUMP, JUMP; APART/UP, APART/UP; APART/UP, DOWN
Beat 1	Jump to forward stride position, (L foot forward, R foot backward)
2	Jump to R foot forward, L foot backward
3-4	Repeat beats 1-2
5	Jump to sideward stride (feet apart)
&	Jump into air clicking heels—legs straight
6-7	Repeat beats 5 & two times
8	Land with feet together
9-16	Repeat Part I, beats 1-8
TO SIMPLIFY	Part I, beats 5-8, JUMP sideward 3 times and then together (leave out the "&" beats).

(continued)

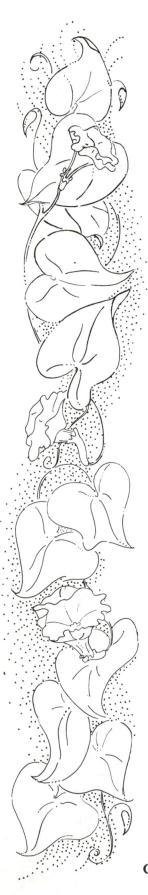

Dučec (continued)

PART II	JUMP, JUMP; JUMP/JUMP, JUMP
Beat 1	Jump to forward stride position (L foot forward, R foot backward)
2	Jump to R foot forward, L foot backward
3	Jump in place
&	Jump in place
4	Jump in place
5-16	Repeat Part II, beats 1-4, three times

RHYTHMIC NOTATION

PART I

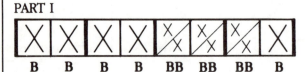

B   B   B   B   BB   BB   BB   B   **REPEAT**

PART II

B   B   BB   B   **REPEAT 3X**

LEAD-UP ACTIVITIES

Practice forward stride JUMPS (one foot forward and one foot backward) alternating feet (individual's tempo).

Practice sideward stride JUMPS, feet apart sideward (individual's tempo).

Practice 3 sideward stride JUMPS followed by a JUMP with feet together (individual's tempo).

Practice moving from forward stride to sideward stride JUMPS.

Practice JUMPS in a rhythmic pattern of 1, 2, 3 &, 4 (individual's tempo).

Practice bringing the feet together in the air between sideward stride JUMPS (individual's tempo).

TEACHING SUGGESTIONS

Practice 4 forward stride JUMPS followed by 3 sideward stride JUMPS and end with a JUMP, feet together: JUMP, JUMP; JUMP, JUMP; SIDE; SIDE; SIDE, TOGETHER; SAY AND DO.

Practice JUMP, JUMP; JUMP/JUMP, JUMP with SAY AND DO.

Put the dance together with SAY AND DO, then add music.

After the dance has been executed successfully, add the APART/UP pattern of Part I.

CHAIR DANCING

Do as described.

The Entertainer*
Novelty
U.S.A.

RECORD	*The Sting* soundtrack MCA 390, Side 2, Band 1
INTRODUCTION	8 beats
FORMATION	Open circle, no hands joined
PART I	FORWARD, 2, 3, 4; RUN/2, 3/4, 5/6, 7... SCISSORS KICK
Beat 1	Step R foot forward counterclockwise
2-4	Step L, R, L foot forward counterclockwise
5-8	Run 7 steps counterclockwise beginning R foot and hold the final beat &
9-16	Repeat beats 1-8 forward clockwise beginning L foot
17-24	Repeat beats 1-8 forward counterclockwise beginning R foot
25-32	Kick legs in—2 kicks for each beat
PART II	SIDE, BACK, SIDE, BACK; SIDE/BACK, SIDE/BACK, SIDE/BACK, SIDE . . . SCISSORS KICK
Beat 1	Step R foot sideward right
2	Step L foot crossing in back of R
3-4	Repeat beats 1-2
5-7	Repeat beats 1-2 three times (5 & 6 & 7 &)
8	Step R foot sideward
9-24	Repeat beats 1-8 sideward left then sideward right again
25-32	Kick legs out—2 kicks for each beat
PART III	HEEL, STEP
Beat 1	Extend R heel in
2	Step R foot in place
3	Extend L heel in
4	Step L foot in place
5-16	Repeat beats 1-4 three times
	TOUCH, STEP
17	Touch R toe out
18	Step R foot in place
19	Touch L toe out
20	Step L foot in place
21-32	Repeat beats 17-20 three times

*Choreographed by Phyllis Weikart.

(continued)

The Entertainer (continued)

	STEP, KICK, STEP, TOUCH
33	Step R foot in place
34	Kick L foot in
35	Step L foot next to R foot
36	Touch R toe out
37-44	Repeat beats 33-36 two times
45-46	Repeat beats 33-34
47-48	Step in place L, R, L, R foot (47 &, 48 &)
49-64	Repeat beats 33-46 beginning L foot and end with 4 steps (R, L, R, L foot)

PART IV	SIDE, CLOSE, SIDE, CLOSE; SIDE/CLOSE, SIDE/CLOSE, SIDE/CLOSE, SIDE . . . SCISSORS KICK
Beat 1	Step R foot sideward right
2	Step L foot next to right
3-4	Repeat beats 1-2
5-7	Repeat beats 1-2 three times (5 &, 6 &, 7 &)
8	Step R foot sideward right
9-24	Repeat beats 1-8 sideward left then sideward right again
25-26	4 kicks in (2 to a beat)
27-28	4 kicks out
29-30	4 kicks in
31-32	3 steps in place L, R, L foot as music retards

RHYTHMIC NOTATION

PART I, II & IV   BEAT 1-24

R   L   R   L   RL   RL   RL   R   REPEAT 2X W/OPP. FTWK.

PART III

(R)   R   (L)   L   (R)   R   (L)   L   REPEAT 3X

BEAT 33-64

R   (L)   L   (R)   R   (L)   L   (R)

R   (L)   L   (R)   R   (L)   LR   LR   REPEAT W/OPP. FTWK.

The Entertainer *(continued)*

LEAD-UP ACTIVITIES	Practice combining single beat and divided beat movement sequences using WALK, RUN combination, SIDE, BACK combination and SIDE, CLOSE combination (individual's tempo).
	Practice HEEL, STEP and TOUCH, STEP patterns (individual's tempo).
	Practice CHARLESTON (STEP, KICK, STEP, TOUCH) with each foot as the starting foot (individual's tempo).
	Practice SCISSORS KICKS IN and OUT (individual's tempo).
TEACHING SUGGESTIONS	Practice Parts I and II with SAY AND DO and add music.
	Practice Part III with SAY AND DO.
	Practice the transition in the CHARLESTON from one foot to the other (individual's tempo).
	Practice Part IV with SAY AND DO.
	Do the entire dance to the music.
CHAIR DANCING	Use SCISSORS KICKS forward instead of backward.
	Do remainder of dance as described using small steps.

Erev Shel Shoshanim*
A Night of Roses
Israel

RECORD	Educational Record #2 *Israeli Dance*
INTRODUCTION	8 beats
FORMATION	Circle facing center, hands joined in "V" position
PART I	WALK, 2, 3, 4; 5, 6, SIDE, TOUCH
Beat 1	Step R foot forward counterclockwise
2	Step L foot forward counterclockwise
3-6	Step R, L, R, L, forward counterclockwise and turn to face center
7	Step R foot sideward right
8	Touch L foot next to R foot
9-16	Repeat Part I, beats 1-8, forward clockwise beginning L foot
TO SIMPLIFY	WALK 8 steps counterclockwise then 8 steps clockwise.
	SIDE, BACK, SIDE, BACK; SIDE, BACK, SIDE, TOUCH
17	Step R foot sideward right
18	Step L foot crossing in back of R foot
19-22	Repeat beats 17-18 two times
23	Step R foot sideward right
24	Touch L foot next to R foot
25-32	Repeat beats 17-24 sideward left beginning L foot
PART II	SWAY, SWAY, SWAY, SWAY; IN, IN, OUT, OUT; SWAY, SWAY, SWAY, SWAY; TURN, 2, 3, 4
Beat 1	Sway right
2-4	Sway left, right, left
5-6	Step R foot, L foot in toward center
7-8	Step R foot, L foot out away from center
9-12	Repeat beats 1-4
13-16	Step R, L, R, L foot turning right (own individual circle)
17-32	Repeat Part II, beats 1-16
BRIDGE	SIDE, TOUCH, SIDE, TOUCH
Beat 1	Step R foot sideward right
2	Touch L foot next to R foot
3-4	Repeat beats 1-2 sideward left beginning L foot
PART I & II	
Beat 1-64	Repeat entire dance

*Choreographed by Phyllis Weikart.

Erev Shel Shoshanim (continued)

ENDING	SIDE, BACK, SIDE, TOUCH; SIDE, BACK, SIDE, TOUCH
Beat 1	Step R foot sideward right
2	Step L foot crossing in back of R foot
3	Step R foot sideward right
4	Touch L foot next to R foot
5-8	Repeat beats 1-4, sideward left beginning L foot

RHYTHMIC NOTATION

PART I

R L R L R L R (L)

REPEAT 3X W/OPP. FTWK.

PART II

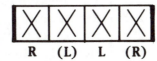

R L R L R L R L

REPEAT 3X

BRIDGE

X X X X

R (L) L (R)

ENDING

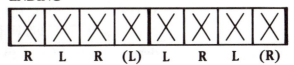

R L R (L) L R L (R)

LEAD-UP ACTIVITIES

Practice walking in one direction, then the other using SIDE, TOUCH as the transition (individual's tempo).

Practice SIDE, BACK in each direction with SIDE, TOUCH as the transition (individual's tempo).

Practice turning to the right in 4 steps without travelling sideward (individual's tempo).

TEACHING SUGGESTIONS

Practice Part I, beats 1-16, with SAY AND DO; add Part I, beats 17-32 with SAY AND DO.

Practice Part II with SAY AND DO and add to the end of Part I. Practice the Bridge and the Ending.

Do the entire dance with the music.

CHAIR DANCING

Do walking steps in place. Substitute SIDE, CLOSE for SIDE, BACK. Substitute 4 steps in place for the TURN.

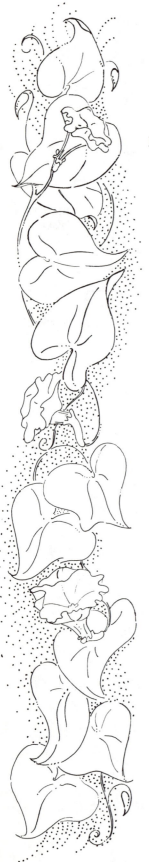

Good Old Days
Novelty
U.S.A.

RECORD	Express 405
INTRODUCTION	8 beats
FORMATION	Partners in double circle facing counterclockwise, inside hands joined. Directions given for person on left, opposite footwork for right-hand person

PART I	HEEL/STEP, HEEL/STEP, OUT/IN, OUT/IN; FORWARD, 2, 3, 4
Beat 1	Extend L heel forward keeping weight on R foot
&	Step L foot next to R foot
2	Extend R heel forward keeping weight on L foot
&	Step R foot next to L foot
3	Weight on both feet—turn heels out
&	Turn heels in (feet are straight)
4 &	Repeat beats 3 &
5	Step L foot forward counterclockwise
6-8	Step R, L, R foot forward counterclockwise
9-16	Repeat Part I, beats 1-8
PART II	STEP, KICK, STEP, TOUCH; STEP, KICK, STEP, TOUCH; HEEL/STEP, HEEL/STEP, OUT/IN, OUT/IN; TURN, 2, 3, 4
Beat 1	Step L foot forward counterclockwise
2	Kick R foot forward counterclockwise
3	Step R foot next to L foot
4	Touch L foot backward
5-8	Repeat beats 1-4
9-12	Repeat Part I, beats 1-4
13-16	Step L, R, L, R foot turning 1/2 circle to the left and return to new partner; right-hand partner step R, L, R, L foot forward to meet new partner
CIRCLE DANCE	Dance left-hand person's part; no R or L foot necessary.
RHYTHMIC NOTATION	PART I

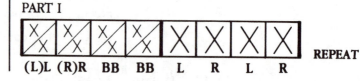

Good Old Days (continued)

PART II

X	X	X	X	X	X	X	X
L	(R)	R	(L)	L	(R)	R	(L)

X	X	X	X	X	X	X	X
(L)L	(R)R	BB	BB	L	R	L	R

LEAD-UP ACTIVITIES

Practice HEEL/STEP (individual's tempo).

Practice turning heels OUT/IN in a steady tempo (individual's tempo).

Practice STEP, KICK, STEP, TOUCH (individual's tempo).

TEACHING SUGGESTIONS

Teach the dance without reference to R foot or L foot using a circle formation.

Practice HEEL/STEP, HEEL/STEP, OUT/IN, OUT/IN with SAY AND DO.

"Add on" FORWARD, 2, 3, 4 taking a full beat as contrasted to the divided beat in the preceding section.

Practice Part I with SAY AND DO.

Practice Part II (STEP, KICK, STEP, TOUCH) in the same tempo as the walking steps (SAY AND DO).

Practice the transition from FORWARD, 2, 3, 4 to the STEP, KICK, STEP, TOUCH.

Practice the transition from the STEP, TOUCH to the HEEL/STEP, HEEL/STEP (SAY AND DO).

Practice the TURN, 2, 3, 4 and go back to the beginning HEEL/STEP, HEEL/STEP (SAY AND DO).

Do the circle version with SAY AND DO then add the music.

Add the partner dance if desired when the dance is reviewed.

CHAIR DANCING

Do as described; substitute steps in place for WALK.

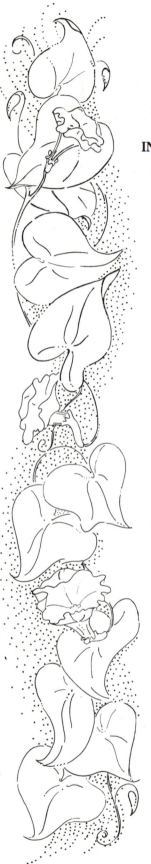

Hasapikos
Butcher's Dance
Greece

RECORD	Tikva 131 *Greek Dance Party*
INTRODUCTION	None or begin after any phrase
FORMATION	Broken circle in "T" position ("W" position may be substituted)

PART I	WALK, WALK; SIDE, LIFT; SIDE, LIFT
Beat 1	Step R foot forward counterclockwise
2	Step L foot forward counterclockwise and turn to face center
3	Step R foot sideward right
4	Lift L foot in front of R leg
5	Step L foot sideward left
6	Lift R foot in front of L leg
VARIATION I	WALK, WALK; STEP, HOP; STEP, HOP
Beat 3-6	Step hop R foot, L foot
VARIATION II	TURN, TURN; SIDE, LIFT; SIDE, LIFT
Beat 1-2	Turn right (R foot, L foot)
VARIATION III	WALK, WALK; SIDE, LIFT; SIDE/CROSS, BACK
Beat 1-4	Repeat Part I, beats 1-4
5	Step L foot sideward left
&	Step R foot crossing in front of L foot
6	Step L foot crossing in back of R foot
VARIATION IV	SIDE, BACK; SIDE/CROSS, BACK; SIDE/CROSS, BACK
Beat 1	Leap R foot sideward right
2	Leap L foot crossing in back of R foot
3	Step R foot sideward right
&	Step L foot crossing in front of R foot
4	Step R foot crossing in back of L foot
5-6	Repeat beats 3-4, beginning L foot
VARIATION V	Repeat Variation IV, substituting SIDE, STAMP for beats 5-6
VARIATION VI	JUMP, HOP; SIDE/CROSS, BACK; SIDE/CROSS, BACK
Beat 1	Jump with feet apart
2	Hop L foot, swinging R foot in
3-6	Repeat Variation IV, beats 3-6

Hasapikos (continued)

RHYTHMIC NOTATION	BASIC 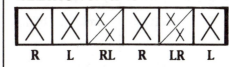

BASIC

X	X	X	X	X	X
R	L	R	(L)	L	(R)

VARIATION IV & VI

X	X	X X	X	X X	X
R	L	RL	R	LR	L

LEAD-UP ACTIVITIES

Practice SIDE, LIFT, SIDE, LIFT (individual's tempo).

Practice WALK, WALK; SIDE, LIFT; SIDE, LIFT (individual's tempo).

Practice SIDE/CROSS, BACK in place (individual's tempo).

TEACHING SUGGESTIONS

Practice WALK, WALK; SIDE, LIFT; SIDE, LIFT with SAY AND DO and add music.

Practice the variation of SIDE/CROSS, BACK with SAY AND DO.

Practice variations with SAY AND DO before adding them to the music.

CHAIR DANCING

Do as described, substituting in-place steps as necessary.

Instant Success*
Novelty
U.S.A.

RECORD	Golden Crest 31031 *More Scott Joplin Rags* "Original Rags"
INTRODUCTION	16 beats
FORMATION	Circle, no hands held
PART I	WALK
Beat 1-32	Walk 32 steps forward counterclockwise
33-64	Walk 32 steps forward clockwise
PART II	SIDE, CLOSE (facing center)
Beat 1	Step R foot sideward right
2	Step L foot next to R foot
3-32	Repeat beats 1-2 fifteen times (beat 32 touch)
33-64	Repeat Part II, beats 1-2, moving sideward left, beginning L foot
PART III	HEEL, STEP
Beat 1	Extend R heel diagonally right
2	Step R foot next to L foot
3	Extend L heel diagonally left
4	Step L foot next to R foot
5-32	Repeat Part III, beats 1-4, seven times
	TOUCH, STEP
Beat 33	Extend R toe out
34	Step R foot next to L foot
35	Extend L toe out
36	Step L foot next to R foot
37-64	Repeat Part III, beats 33-36, seven times
PART IV	SIDE, CLOSE, SIDE, TOUCH
Beat 1	Step R foot sideward right
2	Step L foot next to R foot
3	Step R foot sideward right
4	Touch L foot next to R foot
5-8	Repeat beats 1-4 sideward left, beginning L foot
9-40	Repeat Part IV, beats 1-8, four times
PART V	SIDE, BACK
Beat 1	Step R foot sideward right
2	Step L foot crossing in back of R foot
3-32	Repeat beats 1-2 fifteen times (beat 32 touch)
33-64	Repeat Part V, beats 1-2, sideward left, beginning L foot

*Choreographed by Phyllis Weikart.

Instant Success (continued)

PART VI	STEP, KICK, STEP, TOUCH
Beat 1	Step R foot next to L foot ⎫
2	Kick L foot in ⎪
3	Step L foot next to R foot ⎬ CHARLESTON
4	Touch R foot out ⎪
5-32	Repeat Part VI, beats 1-4, seven times ⎭
	IN, 2, 3, KICK; OUT, 2, 3, TOUCH
Beat 33-35	Step R, L, R foot in toward center of circle
36	Kick L foot in
37-39	Step L, R, L foot out
40	Touch R foot out
41-64	Repeat Part VI, beats 33-40, three times
NOTE	This is designed as a follow-the-leader warm up, and the specific use of R or L foot is not necessary.

RHYTHMIC NOTATION

PART I, II & V

X	X	X	X	**REPEAT 15X**
R	L	R	L	

PART III

X	X	X	X	**REPEAT 15X**
(R)	R	(L)	L	

PART IV

X	X	X	X	**REPEAT 9X W/OPP FTWK.**
R	L	R	(L)	

PART VI   BEAT 1-32

X	X	X	X	**REPEAT 7X**
R	(L)	L	(R)	

PART VI   BEAT 33-64

X	X	X	X	**REPEAT 7X W/OPP. FTWK.**
R	L	R	(L)	

(continued)

Instant Success (continued)

LEAD-UP ACTIVITIES	Do 2-beat movements with the arms in an alternating pattern.
	Practice the various movement sequences found in the dance (individual's tempo).
TEACHING SUGGESTIONS	Have the students practice each movement sequence to be used with SAY AND DO.
	Practice any difficult transitions.
CHAIR DANCING	Substitute steps in place.

Işte Hendek
Dig a Ditch
Turkey

RECORD	Boz-Ok 101
INTRODUCTION	32 beats
FORMATION	Short lines, shoulders touching, hands held down

PART I	FORWARD, FORWARD, IN, HOOK; OUT, TOGETHER, BEND, BOUNCE/BOUNCE
Beat 1	Step R foot diagonally forward right
2	Step L foot diagonally forward right
3	Step R foot in toward center
4	Bend R knee bringing bent L leg behind R knee (lean body out)
5	Step L foot out away from center
6	Step R foot next to L foot and transfer weight to both feet
7	Bend both knees then straighten legs
8 &	Bounce both heels 2 times
VARIATION	FORWARD, FORWARD, HOP/HOP, IN/HOOK; OUT, TOGETHER, BEND, BOUNCE/BOUNCE
Beat 1-2	Repeat Part I, beats 1-2
3 &	Hop twice on L foot bringing straight R leg around to center
4 &	Repeat Part I, beats 3-4, as a divided beat
5-8	Repeat Part I, beats 5-8
PART II	FORWARD, FORWARD, IN, CHUG; OUT, TOGETHER, BEND, BOUNCE/BOUNCE
Beat 1-3	Repeat Part I, beats 1-3
4	Chug R foot out leaning body in, L leg as in Part I, beat 4
5-8	Repeat Part I, beats 5-8
VARIATION	
Beat 1-3	Repeat Variation to Part I, beats 1-3
4 &	Repeat Part II, beats 3-4, as a divided beat

(continued)

İşte Hendek (continued)

RHYTHMIC NOTATION

PART I & II

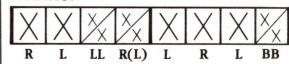

R   L   R   (L)   L   R   L   BB

VARIATION

R   L   LL   R(L)   L   R   L   BB

LEAD-UP ACTIVITIES

Practice BEND, BOUNCE/BOUNCE in the rhythmic pattern of 1, 2 & (individual's tempo).

Practice IN, HOOK (individual's tempo).

Practice IN, CHUG (individual's tempo).

TEACHING SUGGESTIONS

Do IN, HOOK, OUT, TOGETHER beginning R foot (individual's tempo), then group SAY AND DO.

"Precede" the above with FORWARD, FORWARD, and "add on" BEND, BOUNCE/BOUNCE.

Do Part I with SAY AND DO.

Have students understand the change in beat 4 from HOOK to CHUG and point out that the rest of the sequence is the same.

Do the 2 parts with SAY AND DO and then add the music.

Teach the variations whenever it seems desirable—at a session when the dance is reviewed, not during the initial teaching.

CHAIR DANCING

Step in place and substitute a drop of the heels for the BEND of beat 7.

Kendimé
To Myself
Turkey

RECORD	Boz-Ok 101
INTRODUCTION	32 beats
FORMATION	Broken circle, led from right; little fingers held, arms describe small circles forward in time to music
PART I	FORWARD, 2, 3, 4; SIDE, TOUCH, IN, HOOK
Beat 1	Step R foot forward counterclockwise
2	Step L foot forward
3	Step R foot forward
4	Step L foot forward and turn to face center
5	Step R foot sideward right
6	Touch L foot next to R foot
7	Step L foot in toward center
8	Hook R leg behind L knee (bend L knee)

RHYTHMIC NOTATION

R   L   R   L   R   (L)   L   (R)

LEAD-UP ACTIVITIES

Practice stepping and bending the supporting knee while hooking the other leg behind the bent knee (individual's tempo).

Practice walking 4 steps and then taking a step sideward to face center (begin with foot in the direction walking).

TEACHING SUGGESTIONS

Practice SIDE, TOUCH, IN, HOOK (individual's tempo), then SAY AND DO.

"Precede" the practiced pattern with 4 walking steps beginning R foot (individual's tempo), then SAY AND DO.

Practice the transition from the end to the beginning.

CHAIR DANCING

Step in place.

Körtanc
Hungary

RECORD	B and F #S427 *Särkozi Tanc*
INTRODUCTION	None
FORMATION	Single circle or hands joined in front basket with L hand under (move clockwise throughout the dance)

PART I   FORWARD FORWARD; SIDE, CLICK; SIDE, CLICK

Beat 1	Step L foot forward clockwise
2	Step R foot forward and turn to face center
3	Step L foot sideward left
4	Bring R foot to L foot clicking heels and straightening legs or substitute a touch
5	Step R foot sideward right
6	Bring L foot to R foot as in beat 7, or substitute a touch
7-24	Repeat Part I, beats 1-6, three times

NOTE   In Part I, a slight bend of the knee occurs before each step: BEND-STEP.

PART II   SIDE/CROSS, SIDE/CROSS; SIDE/CROSS, SIDE/CROSS; SIDE/HOP, CLOSE/HOLD

Beat 1	Step L foot sideward left
&	Step R foot crossing in front of L foot
2-4	Repeat beats 1-2 three times
5	Step L foot sideward left
&	Hop L foot
6	Step R foot next to L foot
7-24	Repeat Part II, beats 1-6, three times

TO SIMPLIFY   RUN 8 steps clockwise for the 4 SIDE/CROSS steps.

RHYTHMIC NOTATION

PART I

X	X	X	X	X	X	**REPEAT 3X**
L	R	L	(R)	R	(L)	

PART II

X/X	X/X	X/X	X/X	X/L	X	**REPEAT 3X**
LR	LR	LR	LR	LL	R	

Körtanc (continued)

LEAD-UP ACTIVITIES	Practice SIDE, TOUCH, SIDE, TOUCH then change the TOUCH to a HEEL, CLICK (individual's tempo).
	Practice SIDE/CROSS (individual's tempo).
TEACHING SUGGESTIONS	Practice SIDE, TOUCH, SIDE, TOUCH or substitute a CLICK for the TOUCH beginning L foot, SAY AND DO.
	"Precede" the first SIDE, TOUCH with a FORWARD, FORWARD beginning L foot (individual's tempo then SAY AND DO).
	Practice SIDE/CROSS to the left (individual's tempo then SAY AND DO). "Add on" SIDE/HOP, CLOSE/HOLD to 4 SIDE/CROSS steps.
	Practice Part II with SAY AND DO.
	Do the entire dance with SAY AND DO then add the music.
CHAIR DANCING	Substitute steps in place for those moving left.

Limbo Rock*
Novelty
U.S.A.

RECORD	Challenge 59131
INTRODUCTION	3-note pickup
FORMATION	Circle, no hands held
PART I	TOUCH, TOUCH, STEP/STEP, STEP
Beat 1	Touch L foot in
2	Touch L foot out
3-4	3 steps in place L, R, L foot (3 &, 4)
5-8	Repeat beats 1-4 with opposite footwork beginning R foot
9-16	Repeat Part I, beats 1-8
NOTE	No R foot or L foot needs to be specified.
PART II	SWIVEL FEET; SWIVEL FEET; JUMP, CLAP, JUMP, CLAP; JUMP, CLAP, JUMP, CLAP
Beat 1	Swivel toes right
&	Swivel heels right
2-3	Repeat beat 1 & twice
4	Straighten feet
5-8	Repeat beats 1-4 beginning with swivel toes left
9	Jump in
10	Clap
11	Jump out
12	Clap
13-16	Repeat beats 9-12
TO SIMPLIFY	Part II, beats 1-8, WALK 8 steps right or 4 steps right and 4 steps left.

RHYTHMIC NOTATION

PART I

  (L)   (L)   LR   L   (R)   (R)   RL   R   **REPEAT**

PART II

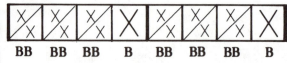

  BB   BB   BB   B   BB   BB   BB   B

*Choreographed by Phyllis Weikart.

Limbo Rock (continued)

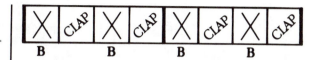

X	CLAP	X	CLAP	X	CLAP	X	CLAP
B		**B**		**B**		**B**	

LEAD-UP ACTIVITIES

Practice STEP/STEP, STEP in place, changing feet with each repetition (individual's tempo).

Practice moving sideward with SWIVEL FEET, moving toes then heels (individual's tempo).

Practice 4-beat sequences of JUMP, CLAP, JUMP, CLAP, moving in and out.

TEACHING SUGGESTIONS

Practice TOUCH, TOUCH, STEP/STEP, STEP (SAY AND DO). Do Part I four times with SAY AND DO.

Practice SWIVEL FEET to the divided beat (individual's tempo) then do the pattern as described for Part II, beats 1-8, with SAY AND DO.

JUMP IN, CLAP, JUMP OUT, CLAP twice with SAY AND DO. Do all of Part II with SAY AND DO.

Practice the entire dance with SAY AND DO and add the music.

CHAIR DANCING

Step in place.

Man in the Hay
Germany

RECORD	Folk Dance MH 1051
INTRODUCTION	8 beats
FORMATION	Square sets
INTRODUCTION	ARM SWING
Beat 1-16	Join hands in circle; swing arms up (bent elbow) on odd beats and down on even beats
PART I	SKIP
Beat 1-16	Skip (16 times) once around clockwise; continue arm swing as in Introduction
CHORUS	SLIDE, 2, 3, STAMP; SLIDE, 2, 3, STAMP; SLIDE, 2, 3, 4; 5, 6, 7, 8; SLIDE, 2, 3, 4; 5, 6, 7, 8
Beat 1-4	Head couples slide 3 times toward one another and Stamp beat 4; men begin L foot, women R foot
5-8	Slide back to place 3 times and Stamp beat 4
9-24	Slide across the set and back, 8 Slides each way; men (L hand partner) pass back to back going over; women (R hand partner) pass back to back returning to place
25-48	Side couples repeat Chorus
PART II	SKIP (ladies)
Beat 1-16	Ladies join hands and skip 16 times once around clockwise
CHORUS	Repeat Chorus, beats 1-48
PART III	SKIP (men)
Beat 1-16	Men join hands and skip 16 times twice around clockwise
CHORUS	Repeat Chorus, beats 1-48
PART IV	BASKET (head couples)
Beat 1-16	Head couples do a basket (men join hands behind ladies' backs and ladies join hands behind men's shoulders)
CHORUS	Repeat Chorus, beats 1-48
PART V	BASKET (side couples)
Beat 1-16	Side couples basket

Man in the Hay (continued)

CHORUS	Repeat Chorus, beats 1-48
PART VI	SKIP
Beat 1-16	Repeat Part I (16 skips) and end dance on last note

RHYTHMIC NOTATION

CHORUS (MEN) BEAT 1-8

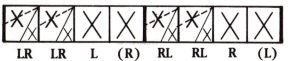

LR   LR   L   (R)   RL   RL   R   (L)

PART I, II, & III

REPEAT 3X

RR   LL   RR   LL

PART IV & V

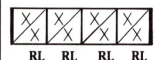
REPEAT 3X

RL   RL   RL   RL

LEAD-UP ACTIVITIES

Practice SLIDE with a partner one way and then the other.

Practice SKIP.

TEACHING SUGGESTIONS

Divide the students into sets of 2 couples (sides and heads) and have each group practice the parts of the dance which can be executed with 4 people.

Form square sets and practice the Chorus then practice each of the verses.

Do the entire dance then add the music.

CHAIR DANCING

May be adapted for wheelchairs.

Plješkavac Kolo
Clap Hands Kolo
Yugoslavia

RECORD	Folk Dancer MH 1009
INTRODUCTION	None or 32 beats
FORMATION	Circle or broken circle, hands joined in "V" position
PART I	IN, IN; STEP/STEP, STEP; OUT, OUT; STEP/STEP, STEP
Beat 1	Step R foot in diagonally right
2	Step L foot in diagonally right
3-4	Step R, L, R in place (3 &, 4)
5	Step L foot out diagonally right
6	Step R foot out diagonally right
7-8	Step L, R, L in place (7 &, 8)
9-16	Repeat Part I, beats 1-8
NOTE	Beats 1, 2; 5, 6 may be changed to STEP HOPS.
PART II	IN, IN; ACCENT/ACCENT, ACCENT; OUT, OUT; CLAP/CLAP, CLAP
Beat 1-2	Step R foot, L foot in toward center
3-4	Step R, L, R foot in place (3 &, 4) accent steps
5-6	Step L foot, R foot out
7-8	Clap hands 3 times (7 &, 8)
9-16	Repeat Part II, beats 1-8

RHYTHMIC NOTATION

PART I

R   L   RL   R   L   R   LR   L   REPEAT

PART II

R   L   RL   R   L   R   REPEAT

LEAD-UP ACTIVITIES

WALK in a rhythmic pattern of 1, 2, 3 &, 4 (individual's tempo), then change the direction to 2 steps IN followed by 3 steps in place then 2 steps OUT and 3 steps in place (individual's tempo).

Practice 2 WALKS, 3 ACCENTS (3 &, 4) and 2 WALKS, 3 CLAPS (3 &, 4), then change to IN and OUT.

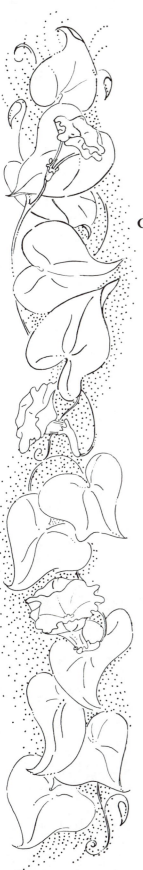

Plješkavac Kolo *(continued)*

TEACHING SUGGESTIONS | WALK 4 steps IN diagonally right and 4 steps OUT diagonally right with SAY AND DO, then change the walking pattern to Part I using SAY AND DO.

Do Part II with SAY AND DO.

Do the entire dance with SAY AND DO and then add the music.

CHAIR DANCING | Do the steps away from and toward the chair.

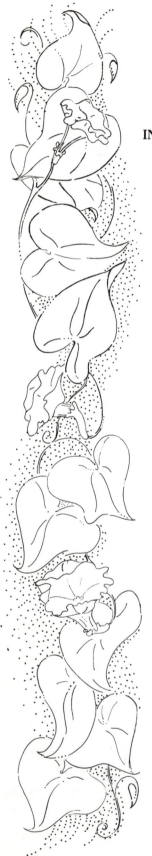

*Popcorn**
Novelty Dance
U.S.A.

RECORD	Musicor Mus 1458
INTRODUCTION	24 beats
FORMATION	Individual
PART I	HEEL, STEP, HEEL STEP; KICK, STEP, KICK, STEP; SIDE, BOUNCE, SIDE, BOUNCE; RUN, 2, 3, 4
Beat 1	Extend R heel
2	Step R foot next to L foot
3	Extend L heel
4	Step L foot next to R foot
5	Kick R foot
6	Step R foot next to L foot
7	Kick L foot
8	Step L foot next to R foot
9-10	Step R foot sideward right and bounce
11-12	Step L foot sideward left and bounce
13-16	Run R, L, R, L foot kicking out
17-32	Repeat Part I, beats 1-16
PART II	UP, STEP, UP, STEP; DOWN, HOLD, UP, HOLD; IN, BOUNCE, OUT, BOUNCE; IN, BOUNCE, OUT, BOUNCE
Beat 1	Raise R knee
2	Step R foot in place
3	Raise L knee
4	Step L foot in place
5-8	Circle knees in bent knee position or substitute down, up
9-10	Step R foot in then bounce
11-12	Step L foot out then bounce
13-14	Step R foot in then bounce,
15-16	Step L foot out then bounce
17-32	Repeat Part II, beats 1-16
NOTE	Repeat dance 3 times plus Part I of fourth repeat.
ENDING	IN, OUT, SIDE, TOGETHER; POP
Beat 1-16	Do Part II, beats 1-8, two times
Final	Step R foot in
Notes	Step L foot out
ritard.	Step R foot sideward right
	Step L foot next to R foot
	Circle knees for final "pop"

*Choreographed by Phyllis Weikart.

Popcorn (continued)

TO SIMPLIFY	Do only one section, or do only two motions per section rather than four. No R foot or L foot is necessary.
RHYTHMIC NOTATION	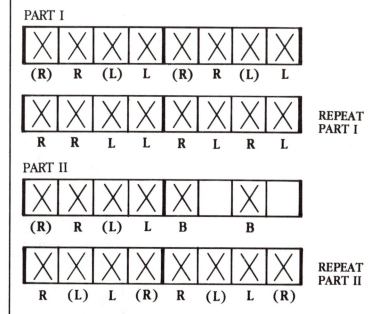
LEAD-UP SUGGESTIONS	Practice the following 2-beat sequences (individual's tempo): HEEL, STEP; KICK, STEP; UP, STEP; SIDE, BOUNCE; IN, BOUNCE; OUT, BOUNCE.
TEACHING SUGGESTIONS	Practice HEEL, STEP, HEEL, STEP; KICK, STEP, KICK, STEP (individual's tempo, then SAY AND DO); "add on" SIDE, BOUNCE, SIDE, BOUNCE; RUN, 2, 3, 4.
	Practice Part I with SAY AND DO.
	Practice Part II UP, STEP, UP, STEP; DOWN, HOLD, UP, HOLD (individual's tempo, then SAY AND DO); "add on" IN, BOUNCE, OUT, BOUNCE; IN, BOUNCE, OUT, BOUNCE.
	Practice Part II with SAY AND DO.
	Do the entire dance with SAY AND DO and add the music.
CHAIR DANCING	Part I—substitute step in place for RUN.

Pravo Horo
Straight Circle Dance
Bulgaria

RECORD	Folk Dancer MH 3057 (there are numerous *Pravo* melodies)
INTRODUCTION	None
FORMATION	Broken circle, hands held in "V" position
PART I	WALK, WALK; SIDE, LIFT; OUT, LIFT
Beat 1	Step R foot forward counterclockwise
2	Step L foot forward counterclockwise
3	Step R foot sideward right
4	Lift L foot in front of R leg
5	Step L foot out
6	Lift R foot in front of L leg
VARIATION	SIDE, CLOSE; SIDE, HOLD; IN, HOLD; OUT, OUT; OUT, HOLD; OUT, HOLD
Beat 1	Step R foot sideward right
2	Step L foot next to R foot
3-4	Step R foot sideward right
5-6	Step L foot in
7-8	Step R foot, L foot out
9-10	Step R foot out
11-12	Step L foot out

RHYTHMIC NOTATION

PART I

X	X	X	X	X	X
R	L	R	(L)	L	(R)

VARIATION

X	X	X		X		X	X
R	L	R		L		R	L

X		X	
R		L	

Pravo Horo (continued)

LEAD-UP ACTIVITIES	Practice SIDE, LIFT, SIDE, LIFT (individual's tempo), then change to SIDE, LIFT, OUT, LIFT (individual's tempo). Practice WALK, WALK, SIDE, LIFT (individual's tempo).
TEACHING SUGGESTIONS	Practice the sequence of Part I first with individual's tempo and then with SAY AND DO. Add the music. Practice the variation with individual's tempo and then SAY AND DO after Part I is secure.
CHAIR DANCING	Step in place.

Spanish Coffee*
Novelty
U.S.A.

RECORD	Polydor PD1-6192 *Music Box Dancer*
INTRODUCTION	6 beats
FORMATION	Circle, hands joined in "W" position

PART I	FORWARD, FORWARD, TOUCH, TOUCH; (Repeat 2 times); FORWARD, FORWARD, SIDE, TOUCH
Beat 1	Step R foot forward counterclockwise (facing diagonally right)
2	Step L foot forward counterclockwise
3	Touch R toe forward in line of direction
4	Touch R toe backward behind and to left of L foot (sweeping motion)
5-12	Repeat beats 1-4 two times
13-14	Step R foot, L foot forward counterclockwise and turn to face center
15	Step R foot sideward right facing center
16	Touch L foot next to R foot
17-32	Repeat Part I, beats 1-16, clockwise beginning L foot
PART II	IN, 2, 3, SWING; OUT, 2, 3, SWING
Beat 1-3	Step R, L, R foot in toward center
4	Swing L foot in raising heel of R foot
5-7	Step L, R, L foot out
8	Swing R foot out raising heel of L foot
9-16	Repeat Part II, beats 1-8
PART III	SIDE, BACK, SIDE, HEEL; SIDE, BACK, SIDE, HEEL (repeat); TURN, 2, 3, HEEL; TURN, 2, 3, HEEL; SIDE, CLOSE, SIDE, CLOSE; SIDE, CLOSE, SIDE, CLOSE
Beat 1	Step R foot sideward right (facing center)
2	Step L foot crossing in back of R foot
3	Step R foot sideward right
4	Extend L heel diagonally left
5-16	Repeat beats 1-4 three times using opposite footwork and direction
17-19	Turn right clockwise beginning R foot (3-step turn)
20	Extend L heel
21-24	Repeat beats 17-20 clockwise beginning L foot
25	Step R foot sideward right (raise R hip)
26	Step L foot next to R foot
27-32	Repeat beats 25-26 three times

*Choreographed by Phyllis Weikart.

Spanish Coffee *(continued)*

RHYTHMIC NOTATION

PART I

| X | X | X | X | REPEAT 2X | | X | X | X | X | REPEAT PART I W/OPP. FTWK. |
| R | L | (R) | (R) | | | R | L | R | (L) | |

PART II & III

| X | X | X | X | X | X | X | X | REPEAT 4X |
| R | L | R | (L) | L | R | L | (R) | |

PART III BEAT 25-32

| X | X | X | X | X | X | X | X |
| R | L | R | L | R | L | R | L |

LEAD-UP ACTIVITIES

Practice FORWARD, FORWARD, TOUCH, TOUCH (individual's tempo) then FORWARD, FORWARD, SIDE TOUCH (individual's tempo).

Practice STEP, STEP, STEP, SWING (IN and OUT using individual's tempo).

Practice SIDE, BACK, SIDE, HEEL (individual's tempo).

Practice 3-step turns followed by HEEL (individual's tempo).

TEACHING SUGGESTIONS

Practice FORWARD, FORWARD, TOUCH, TOUCH (3 times) with SAY AND DO then "add on" FORWARD, FORWARD, SIDE, TOUCH beginning R foot. Repeat in the other direction.

Do all of Part I with SAY AND DO.

Practice Part II with SAY AND DO and then use the music for Parts I and II.

Practice Part III, beats 1-16 (SAY AND DO) then "add on" the TURN, 2, 3, HEEL executed twice and "add on" the SIDE, CLOSE 4 times.

Practice the transitions.

Practice the entire dance with SAY AND DO and then add the music.

CHAIR DANCING PART I

Substitute in-place steps.

PART III

Substitute in-place steps for turns.

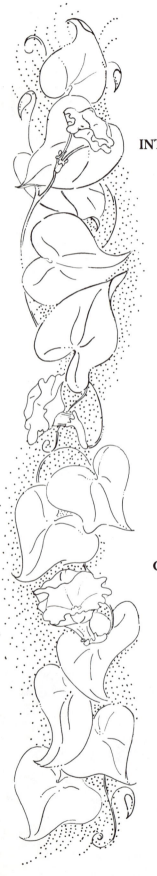

Tant' Hessie
Aunt Hessie
South Africa

RECORD	Folkraft 006X45
INTRODUCTION	8 beats
FORMATION	Double circle, partners facing each other.
ALTERNATE FORMATION	Circle, no partners
PART I	TOWARD, 2, 3, NOD; AWAY, 2, 3, 4
Beat 1-8	Walk 4 steps toward each other until R shoulders adjacent; nod, beat 7
9-16	Walk 4 steps back to place
17-32	Repeat beats 1-16 with L shoulders adjacent
NOTE	The walking steps may be changed to STEP BENDS.
PART II	DO-SA-DO R; DO-SA-DO L
Beat 1-16	Do-sa-do 8 step bends with your partner passing R shoulders first
17-32	Do-sa-do 8 step bends passing L shoulders first
PART III	BUZZ TURN
Beat 1-32	Buzz turn with 16 buzz steps (using shoulder-waist position—double arm-hold, if two girls)
NOTE	At the end of the dance move one place to your left to begin with new partner.
CIRCLE DANCE	
PART I	WALK forward counterclockwise right ending with a TOUCH then backward clockwise
PART II	WALK IN 8 steps and OUT 8 steps
PART III	WALK in own circle 8 steps right and 8 steps left
RHYTHMIC NOTATION	PART I & II

PART I & II

X		X		X		X	
R		**L**		**R**		**L**	

REPEAT 3X EACH PART

PART III

X	X	X	X	X	X	X	X
R	**L**	**R**	**L**	**R**	**L**	**R**	**L**

REPEAT 3X

Tant' Hessie (continued)

LEAD-UP ACTIVITIES

Practice DO-SA-DO with a partner (partner beat).

Practice a slow BUZZ TURN with a partner (partner beat).

TEACHING SUGGESTIONS

Practice Part I with a partner (SAY AND DO).

Practice Part II with a partner (SAY AND DO).

Practice Part III with a partner and practice the transition to a new partner.

Do the entire dance with SAY AND DO and add the music.

For young children or very inexperienced dancers, use the Circle Dance modification.

CHAIR DANCING

May be adapted for wheelchairs.

Tipsy *
Novelty Dance
U.S.A.

RECORD	Educational Activities, AR546 *Movin'*
INTRODUCTION	16 beats
FORMATION	Individuals in free formation (may be done facing a partner)

PART I	TOUCH, STEP; TOUCH, STEP; TOUCH, STEP; TOUCH, STEP; HEEL, STEP; HEEL, STEP; HEEL, STEP; HEEL, STEP
Beat 1-2	Extend R foot out, clap hands beat 1
3-4	Step R foot next to L foot, pat thighs, beat 3
5-8	Repeat beats 1-4 beginning L foot
9-16	Repeat beats 1-8
17-18	Extend R heel in, twisting torso right, snap fingers beat 17 with arms up
19-20	Step R foot next to L foot, pat thighs beat 19
21-24	Repeat beats 17-20 beginning L foot
25-32	Repeat beats 17-24
33-64	Repeat Part I, beats 1-32
NOTE	CLAP and PAT may be omitted and R foot, L foot is not necessary.
PART II	CIRCLE KNEE; CIRCLE KNEE; CIRCLE KNEE; CIRCLE KNEE; SIDE, TOUCH; SIDE, TOUCH
Beat 1-2	Circle R knee right
3-4	Circle L knee left
5-8	Repeat beats 1-4
9-10	Step R foot sideward right
11-12	Touch L foot next to R foot
13-16	Repeat beats 9-12 with opposite footwork
BRIDGE	BEND, STRAIGHTEN; BEND, STRAIGHTEN
Beat 1-2	Bend and straighten knees diagonally right
3-4	Bend and straighten knees diagonally left

*Choreographed by Phyllis Weikart.

Tipsy (continued)

RHYTHMIC NOTATION	

PART I

X		X		X		X	
(R)		R		(L)		L	

REPEAT 3X

PART II

X		X		X		X	
(R)		(L)		(R)		(L)	

X		X		X		X	
R		(L)		L		(R)	

BRIDGE

X	X	X	X
B	B	B	B

LEAD-UP ACTIVITIES

Practice TOUCH, STEP, TOUCH, STEP (individual's tempo).

Practice HEEL, STEP, HEEL, STEP (individual's tempo).

Practice SIDE, TOUCH, SIDE, TOUCH (individual's tempo).

Practice circling knees.

TEACHING SUGGESTIONS

Practice Part I with SAY AND DO—omit hand movements until foot movements are secure.

Practice Part II with SAY AND DO.

Do the entire dance with SAY AND DO and then add the music.

CHAIR DANCING
PART I

Reach foot diagonally backward alongside the chair.

BRIDGE
Beat 1-4

Raise and lower heels.

Twelfth St. Rag
U.S.A.

RECORD	Capitol 6001
INTRODUCTION	8 beats
FORMATION	Free formation or circle or lines
PART I	FORWARD, 2, 3, 4; TOUCH, TOUCH, STEP/STEP, STEP
Beat 1	Step L foot forward counterclockwise
2	Step R foot forward counterclockwise
3-4	Repeat beats 1-2
5	Touch L foot forward
6	Touch L foot sideward in
7-8	Step L, R, L foot in place
9-16	Repeat Part I, beats 1-8 with opposite footwork
NOTE	Beats 7-8 may be made more difficult as follows:
Beat 7	Step L foot crossing in back of R foot
&	Step R foot sideward right
8	Step L foot crossing in front of R foot
PART II	OUT, 2, 3, 4; IN, 2, 3, 4
Beat 1-4	Step L, R, L, R foot moving right out of the circle
5-8	Step L, R, L, R foot moving left in toward the center of the circle
NOTE	Part II may be executed as follows:
Beat 1 &	Cross/side beginning L foot
2-3	Cross/side, cross/side
4	Cross
5-8	Repeat beats 1-4 with opposite footwork
PART III	IN, KICK, OUT, TOUCH; IN, KICK, OUT, TOUCH
Beat 1	Step L foot in
2	Kick R foot in
3	Step R foot out
4	Touch L toe out
5-8	Repeat Part III, beats 1-4
BRIDGE	JUMP, HOLD, JUMP, HOLD; TURN, 2, 3, 4
Beat 1-2	Jump in
3-4	Jump out
5-8	Step L, R, L, R foot turning 360° in place counterclockwise
NOTE	The Bridge is done after each second repetition of the dance.
TO SIMPLIFY	No R or L foot is necessary.

Beats 1-4 of Part III are bracketed with the label CHARLESTON.

Twelfth St. Rag (continued)

RHYTHMIC NOTATION

PART I

REPEAT W/OPP. FTWK.

X	X	X	X	X	X	X/X	X
L	R	L	R	(L)	(L)	LR	L

PART II

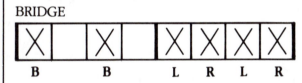

X	X	X	X	X	X	X	X	X
L	R	L	R	L	R	L	R

PART III

REPEAT

X	X	X	X
L	(R)	R	(L)

BRIDGE

X		X		X	X	X	X
B		B		L	R	L	R

LEAD-UP ACTIVITIES

Practice TOUCH, TOUCH, STEP/STEP, STEP (individual's tempo).

Practice walking OUT 4 steps and IN 4 steps.

Practice IN, KICK, OUT, TOUCH (individual's tempo).

TEACHING SUGGESTIONS

Practice TOUCH, TOUCH, STEP/STEP, STEP with SAY AND DO. "Precede" with FORWARD, 2, 3, 4 and SAY AND DO Part I.

Practice OUT, 2, 3, 4; IN, 2, 3, 4 with SAY AND DO and link to Part I.

Practice IN, KICK, OUT, TOUCH with SAY AND DO and "add on" to Part II.

Do the entire dance with SAY AND DO and add the music. After two repetitions "add on" the Bridge.

CHAIR DANCING

PART I   Do the WALKS in place.

PART II   Move feet away from and toward the chair.

PART III Do as described.

BRIDGE   Do the JUMPS and substitute in-place steps for the TURN.

Ugros
Hungary

RECORD	Qualiton LPX 18007 Side A Band 1
INTRODUCTION	8 beats
FORMATION	Open circle, no hands held

PART I	BEND, STRAIGHTEN
Beat 1	Bend knees
2	Straighten knees
3-32	Repeat Part I, beats 1-2, fifteen times
PART II	SIDE, TOUCH
Beat 1	Step R sideward right
2	Touch L foot next to R foot or heel click
3	Step L foot sideward left
4	Touch R foot next to L foot or heel click
5-32	Repeat Part II, beats 1-4, seven times
PART III	SIDE, CLOSE, SIDE, TOUCH
Beat 1	Step R foot sideward right
2	Step L foot next to R foot
3	Step R foot sideward right
4	Touch R foot next to L foot
5-8	Repeat beats 1-4 sideward left beginning L foot
9-32	Repeat Part III, beats 1-8, three times
PART IV	SIDE, LIFT
Beat 1	Step R foot sideward right
2	Lift L foot in front of R leg
3	Step L foot sideward left
4	Lift R foot in front of L leg
5-32	Repeat Part IV, beats 1-4, seven times
PART V	SIDE, STAMP
Beat 1	Step R foot sideward right
2	Stamp L foot next to R foot
3	Step L foot sideward left
4	Stamp R foot next to L foot
5-32	Repeat Part V, beats 1-4, seven times
PART VI	SIDE, LIFT, SIDE, STAMP
Beat 1	Step R foot sideward right
2	Lift L foot in front of R leg
3	Step L foot sideward left
4	Stamp R foot next to L foot
5-32	Repeat Part VI, beats 1-4, seven times

Ugros (continued)

PART VII	STEP/STEP, STEP
Beat 1	Leap R foot sideward right
&	Step L foot slightly behind R foot
2	Step R foot crossing in front of L foot
3	Leap L foot sideward left
&	Step R foot slightly behind L foot
4	Step L foot crossing in front of R foot
5-32	Repeat Part VII, beats 1-4, seven times
TO SIMPLIFY	Leap in place then touch behind.
PART VIII	KICK, KICK, JUMP, HOLD
Beat 1	Kick L foot in
2	Kick R foot in
3-4	Jump in place with feet together
5-32	Repeat Part VIII, beats 1-4, seven times
PART IX	JUMP, JUMP
Beat 1	Jump with feet apart, knees bent
2	Jump with feet together straightening knees (add heel click if desired)
3-32	Repeat Part IX, beats 1-2, fifteen times
NOTE	Part IX may be done with 2 beats for each jump.

RHYTHMIC NOTATION

PART I & IX

X	X	REPEAT 15X
B	**B**	

PART II, IV, V & VI

X	X	X	X	REPEAT 7X
R	**(L)**	**L**	**(R)**	

PART III

X	X	X	X	X	X	X	X	REPEAT 3X
R	**L**	**R**	**(L)**	**L**	**R**	**L**	**(R)**	

PART VII

X/X	X	X/X	X	REPEAT 7X
RL	**R**	**LR**	**L**	

PART VIII

X	X	X		REPEAT 7X
R	**L**	**B**		

LEAD-UP ACTIVITIES Practice the following sequences (individual's tempo): SIDE, TOUCH; SIDE, LIFT; SIDE, STAMP; STEP/STEP, STEP; SIDE, CLOSE, SIDE, TOUCH

(continued)

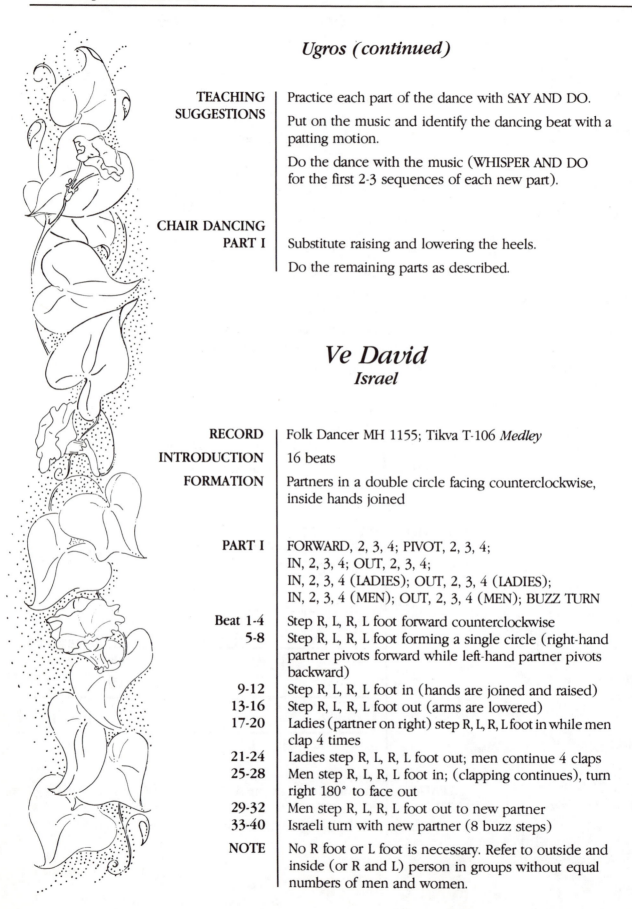

Ugros *(continued)*

TEACHING SUGGESTIONS	Practice each part of the dance with SAY AND DO.
	Put on the music and identify the dancing beat with a patting motion.
	Do the dance with the music (WHISPER AND DO for the first 2-3 sequences of each new part).
CHAIR DANCING PART I	Substitute raising and lowering the heels.
	Do the remaining parts as described.

Ve David
Israel

RECORD	Folk Dancer MH 1155; Tikva T-106 *Medley*
INTRODUCTION	16 beats
FORMATION	Partners in a double circle facing counterclockwise, inside hands joined
PART I	FORWARD, 2, 3, 4; PIVOT, 2, 3, 4; IN, 2, 3, 4; OUT, 2, 3, 4; IN, 2, 3, 4 (LADIES); OUT, 2, 3, 4 (LADIES); IN, 2, 3, 4 (MEN); OUT, 2, 3, 4 (MEN); BUZZ TURN
Beat 1-4	Step R, L, R, L foot forward counterclockwise
5-8	Step R, L, R, L foot forming a single circle (right-hand partner pivots forward while left-hand partner pivots backward)
9-12	Step R, L, R, L foot in (hands are joined and raised)
13-16	Step R, L, R, L foot out (arms are lowered)
17-20	Ladies (partner on right) step R, L, R, L foot in while men clap 4 times
21-24	Ladies step R, L, R, L foot out; men continue 4 claps
25-28	Men step R, L, R, L foot in; (clapping continues), turn right 180° to face out
29-32	Men step R, L, R, L foot out to new partner
33-40	Israeli turn with new partner (8 buzz steps)
NOTE	No R foot or L foot is necessary. Refer to outside and inside (or R and L) person in groups without equal numbers of men and women.

Ve David (continued)

RHYTHMIC NOTATION

REPEAT 3X

LEAD-UP ACTIVITIES

Practice walking IN 4 steps, OUT 4 steps (individual's tempo).

Practice walking with a partner (partner beat).

Practice walking to the music changing direction after each 4 steps.

Practice a GALLOP with the R foot leading (individual's tempo).

Practice a GALLOP turning right in a fairly large circle then narrow the circle—be certain students are leading with the R foot (individual's tempo).

TEACHING SUGGESTIONS

Practice walking with a partner to the music.

Practice the first 16 beats of the dance with SAY AND DO.

"Add on" the next 8 beats for the outside partner then the 8 beats for the inside partner. (Be certain to identify the person to whom the inside partner will be walking before "adding on" those 8 beats.)

Practice the final 8 beats using a WALK and a R elbow hold. (Change to the BUZZ TURN when the dance is reviewed.)

Do the entire dance with group SAY AND DO followed by the music.

CHAIR DANCING

Beat 1-16	Move feet away from and back to the chair
17-24	Clap hands
25-32	Pat thighs
33-40	Pat thighs and clap hands in an alternating pattern
NOTE	May be adapted for wheelchairs.

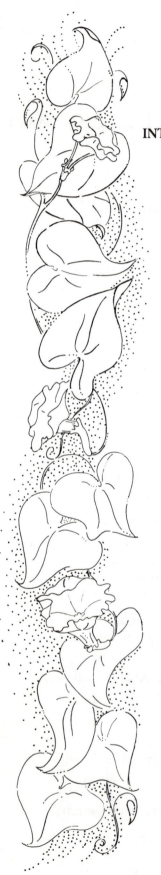

Zemer Atik
Israel

RECORD	Tikva T-100 *Debka*
INTRODUCTION	8 beats
FORMATION	Circle facing counterclockwise, L hand at shoulder, R arm straight, hands joined
PART I	FORWARD/2, 3/4; FORWARD/CLAP, FORWARD/CLAP
Beat 1-2	Step R, L, R, L foot forward counterclockwise and release hand hold
3	Step R foot forward then clap over R shoulder
4	Step L foot forward then clap over L shoulder
5-16	Repeat Part I, beats 1-4, three times
PART II	IN/SNAP, IN/SNAP; OUT/2, 3/4
Beat 1	Step R foot in, sway arms overhead to right (snap fingers after the step)
2	Step L foot in, sway arms left (snap fingers after the step)
3-4	Step R, L, R, L foot out (arms are lowered slowly in front of body)
5-16	Repeat Part II, beats 1-4, three times
NOTE	This is the circle version of *Zemer Atik;* there also is a couple dance. No R foot or L foot is necessary.

RHYTHMIC NOTATION

PART I

PART I rhythmic notation: boxes marked RL RL R L — **REPEAT 3X**

PART II

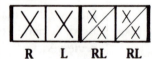

PART II rhythmic notation: boxes marked R L RL RL — **REPEAT 3X**

LEAD-UP ACTIVITIES	WALK, combining 4 quick steps with 2 slow steps: FORWARD/2, 3/4; FORWARD/HOLD, FORWARD/HOLD (individual's tempo).
	Repeat the above with 2 slow steps IN and 4 quick steps OUT (individual's tempo).
	Practice STEP, CLAP several times and STEP, SNAP several times.

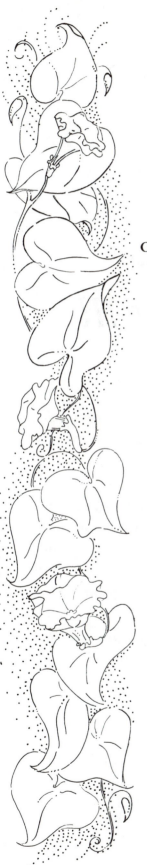

Zemer Atik (continued)

TEACHING SUGGESTIONS	Practice Part I without adding a CLAP—FORWARD/2, 3/4; FORWARD/HOLD, FORWARD/HOLD (SAY AND DO).
	Practice Part II without the SNAPS (SAY AND DO).
	Practice the transitions between the parts.
	Do the dance with the music and "add on" the CLAPS and SNAPS if the group is not having any difficulty— otherwise "add on" during the review of the dance.
CHAIR DANCING PART I	STEP in place then lean right, CLAP, lean left, CLAP.
PART II	STEP away from the chair and toward the chair.

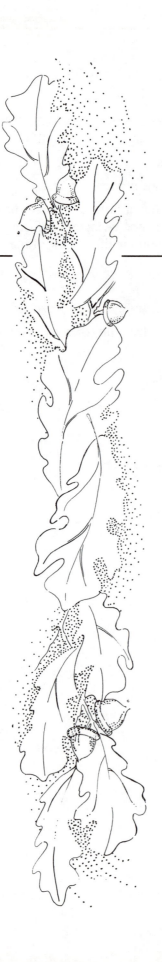

Locomotor Movement III

Characteristics:

1. Quicker footwork may be demanded because the beat of music is faster.

2. There may be several parts to the dance.

3. There are groupings of beats other than in twos and fours. Movement sequences grouped in threes and fives are introduced.

4. The dances may require complex changes of direction.

5. The music may have a more ethnic sound with a less easily defined beat.

Alunelul
Hazelnuts
Romania

RECORD	Folk Dancer MH 1120; *Whole World Dances* EKS
INTRODUCTION	8 beats
FORMATION	Circle, "T" position (shoulder hold)

PART I	SIDE/BACK, SIDE/BACK; SIDE/STAMP, STAMP
Beat 1	Step R foot slightly sideward right (weight on ball of foot)
&	Step L foot crossing in back of R foot
2 &	Repeat beat 1 &
3	Step R foot slightly sideward right
&	Stamp L foot next to R foot
4	Stamp L foot next to R foot
5-8	Repeat beats 1-4 moving left
9-16	Repeat Part I, beats 1-8, moving right then left
PART II	SIDE/BACK, SIDE/STAMP
Beat 1	Step R foot slightly sideward
&	Step L foot in back of R foot
2	Step on R foot sideward right
&	Stamp L foot
3-4	Repeat to left
5-8	Repeat Part II, beats 1-4
PART III	STEP/STAMP, STEP/STAMP; STEP/STAMP, STAMP
Beat 1	Step R foot in place
&	Stamp L foot next to R foot
2	Step L foot in place
&	Stamp R foot next to L foot
3	Step R foot in place
&	Stamp L foot next to R foot
4	Stamp L foot next to R foot
5-8	Repeat Part III, beats 1-4, beginning L foot

(continued)

Alunelul (continued)

RHYTHMIC NOTATION

PART I

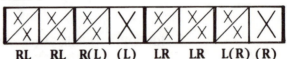

RL   RL   R(L)   (L)   LR   LR   L(R)   (R)   **REPEAT**

PART II

RL   R(L)   LR   L(R)   RL   R(L)   LR   L(R)

PART III

R(L) L(R) R(L) (L)   L(R) R(L) L(R) (R)

LEAD-UP ACTIVITIES

Practice moving SIDE/BACK first one way and then the other—slowly then faster (individual's tempo).

Practice SIDE/BACK, SIDE/HOLD each direction (individual's tempo).

Practice STAMPS without changing weight to the stamping foot (individual's tempo).

TEACHING SUGGESTIONS

Practice STEP/STAMP with each foot (SAY AND DO).

Practice STEP/STAMP, STAMP/HOLD with each foot (SAY AND DO).

Practice SIDE/BACK, SIDE/STAMP with each foot (SAY AND DO).

Practice each part of the dance and then the transitions from one part to the other using SAY AND DO.

CHAIR DANCING

Place the feet one in front of the other for the SIDE/BACK or substitute SIDE/CLOSE.

Bossa Nova
Novelty
U.S.A.

RECORD	Columbia 4-33079
INTRODUCTION	12 beats
FORMATION	Double circle, partners facing each other (directions given for person on inside, outside person uses opposite footwork)

PART I	SIDE/CLOSE, SIDE/TOUCH; SIDE/CLOSE, SIDE/TOUCH; SIDE/CLOSE, SIDE/TOUCH; TURN/2, 3/HOLD
Beat 1	Step L foot sideward left
&	Step R foot next to L foot
2	Step L foot sideward left
&	Touch R foot next to L foot
3-4	Repeat beats 1-2 sideward right beginning R foot
5-6	Repeat beats 1-2
7-8	Step in place 3 steps while turning to face clockwise (partner is now facing counterclockwise)
PART II	OUT/CLOSE, OUT/TOUCH; IN/CLOSE, IN/TOUCH; OUT/CLOSE, OUT/TOUCH; IN/CLOSE, IN/TOUCH
Beat 1-2	Repeat Part I, beats 1-2, sideward away from center of circle beginning L foot
3-4	Repeat Part I, beats 1-2, sideward right toward center of circle beginning R foot.
5-8	Repeat Part II, beats 1-4
PART III	STEP, KICK; STEP, TOUCH; STEP, KICK; STEP, TOUCH
Beat 1	Step L foot forward
2	Kick R foot forward
3	Step R foot backward ⎫ CHARLESTON
4	Touch L foot backward ⎬
5-8	Repeat Part III, beats 1-4 ⎭
PART IV	CROSS, TOUCH; CROSS, TOUCH; CROSS, TOUCH, FORWARD/2, 3/TURN
Beat 1	Step L foot crossing in front of R foot (in)
2	Touch R foot sideward right (in)
3-4	Step R foot crossing in front of L foot and touch L foot sideward left (out)
5-6	Repeat beats 1-2
7-8	Step R, L, R foot forward counterclockwise
&	Turn to face new partner (keep weight on R foot)

(continued)

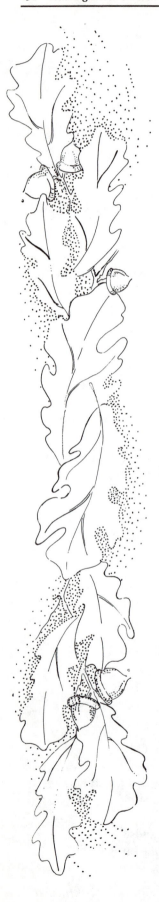

Bossa Nova (continued)

RHYTHMIC
NOTATION

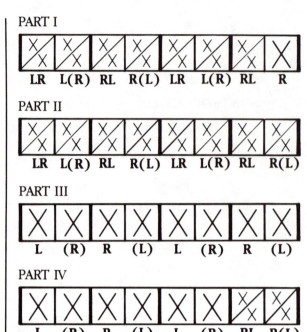

PART I

LR	L(R)	RL	R(L)	LR	L(R)	RL	R

PART II

LR	L(R)	RL	R(L)	LR	L(R)	RL	R(L)

PART III

L	(R)	R	(L)	L	(R)	R	(L)

PART IV

L	(R)	R	(L)	L	(R)	RL	R(L)

LEAD-UP
ACTIVITIES

Practice SIDE/CLOSE, SIDE/TOUCH both directions (individual's tempo).

Practice the CHARLESTON (STEP, KICK, STEP, TOUCH) (individual's tempo).

WALK, crossing the feet in front with each step (individual's tempo).

Practice a pattern of CROSS, TOUCH, crossing the foot in front and touching to the side (individual's tempo).

Bossa Nova (continued)

TEACHING SUGGESTIONS

Use a circle formation and practice 4 SIDE/CLOSE, SIDE/TOUCH steps (OUT and IN) followed by 2 slow CHARLESTON steps in which each beat takes twice the amount of time to execute as the beats in the SIDE/CLOSE, SIDE/TOUCH. Alternate starting foot during the practice (SAY AND DO).

In a circle, practice 2 CHARLESTON steps and continue with CROSS, TOUCH steps. Alternate starting foot during the practice (SAY AND DO).

Using partner formation practice Part I, adding the 1/4 TURN (partner beat).

Link Part II to Part I and practice both parts (partner beat).

Link Part III to Part II and put the first 3 parts together (SAY AND DO).

Link Part IV to Part III and put all 4 parts together (SAY AND DO).

Practice transition from Part IV to Part I.

Be sure students understand that each part begins with the same foot.

CHAIR DANCING

Omit the TURNS and step in place.

*Bulgarian Dance #1**
Bulgaria

RECORD	Educational Record #2
INTRODUCTION	40 beats (begin with vocal)
FORMATION	Circle or broken circle, hands held in "W" position

PART I	WALK, WALK; SIDE, LIFT; OUT, LIFT
Beat 1	Step R foot forward counterclockwise
2	Step L foot forward counterclockwise
3	Step R foot sideward right facing center
4	Lift L foot in front of R leg
5	Step L foot out (away from center)
6	Lift R foot in front of L leg
7-48	Repeat Part I, beats 1-6, seven times
PART II	IN, 2; 3, LIFT; OUT, 2; 3, LIFT; SIDE, CROSS; SIDE, CROSS; SIDE, STAMP; SIDE, STAMP
Beat 1-3	Step R, L, R foot in toward center
4	Lift L foot in front of R leg
5-7	Step L, R, L foot out (away from center)
8	Lift R foot in front of L leg
9	Step R foot sideward right
10	Step L foot crossing in front of R foot
11-12	Repeat beats 9-10
13	Step R foot sideward right
14	Stamp L foot next to R foot
15	Step L foot sideward left
16	Stamp R foot next to L foot
17-48	Repeat Part II, beats 1-16, two times

RHYTHMIC NOTATION

PART I

R   L   R   (L)   L   (R)   **REPEAT 7X**

PART II

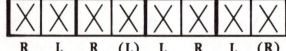

R   L   R   (L)   L   R   L   (R)

R   L   R   L   R   (L)   L   (R)   **REPEAT PART II 2X**

*Choreographed by Phyllis Weikart.

Bulgarian Dance #1(continued)

LEAD-UP ACTIVITIES	Teach the *Hasapikos* (Locomotor Movement II dance) with the basic step before introducing this dance.
	Review the *Hasapikos* basic step (individual's tempo).
	Review STEP, STAMP using one foot then the other (individual's tempo).
	Practice or review SIDE, CROSS each direction (individual's tempo).
	Practice moving in a pattern of WALK, 2, 3, LIFT—use a forward as well as a backward direction (individual's tempo).
TEACHING SUGGESTIONS	Practice the basic step of the *Hasapikos* changing the second SIDE, LIFT to OUT, LIFT (SAY AND DO). Add the music and do several repetitions.
	Practice IN, 2, 3, LIFT; OUT, 2, 3, LIFT (SAY AND DO).
	"Add on" SIDE, CROSS, SIDE, CROSS to the OUT, 2, 3, LIFT then "add on" SIDE, STAMP; SIDE, STAMP (SAY AND DO).
	Do all of Part II 3 times and practice the transition to Part I, SAY AND DO.
	Do the entire dance to the music.
CHAIR DANCING PART I	Do the walking steps in place and the SIDE, LIFT, OUT, LIFT in place.
PART II	Change the SIDE, CROSS to SIDE, CLOSE.

Hole in the Wall
Contra Dance
England

RECORD	Country Dance and Song Society of America, CDS1
INTRODUCTION	12 beats
FORMATION	Longways set; couple #1 dances with couple #2
PART I	#1 couples TURN OUT; #2 couples TURN OUT; DIAGONAL CHANGE; DIAGONAL CHANGE; CIRCLE; CHANGE PLACES
Beat 1-12	#1 couples turn away from partner and walk behind #2 couples; proceed around that couple to center of set, join hands and walk back to place
13-24	#2 couples turn away from partner and walk behind #1 couples; proceed around that couple, join hands, and walk back to place
25-30	#1 men change places with #2 ladies passing R shoulders
31-36	#1 ladies change places with #2 men passing R shoulders
37-42	#1 and #2 couples join hands and circle left to starting position
43-48	#1 couples turn away from partner and walk behind #2 couples changing places with #2 couples; #2 couples walk up the inside of the set to #1 couples' place

RHYTHMIC NOTATION

REPEAT 7X

R L R L R L

LEAD-UP ACTIVITIES	Do progressive circle dances.
	Do other contra dances so students have the concept of a contra and how movement occurs up and down the set.
TEACHING SUGGESTIONS	Beats 1-12, 13-24, and 43-48 should be learned without turning away from partner (WALK straight down or up the set).
	After the parts are learned, put together the contra sets and have students understand the transition for the #1 couples from the end of the dance to the beginning. Students also must understand what happens at each end of the set.
CHAIR DANCING	Dance may be executed in wheelchairs.

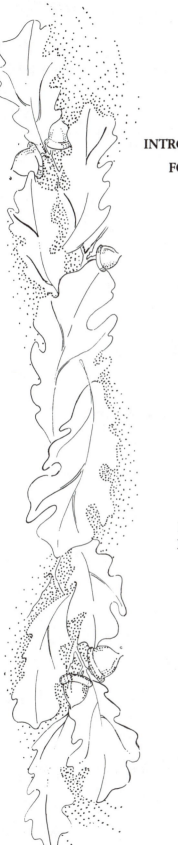

Hora Pe Gheaţa
Hora on the Ice
Romania

RECORD	Nevofoon 15005 "Romanian Folk Dances"
INTRODUCTION	8 beats
FORMATION	Circle, hands joined in "W" position
PART I	FORWARD, 2; 3, 4; SIDE, HOLD; SIDE, HOLD; IN, HOLD; OUT, 2; 3, 4; 5, STAMP
Beat 1-4	Step R, L, R, L foot counterclockwise
5-6	Step R foot counterclockwise, lift L leg, "skate right"
7-8	Step L foot clockwise, lift R leg, "skate left"
9-10	Step R foot in toward center of circle, "skate in"
11-15	Step L, R, L, R, L foot out (as each step is taken the opposite foot rotates outward)
16	Stamp R foot
PART II	IN, 2; 3, 4; OUT, 2; 3, 4
Beat 1-4	Step R, L, R, L foot diagonally in to the right
5-8	Step L, R, L, R foot diagonally out to the right
9-16	Repeat Part II, beats 1-8 (circle is moving counterclockwise)
NOTE	Part II is simplified.

RHYTHMIC NOTATION

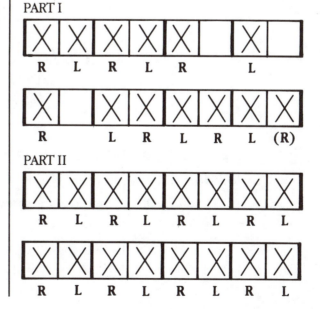

PART I

PART II

(continued)

Hora Pe Gheaṭa (continued)

LEAD-UP ACTIVITIES	Use the imagery of a clock and SKATE to various numerals designated. Each time return to the center of the clock. Use R foot for numerals 1-5, L foot for 7-11.
	Move IN and OUT of the circle using 4 steps IN, 4 steps OUT or 3 steps then HOLD. Change activity to move IN and OUT on a diagonal (individual's tempo).
TEACHING SUGGESTIONS	Do a SIDE, HOLD, SIDE, HOLD, IN, HOLD using the clock imagery moving to the numerals 3, 9, 12 beginning R foot.
	"Precede" the skating pattern with 4 walking steps and "add on" OUT, 2, 3, 4, 5, STAMP. (Use individual's tempo and then SAY AND DO.)
	SAY AND DO Part II.
	Practice the transitions and add the music.
CHAIR DANCING PART I	Substitute steps in place for the 4 FORWARD steps.
PART II	Move away from and toward the chair.

Hot Pretzels
Novelty
U.S.A.

RECORD	Folk Dancer MH 3019
INTRODUCTION	8 beats
FORMATION	Individual or short lines
PART I	HEEL, BACK/SIDE; CROSS, HEEL; BACK/SIDE, CROSS; HEEL, STEP/STEP

Hot Pretzels (continued)

Beat 1	Extend L heel diagonally left (weight on R foot)
2	Step L foot crossing in back of R foot
&	Step R foot sideward right
3	Step L foot crossing in front of R foot
4	Extend R heel diagonally right (weight on L foot)
5	Step R foot crossing in back of L foot
&	Step L foot sideward left
6	Step R foot crossing in front of L foot
7	Extend L heel diagonally left
8	Step L foot next to R foot
&	Step R foot next to L foot

FORWARD, 2; 3, 4; 5, KICK; STEP/STEP, STEP

9-13	Step L, R, L, R, L foot forward
14	Kick R foot (pedal backward)
15-16	Step R, L, R foot in place

RHYTHMIC NOTATION

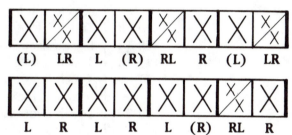

(L)   LR   L   (R)   RL   R   (L)   LR

L   R   L   R   L   (R)   RL   R

LEAD-UP ACTIVITIES

Practice BACK/SIDE, CROSS patterns both directions (individual's tempo).

Practice HEEL, BACK/SIDE, CROSS both directions (individual's tempo).

TEACHING SUGGESTIONS

Practice the first 8 beats (individual's tempo) then SAY AND DO.

Practice beats 9-16 (individual's tempo) then SAY AND DO.

SAY AND DO the entire sequence and add the music.

CHAIR DANCING

Do walking steps in place.

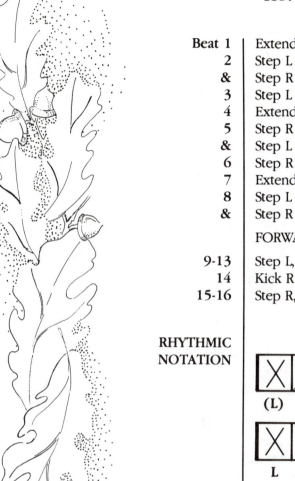

The Hustle
Novelty
U.S.A.

RECORD	H and L Records 4653 *The Hustle*
INTRODUCTION	No introduction or 64 beats
FORMATION	Free formation
PART I	FORWARD, 2, 3, TOUCH; BACKWARD, 2, 3, TOUCH; FORWARD, 2, 3, TOUCH; TOUCH (FORWARD), TOUCH (FORWARD), TOUCH (BACKWARD), TOUCH (BACKWARD); TOUCH (FORWARD), TOUCH (BACKWARD), TOUCH (SIDEWARD), STEP; TOUCH (SIDEWARD), TOUCH (IN PLACE), JUMP, HOP
Beat 1-3	Step L, R, L foot forward
4	Touch R foot forward
5-7	Step R, L, R foot backward
8	Touch L foot backward
9-12	Repeat beats 1-4
13-16	Touch R foot forward twice then backward twice
17-20	Touch R foot forward, backward, sideward, then step next to L foot
21-22	Touch L foot sideward, touch L foot next to R foot
23	Jump turning 1/4 left
24	Hop R foot bringing L foot up in back
RHYTHMIC NOTATION	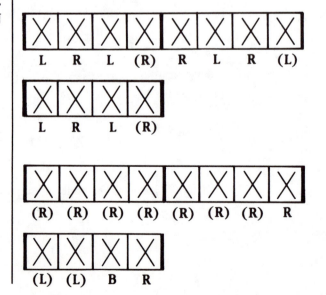

The Hustle (continued)

LEAD-UP ACTIVITIES	Practice balancing on one leg and touching the free foot in front, in back, to the side, etc. (individual's tempo).
	Practice FORWARD, 2, 3, TOUCH; BACKWARD, 2, 3, TOUCH (individual's tempo).
	Practice TOUCH 3 times followed by a STEP (individual's tempo).
	Practice JUMP, HOP executing a 1/4 TURN (individual's tempo).
TEACHING SUGGESTIONS	Begin with the first 12 beats and keep "adding on" the next section of 4 beats. Use individual's tempo, then group SAY AND DO.
	Practice the transition from the end to the beginning.
	Do the entire dance with SAY AND DO and then add the music.
CHAIR DANCING	Do the FORWARD and BACKWARD patterns with small steps away from and toward the chair and omit the TURN at the end.

Jamaican Holiday*
Novelty Mixer
U.S.A.

RECORD	Educational Activities AR546 *Movin'*
INTRODUCTION	16 beats
FORMATION	Partners side by side facing counterclockwise; no hands held
ALTERNATE FORMATION	Circle

PART I	FORWARD, 2, 3, HIT; FORWARD, 2, 3, HIT; TOUCH, TOUCH, TOUCH, STEP; TOUCH, TOUCH, TOUCH, STEP
Beat 1-3	Step R, L, R foot forward counterclockwise
4	Lift L foot and hit inside of L shoe with R hand
5-8	Repeat beats 1-4 beginning L foot
9	Touch R foot sideward right
10	Touch R foot next to L foot
11	Touch R foot sideward right
12	Step R foot next to L foot
13-16	Repeat beats 9-12 beginning L foot (outside person do a 4th touch rather than step)
	TURN, 2, 3, CLAP; TURN, 2, 3, CLAP; BUMP, BUMP, HIT, HIT; CHANGE, 2, 3, 4
17-19	Inside person: 3-step turn to the right beginning R foot crossing behind partner
20	Clap over R shoulder
NOTE	Outside person: 3-step turn to the left beginning L foot in front of partner then clap.
21-24	Repeat beats 17-20 in opposite direction with opposite footwork
25-26	Bump partner twice and turn to face partner
27	Inside person hits partner's hands with a downward motion; outside person hits up
28	Reverse beat 27
29-32	Inside person walks R, L, R, L foot forward to new partner; outside person steps in place or turns in 4 steps
NOTE	Dance may be done without reference to R or L feet. Beats 17-24 may be modified to move sideward rather than turning.

*Choreographed by Phyllis Weikart.

Jamaican Holiday (continued)

CIRCLE DANCE	Dance as inside person and change beats 25-32 to combinations of thigh PATS, CLAPS and SNAPS.
RHYTHMIC NOTATION	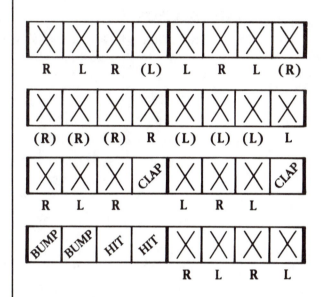

LEAD-UP ACTIVITIES	Practice STEP, STEP, STEP, HIT (individual's tempo).
	Practice TOUCH, TOUCH, TOUCH, STEP (individual's tempo).
	Practice 3-step turn adding a clap on the 4th beat (individual's tempo).
TEACHING SUGGESTIONS	Practice beats 1-16 using individual's tempo and then SAY AND DO.
	Practice TURN, 2, 3, CLAP; TURN, 2, 3, CLAP first with inside person moving and outside person standing still, then with only outside person moving and finally with both people moving simultaneously.
	Practice BUMP, BUMP, HIT, HIT with partner.
	Practice sequence with partner (partner beat then SAY AND DO).
CHAIR DANCING	TURNS—substitute SIDE, CLOSE, SIDE, CLAP.
	BUMP, BUMP, HIT, HIT—substitute thigh PATS and CLAPS or SNAPS.

Joe Clark Mixer*
Novelty
U.S.A.

RECORD	Folkraft 1071
INTRODUCTION	4 beats
FORMATION	Double circle, partners facing each other: man on inside; directions given for inside person; outside person, opposite direction and footwork for Part I
PART I	SIDE, CLOSE, SIDE, TOUCH; SIDE, CLOSE, SIDE, TOUCH; DO-SA-DO
Beat 1	Step L foot sideward left (partners hold both hands)
2	Step R foot next to L foot
3	Step L foot sideward left
4	Touch R foot next to L foot
5-8	Repeat beats 1-4 sideward right beginning R foot
9-16	Do-sa-do partner
17-32	Repeat Part I, beats 1-16, and turn 1/4 right to face clockwise (partner facing counterclockwise)
PART II	FORWARD, 2, 3, HIT; BACKWARD, 2, 3, HIT; FORWARD, 2, 3, HIT; FORWARD, 2, 3, 4; JUMP, KICK, JUMP, KICK; JUMP, KICK, JUMP, KICK; PAT, CLAP, R (hand), CLAP; L (hand), CLAP, BOTH (hands), PAT
Beat 1-3	Walk 3 steps forward clockwise (no R foot or L foot is necessary)
4	Hit both hands with the next outside person
5-7	Walk backward 3 steps
8	Hit both hands with your original partner
9-12	Repeat beats 1-4
13-16	Walk 4 steps forward clockwise to next outside person (you have moved 2 people beyond your partner)
17	Jump (join hands)
18	Hop R foot, kicking L foot across (both persons use same footwork)
19-20	Jump, then hop L foot kicking R foot across
21-24	Repeat beats 17-20
25-26	Pat thighs with both hands, clap own hands
27-28	Hit partner's R hand with your R hand, clap own hands
29-30	Hit partner's L hand with your L hand, clap own hands
31-32	Hit partner's two hands with yours, pat thighs

*Choreographed by Phyllis Weikart.

Joe Clark Mixer (continued)

RHYTHMIC NOTATION

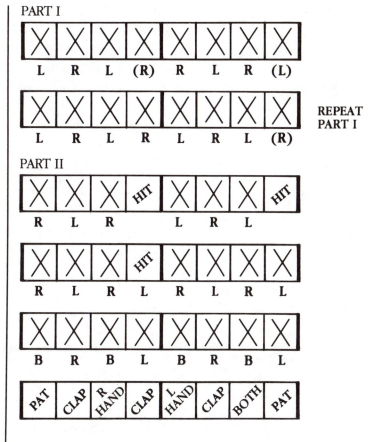

PART I

X	X	X	X	X	X	X	X
L	R	L	(R)	R	L	R	(L)

X	X	X	X	X	X	X	X
L	R	L	R	L	R	L	(R)

REPEAT PART I

PART II

X	X	X	HIT	X	X	X	HIT
R	L	R		L	R	L	

X	X	X	HIT	X	X	X	X
R	L	R	L	R	L	R	L

X	X	X	X	X	X	X	X
B	R	B	L	B	R	B	L

PAT	CLAP	R. HAND	CLAP	L. HAND	CLAP	BOTH	PAT

LEAD-UP ACTIVITIES

Practice SIDE, CLOSE, SIDE, TOUCH (individual's tempo) then with partner (partner beat).

Practice DO-SA-DO with partner (partner beat).

Practice walking FORWARD 4 steps, BACKWARD 4 steps, and FORWARD 8 steps (individual's tempo).

Practice JUMP, KICK (individual's tempo).

Practice "hand-jive" patterns with a partner (partner beat).

(continued)

Joe Clark Mixer (continued)

TEACHING SUGGESTIONS

Practice SIDE, CLOSE, SIDE, TOUCH; SIDE, CLOSE, SIDE, TOUCH with a partner (SAY AND DO) then "add on" the DO-SA-DO and SAY AND DO Part I.

Practice the FORWARD, BACKWARD walking pattern of Part II with SAY AND DO then "add on" the HIT while doing the walking pattern.

Practice the JUMP, KICK with SAY AND DO.

Practice the "hand-jive" pattern of the final 8 beats with SAY AND DO. Do Part II with SAY AND DO.

Practice the transition from the DO-SA-DO into Part II and from the end to the beginning.

Do the entire dance with SAY AND DO and add the music.

CHAIR DANCING PART I

Do the SIDE, CLOSE, SIDE, TOUCH as described and substitute walking the feet away from and toward the chair for the DO-SA-DO.

PART II

WALK the feet in place and PAT the thighs for the HIT. Simulate the "hand-jive" by hitting the air for R hand, L hand, both hands.

NOTE

This dance may be done in wheelchairs.

Mexican Mixer
Mexico

RECORD	Educational Record #2 *Mexican Dance*
INTRODUCTION	4 beats
FORMATION	Partners in a double circle facing counterclockwise, skater's hold
PART I	FORWARD, 2, 3, TURN; BACKWARD, 2, 3, 4
Beat 1-4	Walk 4 steps forward counterclockwise (on 4th step turn 180° to face clockwise)
5-8	Walk 4 steps backward counterclockwise
9-16	Repeat Part I, beats 1-8, moving clockwise
	Keep R hand-hold with partner, release L hand with partner and take neighbor's L hand; men are facing out of circle; women are facing into circle (Alamo position)
NOTE	Part I is a simplification; the actual Part I follows.
Beat 1-4	Men walk L, R, L, R foot
5	Step L foot sideward left (counterclockwise)
6	Step R foot crossing in back of L foot
7	Step L foot sideward left
8	Touch R foot next to L foot
9-16	Repeat beats 1-8 in opposite direction beginning R foot (women use opposite footwork on beats 1-16)
PART II	IN, TOUCH, OUT, TOUCH; TURN, 2, 3, 4
Beat 1-2	Step into the space and touch
3-4	Step out of the space and touch
5-8	Turn 1/2 using 4 steps, keeping R hand-hold with partner (you are now facing the opposite direction)
9-12	Repeat beats 1-4
13-16	Keep holding neighbor's L hand and release partner's R hand; move in 4 steps to a position side by side with neighbor; begin dance from beginning with new partner

RHYTHMIC NOTATION

PART I

X	X	X	X	X	X	X	X	
R	L	R	L	R	L	R	L	**REPEAT**

PART II

X	X	X	X	X	X	X	X	
R	(L)	L	(R)	R	L	R	L	**REPEAT**

(continued)

Mexican Mixer (continued)

LEAD-UP ACTIVITIES	Walk 4 steps FORWARD, turn 180° and walk BACKWARD 4 steps (individual's tempo)—move counterclockwise then execute moving clockwise.
	Practice the above with a partner using skater's hold (partner beat).
TEACHING SUGGESTIONS	Practice Part I with a partner (partner beat then SAY AND DO)—teach the simplification before attempting the actual dance.
	Have the students move into the formation for Part II and execute beats 1-8—SAY "INTO the space, OUT of the space, TURN with your partner" (partners now have changed places)—continue with "INTO the space, OUT of the space, neighbor is your partner."
	Return to original partner and practice Part II until executed successfully.
	Practice the transition from Part I to Part II.
	Do the entire dance with SAY AND DO then add the music.
CHAIR DANCING	May be adapted for wheelchairs.

Pata Pata
South Africa

RECORD	Reprise 0732
INTRODUCTION	16 beats
FORMATION	Individual
PART I	TOUCH, STEP, TOUCH, TOGETHER; TOES OUT, HEELS OUT, HEELS IN, TOES IN; UP, TOUCH, UP, STEP; KICK, TURN, 2, 3

Pata Pata (continued)

Beat 1	Touch R foot sideward right (arms sideward with snap)
2	Step R foot next to L foot (clap)
3	Touch L foot sideward left (arms sideward with snap)
4	Step L foot next to R foot (clap)
5	Turn toes out (raise arms, elbows in)
6	Turn heels out (lower arms)
7	Turn heels in (arms as in beat 5)
8	Turn toes in (arms as in beat 6)
9	Raise R knee in front of body
10	Touch R foot sideward right
11	Raise R knee
12	Step R foot next to L foot
13	Kick L foot in
14-16	Step L, R, L foot turning left (body turns counterclockwise)

RHYTHMIC NOTATION

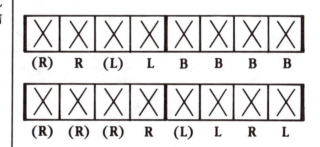

LEAD-UP ACTIVITIES

Practice TOUCH, STEP, TOUCH, TOGETHER (individual's tempo).

Practice moving toes apart, heels apart, heels together, toes together (TOES, HEELS, HEELS, TOES)—individual's tempo. Practice 3-STEP TURNS (individual's tempo).

TEACHING SUGGESTIONS

Do not use any hand motions when teaching the dance the first time. Add motions when dance is secure.

Practice TOUCH, STEP, TOUCH, TOGETHER beginning R foot with SAY AND DO; "add on" TOES, HEELS, HEELS, TOES.

SAY AND DO the first 8 beats then "add on" UP, TOUCH, UP, STEP—(R foot).

SAY AND DO the first 12 beats and "add on" KICK, TURN, 2, 3 or execute the TURN, 2, 3 with 3 steps in place. SAY AND DO the entire dance and add the music.

CHAIR DANCING

Substitute steps in place for the TURN.

Sham Hareh Golan
There They Are the Mountains of Golan
Israel

RECORD	Hadarim III *Back from Israel*
INTRODUCTION	4 beats
FORMATION	Line facing counterclockwise, hands joined
PART I	FORWARD/2, 3/4; CAMEL ROLL; TOUCH, TOUCH; BACKWARD/CLOSE, FORWARD
Beat 1-2	Step R, L, R, L foot forward counterclockwise
3-4	Camel roll backward; step forward on R foot, raise up on R foot and begin to sway backward onto L foot; bend both knees and come forward on R foot again (during the roll the hips make a backward circle)
5-6	Touch L foot forward twice (heel or toe may be touched)
7	Step L foot backward
&	Step R foot next to L foot
8	Step L foot forward counterclockwise
9-16	Repeat Part I, beats 1-8
	Face center
PART II	CROSS, TOUCH; CROSS, TOUCH; CROSS, TOUCH/IN; OUT/2, 3/4
Beat 1	Step R foot crossing in front of L foot (bend both knees)
2	Touch L foot sideward (straighten legs)
3	Step L foot crossing in front of R foot (bend both knees)
4	Touch R foot sideward (straighten legs)
5	Repeat beat 1
6	Touch L foot sideward
&	Step L foot in toward center bending knee
7-8	Step R, L, R, L foot out with small steps
9-16	Repeat Part II, beats 1-8

Sham Hareh Golan (continued)

RHYTHMIC NOTATION

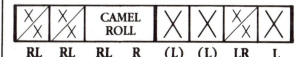

PART I

| X X | X X | CAMEL ROLL | X | X | X X | X | REPEAT |
| RL | RL | RL | R | (L) | (L) | LR | L |

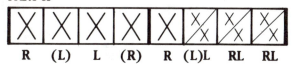

PART II

| X | X | X | X | X | X X | X X | X X | REPEAT |
| R | (L) | L | (R) | R | (L)L | RL | RL |

LEAD-UP ACTIVITIES

Practice or learn the CAMEL ROLL (individual's tempo).

Practice BACKWARD/CLOSE, FORWARD (individual's tempo).

Practice CROSS, TOUCH (individual's tempo).

TEACHING SUGGESTIONS

Practice TOUCH, TOUCH; BACKWARD/CLOSE, FORWARD beginning L foot (individual's tempo then SAY AND DO); "precede" with the CAMEL ROLL and then with the 4 WALKS.

Do Part I with SAY AND DO.

Practice CROSS, TOUCH, CROSS, TOUCH (individual's tempo then SAY AND DO) and "add on" CROSS, TOUCH/IN; OUT/2, 3/4.

Do Part II with SAY AND DO.

Practice the transitions between the parts.

Do the entire dance with SAY AND DO and add the music.

CHAIR DANCING

PART I   Do steps in place and simulate CAMEL ROLL with upper body.

PART II   Do as described.

Tanko Bushi
Coal Miner's Dance
Japan

RECORD	Folk Dancer MH 2010
INTRODUCTION	9 beats
FORMATION	Individual dance often done in an open circle
PART I	DIG, STEP; DIG, STEP; TOE/STEP, TOUCH; TOE/STEP, TOUCH; WALK, WALK; CROSS/BACK, TOGETHER
Beat 1	Weight on L foot, lift R foot in front of L foot (pointed diagonally right); thrust R foot to floor in digging motion (hands apart as if holding a shovel—R hand low)
2	Repeat beat 1 and step on R foot
3-4	Repeat beats 1-2 with weight on R (dig left and step L foot)
5	Touch R foot forward (bring both hands over R shoulder—throwing bag of coal over shoulder)
&	Lower R heel transferring weight to R foot
6	Touch L foot forward (bring hands over L shoulder)
7	Touch L foot backward (bring L arm in back of body with it bent and R arm up to forehead—shielding eyes)
&	Lower L heel to floor transferring weight to L foot
8	Touch R foot backward (switch arms in beat 7)
9	Step R foot forward (push both arms forward—pushing coal car)
10	Step L foot forward (push again)
11	Step R foot crossing in front of L foot (bring arms backward)
&	Step L foot crossing in back of R foot
12	Step R foot next to L foot (weight on both feet); clap hands in front
13-14	Clap hands 2 times
	Repeat dance and add 5 claps

RHYTHMIC NOTATION

X	X	X	X	X/X	X	X/X	X
(R)	R	(L)	L	(R)R	(L)	(L)L	(R)

X	X	X/X	CLAP	CLAP	CLAP
R	L	RL	B		

Tanko Bushi (continued)

LEAD-UP ACTIVITIES	Practice the different arm motions (individual's tempo).
	Practice the 2-beat foot patterns (individual's tempo).
TEACHING SUGGESTIONS	First teach only the foot pattern with SAY AND DO beginning with the TOE/STEP, TOUCH; TOE/STEP, TOUCH in a forward and backward direction.
	"Precede" the above with DIG, STEP, DIG, STEP and SAY AND DO beats 1-8; "add on" the WALK, WALK, CROSS/BACK, TOGETHER.
	Do the entire dance with SAY AND DO and add the music (feet only).
	The second time the dance is presented review the foot movements then the arm sequences. Teach the arm movements visually with very few directions then DO the arm sequence while SAYING the foot patterns (be certain to stand still). When the arm movements are secure against the language of the feet, put the two together.
	Do the entire dance with the arm motions to the music.
CHAIR DANCING	Do the arm motions only or add the feet in place.

Toi Nergis
Armenia

RECORD	Folkraft 1466
INTRODUCTION	16 beats
FORMATION	Men—shoulder hold; women—"W" position, little fingers joined

PART I	Men: FORWARD, FORWARD, SIDE, LIFT; SIDE, TOUCH, STAMP/STAMP, STAMP
Beat 1	Step R foot forward counterclockwise
2	Step L foot forward counterclockwise and turn to face center
3	Step R foot sideward right
4	Lift L foot in front of R leg
5	Step L foot sideward left
6	Touch R foot in
7-8	Stamp R foot next to L foot 3 times (7 &, 8)
	Women: SIDE, CLOSE, SIDE, TOUCH; SIDE, TOUCH, STAMP/STAMP, STAMP
1	Step R foot sideward right (hands move to right)
2	Step L foot next to R foot (hands move to left)
3	Step R foot sideward right (hands move to right)
4	Touch L foot next to R foot (hands move to left)
5	Step L foot sideward left (hands move to right)
6-8	Same as men above (hands move to left on beat 6 and arms move up and down on stamps)

RHYTHMIC NOTATION

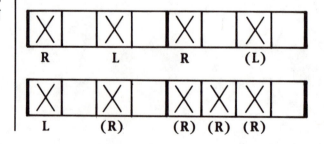

Toi Nergis (continued)

LEAD-UP ACTIVITIES	Practice STAMP/STAMP, STAMP while standing on one foot (individual's tempo).
	Practice SIDE, TOUCH (individual's tempo).
TEACHING SUGGESTIONS	Either teach one part and then the other to everyone or separate the male and female dancers and teach each group its own part.
	Male part—Practice FORWARD, FORWARD, SIDE, LIFT with SAY AND DO and "add on" SIDE, TOUCH and then STAMP/STAMP, STAMP.
	Do the entire sequence with SAY AND DO.
	Female part—Practice SIDE, CLOSE, SIDE, TOUCH with SAY AND DO and then "add on" SIDE, TOUCH and then STAMP/STAMP, STAMP.
	Do the entire arm sequence with SAY AND DO but don't move the feet.
	Do the entire sequence and add the music.
CHAIR DANCING	Step in place for moving steps.

Tsakonikos
Tsakonia, Peloponnesos
Greece

RECORD	Folkraft LP-3 Folkraft 1462X45
INTRODUCTION	No introduction
FORMATION	Open circle, leader at right; escort hold with R under

PART I	FORWARD, 2, 3, 4, DRAW
Beat 1	Step R foot forward moving counterclockwise
2	Step L foot forward moving counterclockwise
3-4	Repeat beats 1-2
5	Draw the R foot up to the L foot without a change of weight
6-40	Repeat Part I seven more times
PART II	FORWARD, 2, 3, HOP/STEP, STEP
Beat 1	Step R foot forward counterclockwise
2	Step L foot forward counterclockwise
3	Step R foot forward counterclockwise
4	Hop R foot (foot barely leaves the floor)
&	Step L foot forward
5	Step R foot forward
6-10	Repeat beats 1-5 with opposite footwork beginning L foot
11-40	Repeat Part II, beats 1-10, three times

RHYTHMIC NOTATION

PART I

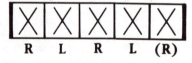

R   L   R   L   (R)   **REPEAT 7X**

PART II

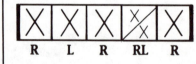

R   L   R   RL   R   **REPEAT 7X W/OPP. FTWK.**

LEAD-UP ACTIVITIES

Practice walking in grouping of 5 beats. Accent beat 1 of each 5 beats (individual's tempo).

Practice 4 steps followed by a TOUCH beginning R foot (individual's tempo).

PAT the rhythm of Part II on the legs.

Practice a pattern of STEP, HOP/STEP, STEP (individual's tempo).

Tsakonikos (continued)

TEACHING SUGGESTIONS	Listen to Part I of the music and identify the grouping of 5 beats using a PAT on the legs.
	Practice Part I with SAY then with SAY AND DO.
	Practice Part II with SAY then practice pattern at individual's tempo followed by SAY AND DO.
	Practice the transitions and add the music.
CHAIR DANCING	
PART I	Move feet away from and toward the chair on each 5 beats.
PART II	Do in place.

Vranjanka (Sano Duso)
Sana, Sweetheart
Yugoslavia (Serbia)

RECORD	EKS 7206 *The Whole World Dances;* Folk Dancer MH 3020
INTRODUCTION	8 measures (24 beats)
FORMATION	Circle, hands held in "W" position, or broken circle
MEASURE I	SIDE, BOUNCE, CROSS
Beat 1	Step R foot sideward right
2	Bounce slightly on R foot carrying L foot across in front of R foot
3	Step L foot crossing in front of R foot
MEASURE II	SIDE, BOUNCE, BOUNCE
Beat 4	Step R foot sideward right
5-6	Touch L foot sideward left and bounce twice on R foot
MEASURE III	SIDE, BOUNCE, BOUNCE
Beat 7	Step L foot sideward left
8-9	Touch R foot sideward right and bounce twice on L foot
MEASURE IV	SIDE, BOUNCE, BOUNCE
Beat 10-12	Repeat Measure II
MEASURE V	SIDE, SIDE, CROSS
Beat 13	Step L foot sideward left
14	Step R foot sideward right
15	Step L foot crossing in front of R foot
RHYTHMIC NOTATION	

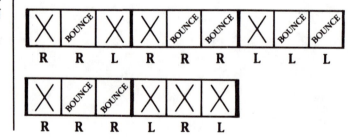

Vranjanka (Sano Duso) (continued)

LEAD-UP ACTIVITIES

Practice a SIDE, BOUNCE pattern (individual's tempo).

Practice SIDE, BOUNCE, CROSS (individual's tempo).

Practice SIDE, SIDE, CROSS (individual's tempo).

WALK in different groupings of 3 beats—WALK all the beats, WALK only the first of each 3 beats, WALK the first and third beats (individual's tempo).

TEACHING SUGGESTIONS

PAT the legs to the music accenting the first PAT of each 3 PATS, PAT only the first beat, PAT beats 1 and 3.

WALK to the music using the same patterns as in the Lead-Up Activities.

Practice SIDE, BOUNCE, BOUNCE with SAY AND DO.

"Precede" 3 patterns of SIDE, BOUNCE, BOUNCE with SIDE, BOUNCE, CROSS (SAY AND DO).

"Add on" the last measure of SIDE, SIDE, CROSS (SAY AND DO).

Practice the transition of measure 5 to measure 1.

Practice the entire dance with SAY AND DO then add the music.

CHAIR DANCING

Do steps in place.

Even Dance Steps

Characteristic:
Each movement in the sequence takes the same amount of time to execute.

Cherkessiya
Israel

RECORD	Tikva T-106 *Medley*
INTRODUCTION	16 beats
FORMATION	Single circle, facing center
CHORUS Beat 1-16	CHERKESSIYA Do 4 Cherkessiya steps beginning R foot
TO SIMPLIFY	Substitute 4 steps in place (body low) and 4 steps in place (body tall) for the CHERKESSIYA steps. This sequence is done twice. No R or L foot is necessary. Further simplification: 8 steps (body low), 8 steps (body tall).
PART I Beat 1-16	JUMP Jump 16 times in place
CHORUS	Repeat Chorus, beats 1-16
PART II Beat 1-16	SKIP Skip 8 times forward counterclockwise beginning R foot
CHORUS	Repeat Chorus, beats 1-16
PART III Beat 1-16	SCISSORS IN Scissors kicks in (16 leg kicks)
CHORUS	Repeat Chorus, beats 1-16
PART IV Beat 1 2 3-16	SIDE, BACK Step R foot sideward right Step L foot crossing in back of R foot (bending knees) Repeat beats 1-2 seven times
CHORUS	Repeat Chorus, beats 1-16
PART V Beat 1-16	SCISSORS OUT Scissors kicks out (16 leg kicks)
CHORUS	Repeat Chorus, beats 1-16
PART VI Beat 1-16	TOES, HEELS (SWIVEL STEPS) Move toes right, then move heels right; keep feet together; repeat 7 times
CHORUS	Repeat Chorus, beats 1-16
PART VII Beat 1-16	TROT Horse trot 16 times forward counterclockwise beginning R foot
CHORUS	Repeat Chorus, beats 1-16
PART VIII Beat 1-16	LOCOMOTIVE Walk 16 steps forward counterclockwise 4 steps with body low and knees bent, (4 steps with body tall and legs straight); repeat 4 low and 4 tall

(continued)

Cherkessiya *(continued)*

RHYTHMIC NOTATION

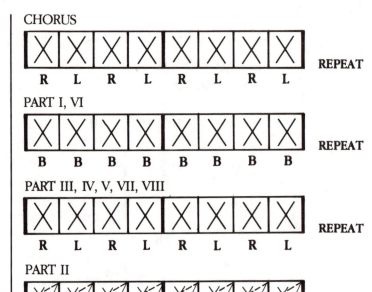

CHORUS

| X | X | X | X | X | X | X | X | REPEAT
| R | L | R | L | R | L | R | L |

PART I, VI

| X | X | X | X | X | X | X | X | REPEAT
| B | B | B | B | B | B | B | B |

PART III, IV, V, VII, VIII

| X | X | X | X | X | X | X | X | REPEAT
| R | L | R | L | R | L | R | L |

PART II

| X | X | X | X | X | X | X | X | REPEAT
| RR | LL | RR | LL | RR | LL | RR | LL |

LEAD-UP ACTIVITIES

Step in place with the body low then with the body tall—do 4 low and 4 tall (individual's tempo).

SKIP, HORSE TROT, JUMP (individual's tempo).

KICK the legs IN, KICK the legs OUT (individual's tempo).

Move in a SIDE, BACK pattern (individual's tempo).

Move with SWIVEL STEPS (individual's tempo).

TEACHING SUGGESTIONS

Practice the CHERKESSIYA step beginning with 4 steps in place accenting the first of each 4 steps then step IN on the first of each 4 steps (SAY AND DO).

If simplifying the CHERKESSIYA, move in a pattern of 4 steps in place with body bent over and 4 steps with arms overhead.

Practice the verses or use other movement ideas.

Do the dance with the music.

CHAIR DANCING

Change the verses to include arm movements.

Ciocarlanul
Romania

RECORD	Folk Dancer MH 1122
INTRODUCTION	8 beats
FORMATION	Circle, hands joined, face center
PART I	CHERKESSIYA; CHERKESSIYA; CHERKESSIYA; STEP/STEP, STEP, STEP/STEP, STEP
Beat 1-4	Cherkessiya beginning R foot (cross R foot in front of L foot, lifting L foot behind, beat 1)
5-12	Repeat Cherkessiya beginning R foot 2 times
13	Step R foot next to L foot
&	Step L foot next to R foot or cross slightly in front of R foot
14	Step R foot next to L foot or cross in back of L foot
15-16	Repeat beats 13-14 beginning L foot
17-32	Repeat Part I, beats 1-16
PART II	SIDE, BACK, SIDE, BACK; SIDE, STAMP, STAMP, HOLD
Beat 1	Step R foot sideward right (ball of foot)
2	Step L foot crossing in back of R foot
3	Step R foot sideward right
4	Step L foot crossing in back of R foot
5	Step R foot sideward right
6-7	Stamp L foot next to R foot 2 times
8	Hold
9-16	Repeat Part II, beats 1-8, sideward clockwise beginning L foot
17-32	Repeat Part II, beats 1-16

RHYTHMIC NOTATION

PART I

X	X	X	X	**REPEAT 2X**
R	L	R	L	

PART I BEAT 13-16

X/X	X	X/X	X	**REPEAT PART I**
RL	R	LR	L	

PART II

X	X	X	X	X	X	X	**REPEAT 3X W/OPP. FTWK.**
R	L	R	L	R	(L)	(L)	

(continued)

Ciocarlanul (continued)

LEAD-UP ACTIVITIES	Review CHERKESSIYA step (individual's tempo).
	PAT the legs in an even beat and say "Bumble Bee" for each 2 PATS then do "Bumble Bee" with the feet (STEP/STEP, STEP) in place (individual's tempo).
	Practice SIDE, BACK steps each direction (individual's tempo).
	Practice STAMPS without changing weight, then SIDE, STAMP, STAMP, HOLD each direction. (individual's tempo).
TEACHING SUGGESTIONS	PAT the rhythm of Part I then add the language of Part I (IN, OUT, OUT, IN; IN, OUT, OUT, IN; IN, OUT, OUT, IN; BUMBLE BEE, BUMBLE BEE).
	SAY AND DO the sequence of Part I.
	SAY the language of Part II, then SAY AND DO.
	Practice the transitions from Part I to Part II and back to the beginning.
CHAIR DANCING	Substitute SIDE, CLOSE for SIDE, BACK in Part II.

Mechol Hagat
Dance of the Winepressers
Israel

RECORD	Tikva T-106 *Medley*
INTRODUCTION	8 beats
FORMATION	Closed circle, L hand carried at L shoulder, R arm straight
CHORUS	SHUFFLE
Beat 1-32	Shuffle 32 steps forward counterclockwise beginning R foot, body leans slightly backward
PART I	CHERKESSIYA (4); CHERKESSIYA; TURN 2, 3, 4; CHERKESSIYA; TURN, 2, 3, 4

Mechol Hagat (continued)

Beat 1-16	Cherkessiya 4 times beginning R foot (facing center)
17-20	Cherkessiya beginning R foot
21-24	Turn right with 4 steps beginning R foot (full turn)
25-28	Cherkessiya beginning R foot
29-32	Turn right with 4 steps beginning R foot
CHORUS	Repeat Chorus, beats 1-32
PART II	CHERKESSIYA; ACCENT, 2, 3, 4
Beat 1-4	Cherkessiya beginning R foot
5-8	Accent R, L, R, L foot, body low
9-32	Repeat Part III, beats 1-8, three times
CHORUS	Repeat Chorus, beats 1-32
PART III	CHERKESSIYA (4); DOWN, 2, 3, 4; UP, 2, 3, 4; DOWN, 2, 3, 4; UP, 2, 3, 4
Beat 1-16	Cherkessiya 4 times beginning R foot
17-20	Accent R, L, R, L foot, body low
21-24	Accent R, L, R, L foot, body high
25-32	Repeat beats 17-24
	Repeat dance from the beginning.

RHYTHMIC NOTATION	CHORUS AND ALL PARTS

REPEAT 7X

LEAD-UP ACTIVITIES	Practice SHUFFLE step (individual's tempo). Practice CHERKESSIYA (individual's tempo). Practice turning in 4 steps (individual's tempo).
TEACHING SUGGESTIONS	Put on the music and identify the beat then SHUFFLE to it. Practice Part II (SAY AND DO). Practice Part III (SAY AND DO) then do Part II again. Practice Part IV (SAY AND DO) then do Parts II and III again. Help students understand the format of the dance with Chorus repeated in between the parts (rondo).
CHAIR DANCING PART I	SHUFFLE feet in place.
PART II	Use steps in place for the TURN.

Armenian Misirlou
Armenia

RECORD	Festival 3505 *Misirlou,* begin with vocal
INTRODUCTION	20 beats, begin with vocal
FORMATION	Circle, little fingers joined

PART I	TOUCH, TOUCH; TOUCH, TOUCH; CROSS, CROSS; CROSS/SIDE, BACK/SIDE
Beat 1	Touch L foot in toward center
2	Touch L foot to the left side
3	Touch L foot in toward center
4	Touch L foot to the left side
5	Step L foot crossing in front of R foot
6	Step R foot crossing in front of L foot
7	Step L foot crossing in front of R foot
&	Step R foot sideward right
8	Step L foot crossing in back of R foot
&	Step R foot sideward right

RHYTHMIC NOTATION

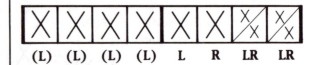

LEAD-UP ACTIVITIES	Practice standing on one foot and touching the free foot 4 times (individual's tempo).
	Practice stepping several times using a CROSS (individual's tempo).
	Practice a GRAPEVINE beginning L foot
TEACHING SUGGESTIONS	Practice CROSS/SIDE, BACK/SIDE beginning L foot with SAY AND DO then "precede" with CROSS, CROSS.
	Practice beats 5-8 with individual's tempo then SAY AND DO.
	"Precede" beats 5-8 with TOUCH, TOUCH, TOUCH, TOUCH and SAY AND DO the entire dance.
	Add the music.
CHAIR DANCING	Do in place steps substituting a CHERKESSIYA for the GRAPEVINE (CROSS/SIDE, BACK/SIDE).

Corrido
Mexico

RECORD	EKS 7206 *Whole World Dances*
INTRODUCTION	None
FORMATION	Couples in a double circle, men with backs to center, closed dance position; footwork given for men, women use opposite footwork
ALTERNATE FORMATION	Circle
PART I	SIDE, CLOSE
Beat 1	Step R foot sideward right
2	Step L foot next to R foot
3-20	Repeat Part I, beats 1-2, nine times
PART II	GRAPEVINE
Beat 1-4	Grapevine counterclockwise, begin crossing R foot in front of L foot
5-32	Repeat Part II, beats 1-4, seven times
BRIDGE	SIDE, CLOSE, SIDE, CLOSE
Beat 1-4	Repeat Part I, beats 1-2, two times
PART III	IN, 2, 3, 4; OUT, 2, 3, 4
Beat 1-4	Step R, L, R, L foot diagonally in toward center
5-8	Step R, L, R, L foot diagonally out
9-32	Repeat Part III, beats 1-8, three times
NOTE	Double circle is moving counterclockwise.
PART IV	GRAPEVINE
Beat 1-32	Repeat Part II, beats 1-32, eight times
NOTE	Hand-hold may be substituted for closed dance position.
CIRCLE DANCE	Dance women's part beginning L foot
RHYTHMIC NOTATION	PART I-V

R L R L R L R L

Corrido (continued)

LEAD-UP ACTIVITIES	Practice SIDE, CLOSE both directions (individual's tempo).
	Practice GRAPEVINE starting with one foot for several repetitions and then the other foot (individual's tempo).
	Practice walking diagonally IN 4 steps and diagonally OUT 4 steps (individual's tempo).
TEACHING SUGGESTIONS	Partners practice SIDE, CLOSE (partner beat)—move same direction.
	Partners practice GRAPEVINE moving same direction (partner beat).
	Partners move IN and OUT of the circle with 4 steps each and then execute on the proper diagonal (partner beat).
	Put dance together with SAY AND DO; then add music.
NOTE	Substitute a sequential count for one of the words, i.e., SIDE, CLOSE, 2 CLOSE, 3 CLOSE, 4 CLOSE, etc. when sequences occur in high repetition.
CHAIR DANCING	Substitute CHERKESSIYA steps for GRAPEVINE steps.
	Substitute steps in place for SIDE, CLOSE or use a SIDE, TOUCH; SIDE, TOUCH pattern.
	Move feet away from and toward the chair for IN, 2, 3, 4; OUT, 2, 3, 4

Debka Le Adama
Debka of the Soil
Israel

RECORD	Tikva T-98 *Dance with Rivka*
INTRODUCTION	8 beats
FORMATION	Line facing right, hands joined with L arm behind back

PART I	WALK
Beat 1-8	Walk 8 steps forward counterclockwise beginning L foot
9-16	Walk 8 steps backward beginning L foot (move clockwise)
PART II	IN, CLOSE, IN, TOUCH; HOP, HOP, STEP/STEP, STEP
Beat 1	Step L foot sideward (toward the center) with accent
2	Step R foot next to L foot
3	Step L foot sideward with accent
4	Touch R foot next to L foot
5	Hop L foot sideward right (away from center)
6	Hop L foot sideward right
7-8	Step R, L, R foot in place (substitute Yemenite beginning R foot for more experienced dancers)
9-16	Repeat Part II, beats 1-8
PART III	FORWARD, 2, 3, 4; GRAPEVINE (7)
Beat 1-4	Step L, R, L, R foot forward counterclockwise
5-8	Grapevine counterclockwise beginning L foot crossing in front of R foot
9-32	Repeat Grapevine 6 times; accelerate slightly and turn steps of Grapevine into leaping steps

RHYTHMIC NOTATION

PART I

X	X	X	X	X	X	X	X	REPEAT
L	R	L	R	L	R	L	R	

PART II

X	X	X	X	X	X	X/X	X	REPEAT
L	R	L	(R)	L	L	RL	R	

PART III

X	X	X	X	X	X	X	X	REPEAT 3X
L	R	L	R	L	R	L	R	

(continued)

Debka Le Adama *(continued)*

LEAD-UP ACTIVITIES	Walk FORWARD 8 steps and BACKWARD 8 steps. Use different starting foot (individual's tempo).
	Practice hopping on one foot SIDEWARD, moving in the direction opposite to the hopping foot (individual's tempo).
	Practice SIDE, CLOSE, SIDE, TOUCH each direction (individual's tempo).
	Practice GRAPEVINES in one direction then the other (individual's tempo).
TEACHING SUGGESTIONS	Walk FORWARD 8 steps and BACKWARD 8 steps beginning L foot. Add IN, CLOSE, IN, TOUCH sideward left beginning L foot (SAY AND DO).
	Practice HOP, HOP, STEP/STEP, STEP moving sideward right hopping on the L foot. Put this sequence together with the IN, CLOSE, IN, TOUCH (SAY AND DO).
	Practice Part III moving from the WALK to the GRAPEVINE (SAY AND DO).
	Practice the transition from Part II to Part III and from Part III to Part I.
	Practice the entire dance with SAY AND DO and then add music.
CHAIR DANCING **PART I**	Substitute steps in place or away from and toward the chair.
PART II	Move to the left and to the right.
PART III	Substitute CHERKESSIYA steps for the GRAPEVINE steps.

Dimna Juda Mamo
Macedonia

RECORD	Festival 4001, *Kopacka*—1st half
INTRODUCTION	4 beats
FORMATION	Broken circle, leader at right. Hands joined in front basket with R hand under

Dimna Juda Mamo (continued)

PART I	WALK
Beat 1-40	Walk 40 steps forward counterclockwise beginning R foot Turn to face center on beat 40
PART II	SIDE, CROSS; SIDE, BACK; SIDE, LIFT; SIDE, LIFT; SIDE, LIFT
Beat 1	Step R foot sideward right
2	Step L foot crossing in front of R foot
3	Step R foot sideward right
4	Step L foot crossing in back of R foot
5	Step R foot sideward right
6	Lift L foot in front of R leg (keep lift low to floor)
7-10	Repeat beats 5-6 two times alternating footwork
11-20	Repeat beats 1-10 to the left beginning L foot
21-40	Repeat Part II, beats 1-20

RHYTHMIC NOTATION

PART I

PART II

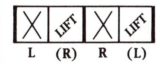

LEAD-UP ACTIVITIES

Practice SIDE, LIFT (individual's tempo).

Practice SIDE, CROSS, SIDE, BACK (individual's tempo).

TEACHING SUGGESTIONS

WALK to the music.

Practice SIDE, CROSS, SIDE, BACK several times each direction (SAY AND DO).

Do 1 pattern of SIDE, CROSS, SIDE, BACK and "add on" 3 SIDE, LIFT patterns. Practice each direction with SAY AND DO.

CHAIR DANCING

PART I WALK in place.

PART II Do as described keeping steps small.

Dirlada
Greece

RECORD	Peters International *Greek Dances* or Nina 2505 *Oh Dirlada*
INTRODUCTION	16 beats
FORMATION	Free formation
PART I	SIDE, BACK, SIDE, CROSS; SIDE, LIFT, SIDE, HIT; STEP, HIT, TURN, CLAP
Beat 1	Step R foot sideward right
2	Step L foot crossing in back of R foot
3	Step R foot sideward right
4	Step L foot crossing in front of R foot
5	Step R foot sideward right
6	Lift L foot in front of R leg
7	Step L foot sideward left
8	Raise R foot, knee bent, in back of L foot, hit R shoe with L hand
9	Step R foot next to L foot
10	Lift L foot in front of R leg and hit inside of L shoe with L hand
11	Step L foot turning 1/4 left
12	Raise R leg and clap under R leg

RHYTHMIC NOTATION

R   L   R   L   R   (L)   L   (R)

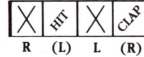

R   (L)   L   (R)

Dirlada (continued)

LEAD-UP ACTIVITIES

Practice GRAPEVINE patterns each direction (individual's tempo).

Practice STEP, HIT hitting free foot in back, then practice hitting free foot in front, then practice clapping under free leg (individual's tempo).

TEACHING SUGGESTIONS

Practice SIDE, LIFT, SIDE, HIT beginning R foot (SAY AND DO), "add on" STEP, HIT and practice beats 5-10 then "add on" TURN, CLAP (SAY AND DO).

"Precede" sequence with beats 1-4 (SAY AND DO).

Do entire dance and add music.

CHAIR DANCING

Omit TURN and step in place. Do other beats as described.

Hora Medura
Hora Around the Campfire
Israel

RECORD	Tikva T-106 *Medley*
INTRODUCTION	12 beats
FORMATION	Single circle facing center, hands joined
PART I	SIDE, CLOSE, SIDE, CLOSE; SIDE, CLOSE, SIDE, CLOSE; IN, 2, 3, 4; OUT, 2, 3, 4
Beat 1	Step R foot sideward right
2	Step L foot next to R foot
3-8	Repeat beats 1-2 three times
9-12	Step R, L, R, L foot in toward center of circle, raise arms
13-16	Step R, L, R, L foot out, lower arms
17-32	Repeat Part I, beats 1-16
TO SIMPLIFY	RUN 8 steps forward counterclockwise beats 1-8.
PART II	GRAPEVINE; RUN, 2, 3, 4; GRAPEVINE; HEEL, HOLD, HEEL, HOLD
Beat 1-4	Grapevine beginning R foot crossing in front of L foot
5-8	Run R, L, R, L foot forward clockwise
9-12	Grapevine beginning R foot
13	Stamp R heel (raise arms overhead)
14	Hold (lower arms)
15-16	Repeat beats 13-14
17-32	Repeat Part II, beats 1-16
TO SIMPLIFY	
Beat 1-12	Run 12 steps forward clockwise

Hora Medura *(continued)*

RHYTHMIC NOTATION

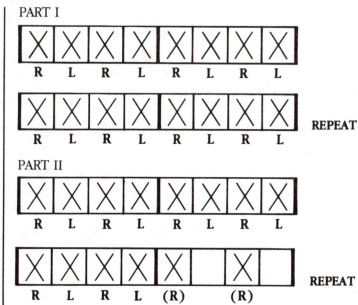

PART I

X	X	X	X	X	X	X	X
R	L	R	L	R	L	R	L

X	X	X	X	X	X	X	X
R	L	R	L	R	L	R	L

REPEAT

PART II

X	X	X	X	X	X	X	X
R	L	R	L	R	L	R	L

X	X	X	X	X		X	
R	L	R	L	(R)		(R)	

REPEAT

LEAD-UP ACTIVITIES

Practice SIDE, CLOSE (individual's tempo).

Practice GRAPEVINES if actual dance rather than simplification is to be taught.

Practice IN, 2, 3, 4; OUT, 2, 3, 4 followed by a running step clockwise.

TEACHING SUGGESTIONS

Practice Part I with SAY AND DO.

Practice simplification of Part II with SAY AND DO.

If using actual Part II, practice sequence of GRAPEVINE; RUN 4; GRAPEVINE with individual's tempo before SAY AND DO "adding on" the HEEL, HOLD, HEEL, HOLD.

Practice the transitions from Part I to Part II and back to Part I, then add the music.

CHAIR DANCING PART II

Do the steps in place.

Mayim
Water
Israel

RECORD	Israeli Music Foundation LP 5/6
INTRODUCTION	40 beats
FORMATION	Single circle facing center, hands joined
PART I	GRAPEVINE
Beat 1-16	Grapevine 4 times moving clockwise, beginning R foot crossing in front of L foot
PART II	IN, 2, 3, 4; OUT, 2, 3, 4; IN, 2, 3, 4; OUT, 2, 3, 4
Beat 1-4	Run R, L, R, L foot in to center of circle (raise arms)
5-8	Run R, L, R, L foot out backing up (lower arms), a clap on beat 5 may be added
9-16	Repeat Part II, beats 1-8
PART III	FORWARD, 2, 3, HOP; HOP 2, 3, 4; 5, 6, 7, 8; HOP, 2, 3, 4; 5, 6, 7, 8
Beat 1-3	Run R, L, R foot forward clockwise
4	Hop R foot turning to face center, bringing L foot in
5	Hop on R foot touching L foot in front of R foot
6	Hop on R foot touching L foot to left side
7-12	Repeat beats 5-6 three times
13	Hop on L foot and touch R foot in front
14	Hop on L foot touching R foot to right side
15-20	Repeat beats 13-14 three times
NOTE	If desired, release hands on Part III, beats 13-20, and clap hands in front of body each time foot touches in front.

Mayim (continued)

RHYTHMIC NOTATION

PART I & II

X	X	X	X	X	X	X	X
R	L	R	L	R	L	R	L

REPEAT

PART III

X	X	X	X	X	X	X	X
R	L	R	R	R	R	R	R

X	X	X	X
R	R	R	R

X	X	X	X	X	X	X	X
L	L	L	L	L	L	L	L

LEAD-UP ACTIVITIES

Practice GRAPEVINE (individual's tempo).

Practice touching the free foot forward and sideward while hopping (individual's tempo).

Practice combining GRAPEVINES with IN 4 steps and OUT 4 steps (individual's tempo).

TEACHING SUGGESTIONS

Practice 4 GRAPEVINE steps moving clockwise (SAY AND DO).

Do Parts I and II with SAY AND DO.

Practice FORWARD, 2, 3, HOP moving clockwise beginning R foot and bringing the L foot toward the center on the HOP. "Add on" 8 HOPS on the R foot followed by 8 HOPS on the L foot—add the TOUCH after the sequence has been learned without it (SAY AND DO).

Do Part III with SAY AND DO.

Do the entire dance with SAY AND DO and add the music.

CHAIR DANCING

PART I Do as described with small steps using CHERKESSIYA.

PART II Move feet away from and toward the chair.

PART III Do in place.

Romanian Hora
Triple Hora
Romania

RECORD	Folkraft 010X45 and LP-12
INTRODUCTION	8 beats
FORMATION	Circle facing center, arms in "T" position
PART I	GRAPEVINE; GRAPEVINE; GRAPEVINE; CROSS, SIDE, JUMP, JUMP
Beat 1-4	Grapevine moving counterclockwise beginning L foot
5-12	Repeat beats 1-4 two times
13	Step L foot crossing in front of R foot
14	Step R foot sideward right
15-16	Jump two times
17-32	Repeat Part I, beats 1-16, beginning R foot moving clockwise
TO SIMPLIFY	RUN 14 steps followed by 2 JUMPS counterclockwise then clockwise.
PART II	SIDE, BACK, SIDE, HOP
Beat 1	Step R foot sideward right
2	Step L foot crossing in back of R foot
3	Step R foot sideward right
4	Hop R foot swinging L foot in front of R leg
5-8	Repeat beats 1-4 beginning L foot sideward left
9-32	Repeat Part II, beats 1-8
PART III	LEAP, HOLD, LEAP, HOLD; SCISSORS, 2, 3, 4
Beat 1-2	Leap on R foot in place extending L heel in
3-4	Leap on L foot in place extending R heel in
5-8	Leap on R, L, R, L foot in place (scissors)
9-24	Repeat Part III, beats 1-8 two times
25-28	Repeat beats 1-4
29-32	Leap on R, L, R foot in place, hold beat 32

RHYTHMIC NOTATION

PART I

X	X	X	X	X	X	X	X
L	R	L	R	L	R	L	R

X	X	X	X	X	X	X	X
L	R	L	R	L	R	B	B

REPEAT W/OPP. FTWK.

Romanian Hora (continued)

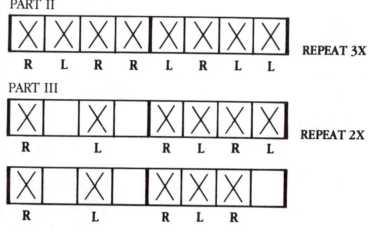

PART II

X	X	X	X	X	X	X	X
R	L	R	R	L	R	L	L

REPEAT 3X

PART III

X		X		X	X	X	X
R		L		R	L	R	L

REPEAT 2X

X		X		X	X	X	
R		L		R	L	R	

LEAD-UP ACTIVITIES

Practice 14 RUNS followed by 2 JUMPS in place (SAY AND DO).

Practice GRAPEVINES each direction (individual's tempo).

Practice SIDE, BACK, SIDE, HOP each direction (individual's tempo).

Practice SCISSORS KICKS.

TEACHING SUGGESTIONS

Practice GRAPEVINES with SAY AND DO.

Practice CROSS, SIDE, JUMP, JUMP with SAY AND DO.

Do Part I with SAY AND DO and add music before teaching Parts II and III.

Practice Part II with SAY AND DO.

Practice LEAP, HOLD, LEAP, HOLD with SAY AND DO and "add on" 4 SCISSORS IN.

Do Part III with SAY AND DO.

Practice the transitions between parts.

Do the dance with SAY AND DO and add the music.

CHAIR DANCING
PART I

Substitute CHERKESSIYA steps for GRAPEVINE steps.

PART II

Do as described.

PART III

Do as described.

The Stars and Stripes Forever*
Novelty
U.S.A.

RECORD	Boston Pops, RCA LSC-3200, *All American Favorites*
INTRODUCTION	8 beats
FORMATION	Short lines of 4-6 dancers standing side by side.
	At end of Introduction, TURN 1/4 left to face one behind the other
PART I	FORWARD, 2, 3, 4; BACKWARD, 2, 3, TURN; FORWARD, 2, 3, 4; BACKWARD, 2, 3, TURN; IN, 2, 3, 4; OUT, 2, 3, 4; OUT, 2, 3, 4; IN, 2, 3, 4
Beat 1-4	Step L, R, L, R foot forward
5-8	Step L, R, L, R foot backward and turn 1/2 to face opposite direction
9-16	Repeat beats 1-8 and end facing original position side by side
17-20	Step L, R, L, R foot IN or OUT (1/2 line moves IN; other 1/2 OUT)
21-24	Step L, R, L, R foot OUT or IN (opposite direction from beats 17-20)
25-28	Step L, R, L, R foot the same direction as beats 21-24
29-32	Step L, R, L, R foot the same direction as beats 17-20
33-64	Repeat Part I
TO SIMPLIFY	Don't divide line for beats 17-32.
PART II	UP, TOUCH, KICK, STEP; UP, TOUCH, KICK, STEP; KICK, STEP, KICK, STEP; KICK, STEP, KICK, TOUCH
Beat 1	Raise L knee up in front
2	Touch L foot next to R foot
3	Kick L foot in front
4	Step L foot next to R foot
5-8	Repeat beats 1-4 using R foot
9-16	Repeat beats 3-4 four times, end with a touch R foot
17-32	Repeat Part II, beats 1-16, beginning R foot
33-64	Repeat Part II, beats 1-32
PART III	CHERKESSIYA; CHERKESSIYA; CROSS, SIDE, BACK, SIDE; CROSS, SIDE, CLOSE, HOLD

*Choreographed by Phyllis Weikart.

The Stars and Stripes Forever *(continued)*

Beat 1-8	Cherkessiya step two times beginning L foot
9-12	Grapevine moving right beginning L foot
13	Step L foot crossing in front of R foot
14	Step R foot sideward right
15	Step L foot next to R foot
16	Hold
17-32	Repeat Part III, beats 1-16, beginning R foot
33-64	Repeat Part III, beats 1-32
PART IV	SIDE, CLOSE, SIDE, CLOSE; TURN, 2, 3, 4; (repeat 3 times); TOUCH, STEP, STEP, STEP; (repeat 3 times)
Beat 1-4	Side, close two times beginning L foot
5-8	Step L, R, L, R foot turning 1/4 left
9-32	Repeat beats 1-8 moving in a square pattern
33	Touch L foot in front of the body
34	Step L next to R foot
35-36	Step R foot, L foot in place
37-40	Repeat beats 33-36
41-48	Repeat beats 33-40
PART III **Beat 1-64**	Repeat Part III, beats 1-64
PART IV **Beat 1-48**	Repeat Part IV, beats 1-48
PART III **Beat 1-64**	Repeat Part III, beats 1-64 increasing intensity; end with a jump on both feet

(continued)

The Stars and Stripes Forever (continued)

RHYTHMIC NOTATION

PART I

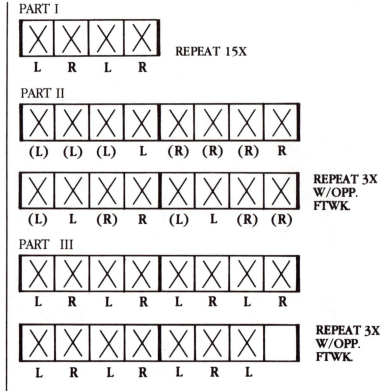

PART I

X	X	X	X
L	R	L	R

REPEAT 15X

PART II

X	X	X	X	X	X	X	X
(L)	(L)	(L)	L	(R)	(R)	(R)	R

X	X	X	X	X	X	X	X
(L)	L	(R)	R	(L)	L	(R)	(R)

REPEAT 3X W/OPP. FTWK.

PART III

X	X	X	X	X	X	X	X
L	R	L	R	L	R	L	R

X	X	X	X	X	X	X	
L	R	L	R	L	R	L	

REPEAT 3X W/OPP. FTWK.

LEAD-UP ACTIVITIES

Practice walking different directions beginning L foot (individual's tempo).

Practice UP, TOUCH and KICK, STEP and practice combining them (individual's tempo).

Practice CHERKESSIYA step and GRAPEVINE step.

The Stars and Stripes Forever (continued)

TEACHING SUGGESTIONS	Practice Part I with SAY AND DO using the simplification for beats 17-32 then add the music for Part I.
	Practice UP, TOUCH, KICK, STEP with SAY AND DO then KICK, STEP with SAY AND DO.
	Do Part II with SAY AND DO then add music for Part I and II.
	Practice Part III, using individual's tempo then SAY AND DO.
	Practice the square pattern of Part IV with SAY AND DO then "add on" the TOUCH, STEP, STEP, STEP sequence with SAY AND DO.
	Do Part III followed by Part IV with SAY AND DO.
	Recall Part I and II and do the dance to the music.
CHAIR DANCING **PART I**	Substitute a diagonal pattern away from and toward the chair for FORWARD and BACKWARD.
PART II	Do as described.
PART III	Do as described.
PART IV	Substitute in-place steps for 1/4 TURNS.
	May be designed as a wheelchair routine.

Sweet Girl
Armenia

RECORD	Folkraft 1528X45 (may be done to the Beatles' song—*A Little Help From My Friends*)
INTRODUCTION	16 beats
FORMATION	Line, little fingers joined in "W" position
PART I	TWO-STEP; TWO-STEP; SIDE, BACK; 1/2 TURN, SIDE; BACK, 1/2 TURN; SIDE, BACK
Beat 1-4	Two-step beginning R foot, L foot
5	Step R foot sideward right (facing center)
6	Step L foot crossing in back of right (lean body out)
7	Step R foot sideward with 1/2 turn to the right
8	Step L foot sideward left (facing out)
9	Step R foot crossing in back of L foot (clap and lean forward)
10	Step L foot sideward with 1/2 turn to left
11	Step R foot sideward right (facing in)
12	Step L foot crossing in back of R foot
TO SIMPLIFY **Beats 1-4**	Walk R, L, R, L foot
RHYTHMIC NOTATION	

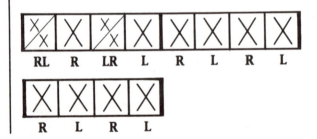

Sweet Girl (continued)

LEAD-UP ACTIVITIES

Practice stepping R foot with a 1/2 TURN right then L foot with a 1/2 TURN left. The movement direction is counterclockwise (individual's tempo). Encourage students to take large steps.

Practice moving counterclockwise with a series of SIDE, BACK, 1/2 TURN patterns. Make sure students balance themselves on the TURN and don't step down on the free foot until the SIDE step (individual's tempo).

Practice quick TWO-STEPS before the change from the simplified 4 WALKS to the 2 TWO-STEPS (individual's tempo).

TEACHING SUGGESTIONS

Practice FORWARD, 2, 3, 4; SIDE, BACK beginning R foot moving counterclockwise (individual's tempo then SAY AND DO).

"Add on" the 1/2 TURN following the SIDE, BACK, then "add on" another SIDE, BACK, 1/2 TURN. Note for the students that they have their backs to the center of the circle on this second SIDE, BACK, 1/2 TURN. Finally, "add on" the SIDE, BACK, of beats 11-12.

Do not add the claps until the dance is comfortable.

Do the entire dance with SAY AND DO and then add the music.

CHAIR DANCING

Beat 1-4 Do the four WALKS or the 2 TWO-STEPS in place.

Beat 5-10 Substitute a side-to-side stepping pattern. (SIDE, BACK, SIDE—SIDE, BACK, SIDE—SIDE, BACK).

Branle Normand
France

RECORD	Folkraft 337-002
INTRODUCTION	4 beats
FORMATION	Circle, hands held at shoulder level, "W" position
PART I	STEP/BEND, STEP/BEND; STEP/BEND, STEP/BEND; STEP/HOP, STEP/HOP; STEP/HOP, STEP/HOP
Beat 1	Step bend R foot forward counterclockwise
2	Step bend L foot forward counterclockwise
3-4	Repeat beats 1-2 and turn to face center
5	Step Hop R foot in place kicking L foot in
6	Step Hop L foot in place kicking R foot out
7-8	Repeat beats 5-6
	STEP/BEND, STEP/BEND; STEP/BEND, STEP/BEND; STEP/HOP, STEP/HOP; STEP/HOP, STEP/HOP; SIDE/HOP, SIDE/HOP; SIDE/HOP, SIDE/HOP
9-16	Repeat beats 1-8
17	Side Hop R foot sideward right (bring L foot to R calf with knee turned out)
18	Side Hop L foot sideward left (bring R foot to L calf with knee turned out)
19-24	Repeat beats 17-18 three times

RHYTHMIC NOTATION

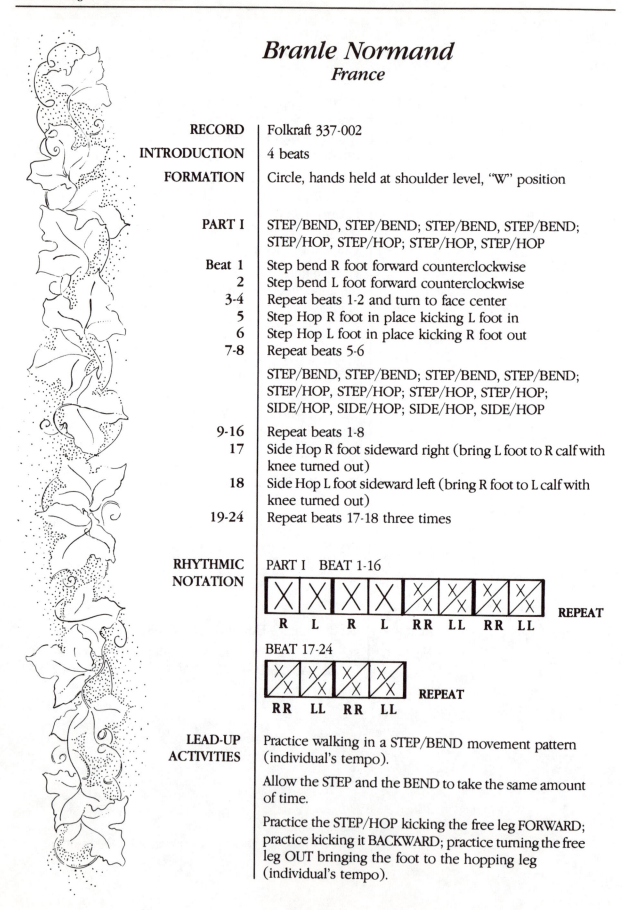

PART I   BEAT 1-16

R L R L RR LL RR LL   **REPEAT**

BEAT 17-24

RR LL RR LL   **REPEAT**

LEAD-UP ACTIVITIES	Practice walking in a STEP/BEND movement pattern (individual's tempo).
	Allow the STEP and the BEND to take the same amount of time.
	Practice the STEP/HOP kicking the free leg FORWARD; practice kicking it BACKWARD; practice turning the free leg OUT bringing the foot to the hopping leg (individual's tempo).

Branle Normand (continued)

TEACHING SUGGESTIONS	Practice the STEP/BEND to the music.
	Practice the STEP/HOP to the music.
	Practice swinging the L leg FORWARD when the R foot is doing the STEP/HOP and the R leg BACKWARD when the L foot is doing the STEP/HOP. Add this to music.
	Do the side-to-side SIDE/HOP bringing the free foot to the calf of the hopping leg.
	Practice the transition of the STEP/HOP with the free leg swinging FORWARD then BACKWARD to the SIDE/HOP.
	Put the dance sequence together with SAY AND DO then add music.
CHAIR DANCING	Substitute a lifting of the free leg for the BEND of the supporting leg.
	Do the STEP/HOP with leg swing on the diagonal and the SIDE/HOP with the knee turned OUT slightly.

Debka Kurdit
Debka of the Kurds
Israel

RECORD	Tikva T-117 "Potpourri"
INTRODUCTION	16 beats
FORMATION	Short lines in shoulder hold, "T" position
PART I	IN, BEND, OUT, BEND
Beat 1	Step L foot in (lift R leg in back with knee bent)
2	Bend L knee
3	Step R foot out (lift L leg in front with knee bent)
4	Bend R knee
5-16	Repeat Part I, beats 1-4, three times

(continued)

Debka Kurdit (continued)

PART II	IN, HOP, OUT, HOP
Beat 1-2	Step Hop L foot in (lift R leg in back—higher, bigger motion)
3-4	Step Hop R foot out (lift L leg in front—higher, bigger motion)
5-16	Repeat Part II, beats 1-4, three times
NOTE	Stay on R foot to begin Part III.
PART III	BOUNCE, 2, 3, IN
Beat 1-3	Bounce 3 times on R foot with L leg reaching in front of body
4	Step L foot in with accent
5-8	Repeat beats 1-4 bouncing L foot and stepping R foot in
9-16	Repeat Part III, beats 1-8
PART IV	IN, HOLD, OUT/OUT, OUT
Beat 1-2	Step L foot in then hold beat 2
3-4	Step R, L, R foot out (3 &, 4)
5-16	Repeat Part IV, beats 1-4, three times
PART V	IN, BEND, OUT, BEND
Beat 1-16	Repeat Part I, beats 1-16
PART VI	CROSS, SIDE
Beat 1	Step L foot crossing in front of R foot
2	Step R foot sideward right
3-16	Repeat Part VI, beats 1-2, seven times
NOTE	Keep body low with straight back.

RHYTHMIC NOTATION

PART I & V

L   R   **REPEAT 3X**

PART II

L   L   R   R   **REPEAT 3X**

PART III

R   R   R   L   L   L   R   **REPEAT**

PART IV

L   RL   R   **REPEAT 3X**

Debka Kurdit (continued)

PART VI

REPEAT 3X

L	R	L	R

LEAD-UP ACTIVITIES	Practice rocking FORWARD and BACKWARD—one foot FORWARD and opposite one BACKWARD (individual's tempo).
	Practice STEP HOP in place. Practice STEP HOP FORWARD and BACKWARD, then do one FORWARD, one BACKWARD (individual's tempo).
	Practice balancing on one foot for 3 beats, then change feet on 4th beat (individual's tempo).
	Pat the legs with both hands in a pattern of "1, 2, 3 &, 4" (group beat). WALK pattern (individual's tempo).
	Practice a CROSS, SIDE pattern (individual's tempo).
TEACHING SUGGESTIONS	Practice IN, BEND, OUT, BEND (rocking pattern).
	Substitute a HOP for the BEND to create IN, HOP, OUT, HOP—begin L foot (SAY AND DO).
	Practice balancing on the R foot for 3 beats while extending the L foot IN (BOUNCE, 2, 3, STEP)—change feet beat 4 and repeat. Do this pattern several times (SAY AND DO).
	Practice the transition from OUT, HOP (R foot) to Part III.
	Practice Part IV (IN, HOLD, OUT/OUT, OUT) several times (SAY AND DO).
	Practice the transition from Part III to Part IV.
	Practice Part VI CROSS, SIDE moving right beginning R foot (SAY AND DO).
	Practice the transition from Part VI to Part I.
	Put the dance together with SAY AND DO, then add music.
CHAIR DANCING	
PARTS I & II	Step FORWARD and BACKWARD on a diagonal.
PARTS III & IV	Do in place.
PART IV	Step in place with one foot in front of the other.

D'Hammerschmiedsgsell'n
The Journeyman Blacksmith
Germany

RECORD	Folkraft 1485X45
INTRODUCTION	4 measures, 3/4 meter
FORMATION	Groups of four, two facing two
ALTERNATE FORMATION	Pairs scattered about the space
CHORUS	PAT, HIT, CLAP; R HAND, L HAND, BOTH HANDS (ME, ME, ME; YOU, YOU, YOU)
Beat 1	Pat thighs (both hands)
2	Hit chest with both hands
3	Clap own hands
4	Hit opposite's R hand with your R hand
5	Hit opposite's L hand with your L hand
6	Hit opposite's two hands with your two hands
7-48	Repeat beats 1-6 seven times
TO SIMPLIFY	CLAP hands or PAT thighs 3 times and HIT partner's hands 3 times.
NOTE	In groups of 4, work diagonally across from partner— 1's beginning with beat 1 and 2's beginning with beat 4 simultaneously.
	Join hands in circle of 4 dancers
PART I	STEP, HOLD, HOP
Beat 1	Step R foot forward clockwise
2	Hold
3	Hop R foot in place
4	Step L foot forward clockwise
5	Hold
6	Hop L foot in place
7-24	Repeat beats 1-6, three times
25-48	Repeat Part I, beats 1-6, moving counterclockwise
NOTE	No R foot or L foot is necessary.
CHORUS	Repeat Chorus, beats 1-48
PART II	
Beat 1-48	Repeat Part II substituting R hand Star and L hand Star
CHORUS	Repeat Chorus, beats 1-48
PART III	
Beat 1-48	Repeat Part I

D'Hammerschmiedsgsell'n *(continued)*

RHYTHMIC NOTATION

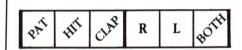

LEAD-UP ACTIVITIES

Practice using music in 3/4 meter—PAT thighs 3 times then CLAP 3 times.

Practice a sequence of PAT thighs, HIT chest, CLAP hands several times.

Practice a sequence of pushing R hand FORWARD, L hand FORWARD, both hands FORWARD.

Practice walking in this meter, accenting the first WALK (individual's tempo).

Practice hopping—3 on one foot and 3 on the other (individual's tempo).

Practice WALK, HOP, HOP then WALK, HOLD, HOP (individual's tempo).

TEACHING SUGGESTIONS

Have students work in pairs on the Chorus to their own tempo. Do the Chorus to a group tempo (SAY AND DO).

Have students work on Part I with their partner. Do Part I to a group tempo (SAY AND DO).

Do the dance with SAY AND DO and then add music.

Add groups of 4 the second time the dance is presented.

CHAIR DANCING
PART I

Do facing a partner.

PART II

Do in place holding hands with the partner or substitute arm motions.

Hora
Israel

RECORD	Educational Record #2 *Hora* and others
INTRODUCTION	Begin dance with vocal
FORMATION	Single circle facing center, "T" position or hands held down
NOTE	A double circle may be used with one circle moving in the opposite direction.
PART I	SIDE, BACK; SIDE, HOP; SIDE, HOP
Beat 1	Step L foot sideward left
2	Step R foot crossing in back of L foot
3	Step L foot sideward left
4	Hop L foot while swinging R foot in toward center
5	Step R foot sideward right
6	Hop R foot and swing L foot
NEW HORA	SIDE, CROSS; JUMP, HOP; STEP/STEP, STEP

RHYTHMIC NOTATION

PART I

VARIATION

LEAD-UP ACTIVITIES	Practice STEP HOP in place (individual's tempo).
	Practice SIDE, BACK, SIDE, HOP (individual's tempo).
TEACHING SUGGESTIONS	Teach the *Hasapikos* first and relate this dance to it.
	Practice the sequence with SAY AND DO and add music.
CHAIR DANCING	Do steps in place.

Machar
Tomorrow
Israel

RECORD	Tikva T-117 *Potpourri*
INTRODUCTION	16 beats
FORMATION	Groups of 3 side by side, facing counterclockwise
PART I	FORWARD, 2, 3, 4; STEP HOP, STEP HOP
Beat 1-4	Run R, L, R, L foot forward counterclockwise
5-6	Step Hop R foot crossing in front of L foot
7-8	Step Hop L foot crossing in front of R foot
9-32	Repeat Part I, beats 1-8, three times
NOTE	Omit the crossing over STEP HOP when learning the dance.
PART II	Middle dancer and R hand dancer face each other SWAY, CLAP, SWAY, CLAP; R ELBOW; L ELBOW
Beat 1-2	Both dancers sway right, then clap near R shoulder on beat 2
3-4	Repeat sway and clap to left (partner on left may do same action)
5-8	Middle dancer and R dancer hook R elbows and turn with 4 steps
9-16	Middle dancer and L dancer hook L elbows and turn with 8 steps; middle dancer ends facing L dancer
17-24	Repeat Part II, beats 1-8, with L dancer
25-28	Middle dancer hooks L elbow with R dancer and turns in 4 steps
29-32	Middle dancer moves forward in 4 steps to join 2 new dancers
NOTE	No R foot or L foot needs to be specified in Part II.
RHYTHMIC NOTATION	

PART I

X	X	X	X	X	X	X	X	
R	L	R	L	R	R	L	L	**REPEAT 3X**

PART II

X	CLAP	X	CLAP	X	X	X	X
R		L		R	L	R	L

X	X	X	X	X	X	X	X	
R	L	R	L	R	L	R	L	**REPEAT**

(continued)

Machar (continued)

LEAD-UP ACTIVITIES	Practice combinations of running steps and STEP HOPS (individual's tempo).
	Groups of 3 dancers practice R and L elbow turns with the middle person working with the 2 persons on each side.
TEACHING SUGGESTIONS	Have groups of 3 dancers practice the sequence in Part I at a tempo agreed upon by the 3.
	Do Part I with SAY AND DO then add the music for this part.
	Have the groups review the beat structure and movement sequence for Part II and practice in their groups of 3.
	Do Part II with SAY AND DO.
	Do the entire dance with SAY AND DO and add the music.
CHAIR DANCING **PART I**	Do in place
PART II Beat 1-8	Do in place
9-16	Do HEEL, STEP 4 times
17-32	Repeat beats 1-8
	Dance may be executed in wheelchairs.

Makazice Kolo
Scissors
Yugoslavia

RECORD	Folk Dancer MH 3023
INTRODUCTION	None
FORMATION	Circle of dancers, hands held in "V" position (kolo hold), face center
PART I	SIDE/BACK, SIDE/BACK; SIDE, BACK/STEP, HOP
Beat 1	Step R foot sideward right
&	Step L foot crossing in back of R foot
2-3	Repeat beat 1 & two times
4 &	Step Hop R foot
5-8	Repeat Part I, beats 1-4, sideward left beginning L foot

Makazice Kolo (continued)

PART II	IN, CROSS, CHUG/APART, TOGETHER
Beat 1	Step R foot in toward center of circle
2	Cross L foot over R foot (weight on both feet)
3	Chug out, keep weight on balls of feet
&	Uncross L foot placing weight on both feet (toes-in, heels-out position)
4	Bring feet together lowering heels
5-8	Repeat Part II, beats 1-4
STYLE NOTE	In Part II a bouncing motion occurs on each beat.

RHYTHMIC NOTATION

PART I

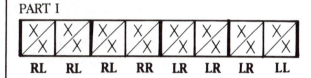

RL   RL   RL   RR   LR   LR   LR   LL

PART II

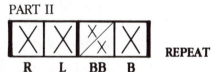

R   L   BB   B   **REPEAT**

LEAD-UP ACTIVITIES

Practice SIDE/BACK (individual's tempo).

Practice jumping with feet slightly apart toes IN then bring them together; stand with the L foot crossed over the R foot before jumping to the toes IN position (individual's tempo).

Practice chugging backward (individual's tempo).

TEACHING SUGGESTIONS

Practice 3 SIDE/BACK steps with SAY AND DO then "add on" the STEP HOP.

Do Part I with SAY AND DO.

Practice Part II with individual's tempo and then SAY AND DO beginning with CHUG/APART, TOGETHER and then "preceding" that pattern with IN, CROSS.

Do the entire dance with SAY AND DO and then add the music.

CHAIR DANCING   Do as described.

Niguno Shel Yossi
Israel

RECORD	Tikva T-100 *Debka*
INTRODUCTION	16 beats
FORMATION	Partners in a single circle, hands joined
PART I	STEP, HOP, STEP, HOP; IN, 2, 3, 4; STEP, HOP, STEP, HOP; OUT, 2, 3, 4
Beat 1-2	Step Hop R foot kicking L foot in
3-4	Step Hop L foot kicking R foot in
5-8	Step R, L, R, L foot in (raise arms)
9-12	Repeat beats 1-4
13-16	Step R, L, R, L foot out (lower arms)
17-32	Repeat Part I, beats 1-16, and turn to face partner
NOTE	Omit the KICK with the STEP HOP when learning the dance.
PART II	STEP, STAMP, STEP, STAMP; FORWARD, 2, 3, 4; BUZZ TURN
Beat 1	Step R foot slightly sideward right
2	Stamp L foot next to R foot (clap hands over shoulder)
3	Step L foot slightly sideward left
4	Stamp R foot (clap over L shoulder)
5-8	Step R, L, R, L foot forward passing R shoulders with partner
9-16	Israeli turn with new partner, use 8 buzz steps
17-32	Repeat Part II, beats 1-16, progressing to a second new person; end Part II facing center to begin dance again

RHYTHMIC NOTATION

PART I

X	X	X	X	X	X	X	X	
R	R	L	L	R	L	R	L	**REPEAT 3X**

PART II

X	X	X	X	X	X	X	X
R	(L)	L	(R)	R	L	R	L

X X	X X	X X	X X	X X	X X	X X	X X	
RL	RL	RL	RL	RL	RL	RL	RL	**REPEAT PART II**

Niguno Shel Yossi (continued)

LEAD-UP ACTIVITIES	Practice STEP HOPS (individual's tempo).
	Practice combining 2 STEP HOPS with 4 steps IN and with 4 steps OUT (individual's tempo).
	Practice STEP, STAMP, STEP, STAMP; FORWARD, 2, 3, 4 (individual's tempo).
	Practice BUZZ TURN with partner (partner beat).
TEACHING SUGGESTIONS	Do Part I with SAY AND DO.
	Practice Part II up to the BUZZ TURN with SAY AND DO then "add on" the TURN.
	Practice the transition from Part II to the repeat of Part II to be certain everyone is travelling in the correct direction.
	Practice the transition from Part II back to the beginning.
	Do the entire dance with SAY AND DO then add the music.
CHAIR DANCING PART II	Substitute steps in place for the FORWARD steps and TURN or further substitute PAT, CLAP for the TURN.
	May be adapted for wheelchairs.

Shibolet Basadeh
A Sheaf in the Field
Israel

RECORD	EKS 7206 *The Whole World Dances;* Folk Dancer MH 1150
INTRODUCTION	12 beats
FORMATION	Circle facing center, hands joined
PART I	SIDE, CLOSE; SIDE, CLOSE; SIDE, CLOSE; SIDE, HOP
Beat 1	Step R foot sideward right moving counterclockwise
2	Step L foot next to R foot
3-6	Repeat beats 1-2 two times
7	Step R foot sideward right
8	Hop R foot turning 1/2 clockwise to face out of circle
9-16	Repeat beats 1-8 with opposite footwork, end facing center (continue to move counterclockwise around the circle)
17-32	Repeat beats 1-16
PART II	FORWARD, HOP; FORWARD, HOP; BACKWARD, HOP; BACKWARD, HOP; REPEAT; IN, HOP; IN, HOP; OUT, HOP; OUT, HOP; OUT, HOP; OUT, HOP
Beat 1	Step R foot forward counterclockwise
2	Hop R foot
3	Step L foot forward counterclockwise
4	Hop L foot turning 1/2 counterclockwise to face clockwise
5-8	Repeat beats 1-4 backward counterclockwise, end facing counterclockwise
9-16	Repeat beats 1-8
17-20	Step Hop R foot, L foot in (large Step Hops raising arms up)
21-28	Step Hop R, L, R, L foot out (small Step Hops lowering arms)
RHYTHMIC NOTATION	PART I

PART I

X	X	X	X	X	X	X	X	**REPEAT 3X W/OPP. FTWK.**
R	L	R	L	R	L	R	R	

PART II

X	X	X	X
R	R	L	L

Shibolet Basadeh (continued)

LEAD-UP ACTIVITIES	Practice sliding then execute 1/2 TURNS in the moving direction (individual's tempo). Practice SIDE, CLOSE (individual's tempo). Practice STEP HOP (individual's tempo). Practice STEP HOP and execute a 1/2 TURN on the HOP (individual's tempo).
TEACHING SUGGESTIONS	Practice 3 SIDE, CLOSE steps (individual's tempo then SAY AND DO) and "add on" the SIDE, HOP turning 1/2 in the moving direction (counterclockwise). Practice Part I with SAY AND DO. Practice moving FORWARD with 2 STEP HOPS beginning R foot then BACKWARD with 2 STEP HOPS turning 1/2 after each 2 STEP HOPS (individual's tempo then SAY AND DO). "Add on" 2 STEP HOPS IN and 4 STEP HOPS OUT. Do the entire dance with SAY AND DO and then add the music.
CHAIR DANCING **PART I**	Do in place beginning with feet off to the left and omit TURN (feet move back and forth across in front of the chair).
PART II	Do in place without the TURN moving feet away and toward the chair for IN and OUT.

Sicilian Tarantella
Italy

RECORD	Folkraft 1173X45
INTRODUCTION	4 beats
FORMATION	Groups of four, two facing two (if couples, men on the same side)

PART I	STEP HOP, STEP HOP; RUN, 2, 3, 4
Beat 1-2	Step Hop R foot; clap hands overhead on hop
3-4	Step Hop L foot; clap hands overhead on hop
5-8	Run R, L, R, L foot in place (snap fingers overhead each beat)
9-32	Repeat Part I, beats 1-8, three times
PART II	IN, 2, 3, 4; OUT, 2, 3, 4
Beat 1-4	Run R, L, R, L foot right diagonally in; (clap on beat 4)
5-8	Run R, L, R, L foot left diagonally out; (clap on beat 8)
9-16	Repeat beats 1-8 diagonally left in and right out
17-32	Repeat Part II, beats 1-16
PART III	R ELBOW; L ELBOW; R DO-SA-DO; L DO-SA-DO
Beat 1-8	2 people on right do a R elbow turn
9-16	2 people on left do a R elbow turn
17-32	Repeat with L elbow turns
33-48	Repeat with R shoulder Do-sa-do
49-64	Repeat with L shoulder Do-sa-do
PART IV	SKIP COUNTERCLOCKWISE; STAR CLOCKWISE
Beat 1-8	Skip 8 times counterclockwise in circle of 4 persons, hands on hips
9-16	Walk 8 steps clockwise using R hand Star
17-32	Repeat Part IV, beats 1-16

Sicilian Tarantella *(continued)*

RHYTHMIC NOTATION	**PART I** 

PART I

$$\boxed{X}\ \boxed{X}\ \boxed{X}\ \boxed{X}\ \boxed{X}\ \boxed{X}\ \boxed{X}\ \boxed{X}$$
R   R   L   L   L   R   L   R   L   **REPEAT 3X**

PART II & III

$$\boxed{X}\ \boxed{X}\ \boxed{X}\ \boxed{X}$$
R   L   R   L   **REPEAT 7X**

PART IV

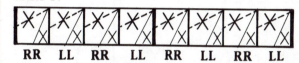
RR   LL   RR   LL   RR   LL   RR   LL

$$\boxed{X}\ \boxed{X}\ \boxed{X}\ \boxed{X}\ \boxed{X}\ \boxed{X}\ \boxed{X}\ \boxed{X}$$
R   L   R   L   R   L   R   L   **REPEAT PART IV**

LEAD-UP ACTIVITIES	Practice the STEP HOP (individual's tempo) swinging the free leg IN on the HOP.
	Practice running, kicking the feet UP behind (individual's tempo).
	Practice R and L elbow turns and DO-SA-DO patterns with a partner (partner beat).
TEACHING SUGGESTIONS	Practice Part I with SAY AND DO—leave out the CLAP and SNAP while learning.
	Practice Part II with SAY AND DO then add the CLAP.
	Practice Parts I and II in the dance formation and add music.
	Practice Parts III and IV in the dance formation.
	Do the entire dance with SAY AND DO and add the music.
CHAIR DANCING	Do in place.
	May be adapted for wheelchairs.

Bekendorfer Quadrille
Germany

RECORD	Folkraft 007
INTRODUCTION	8 beats
FORMATION	Square sets

PART I	STEP HOP (CIRCLE)
Beat 1-16	Step Hop 8 times forward clockwise, beginning R foot (hands joined in circle)
17-32	Step Hop 8 times forward counterclockwise, beginning R foot (hands joined in circle)
CHORUS	STEP, HOLD; STEP, HOLD; STEP, HOLD; CLAP, CLAP; STEP HOP; STEP HOP; STEP HOP; STEP HOP
Beat 1-6	Heads move toward each other with 3 slow steps
7-8	Clap own hands twice
9-16	Heads move back to place with 4 step hops
17-32	Sides repeat Chorus, beats 1-16
	SCHOTTISCHE; SCHOTTISCHE; SCHOTTISCHE; SCHOTTISCHE
33-36	Heads Schottische diagonally left
37-40	Heads Schottische diagonally right passing back to back with opposite couple
41-44	Heads Schottische diagonally left passing face to face with opposite couple
45-48	Heads Schottische backward to place
49-64	Sides repeat Schottische figure, beats 33-48
	STEP HOP
65-80	All Step Hop 16 times in a Grand right and left
PART II	STEP HOP (STAR)
Beat 1-16	Step Hop 8 times forward clockwise (partners R hand star)
17-32	Step Hops 8 times backward counterclockwise
CHORUS	Repeat Chorus, beats 1-80
PART III	STEP HOP (PARTNER)
Beat 1-16	Step Hop 8 times forward clockwise, partners join hands, R hips adjacent
17-32	Step Hop 8 times forward counterclockwise (L hips adjacent)

Bekendorfer Quadrille (continued)

CHORUS	Repeat beats 1-80 of Chorus
PART I	Repeat Part I, beats 1-32

RHYTHMIC NOTATION

CHORUS

PART I, II & III   BEAT 1-32

R   R   L   L   R   R   L   L   **REPEAT 3X**

LEAD-UP ACTIVITIES

Practice STEP HOP in all directions (individual's tempo).

Practice SCHOTTISCHE in all directions (individual's tempo).

Practice Grand right and left using a WALK.

TEACHING SUGGESTIONS

Learn the parts of the dance in a full circle of partners so the floor pattern of the partner movements and the floor pattern of the Chorus can be made clear.

Form square sets and work on the Chorus. Walk through the sequence before adding the SCHOTTISCHE.

Do the Grand right and left by walking through the pattern before adding the STEP HOP.

CHAIR DANCING

Do the same steps in place.

Move the feet away from and toward the chair on the Chorus.

NOTE

No R foot and L foot is necessary.

Carnavalito
Bolivia

RECORD	Folk Dancer MH 1130
INTRODUCTION	14 beats after full instrumentation begins
FORMATION	Broken circle, hands joined in "V" position
PART I	SCHOTTISCHE
Beat 1-4	Schottische R foot forward counterclockwise (body bent over)
5-8	Schottische L foot forward counterclockwise (body straightens)
9-64	Repeat Part I, beats 1-8, seven times
PART II	STEP HOP
Beat 1-2	Step Hop R foot forward counterclockwise (swing arms in)
3-4	Step Hop L foot forward counterclockwise (swing arms out)
5-32	Repeat beats 1-4 seven times
33-64	Repeat Part II, beats 1-32, forward clockwise 8 times
NOTE	On third (last) sequence of the dance do 8 SCHOTTISCHES instead of 16.
RHYTHMIC NOTATION	PART I BEAT 1-64

PART I   BEAT 1-64

X X X X X X X X   REPEAT 7X
R L R R L R L L

PART II   BEAT 1-64

X X X X   REPEAT 15X
R R L L

Carnavalito (continued)

LEAD-UP ACTIVITIES	Practice walking in sets of 4 steps bending over during one set of 4 and straightening up during the alternate set of 4 steps (individual's tempo).
	Practice the SCHOTTISCHE adding the bending and straightening (individual's tempo).
	Practice the STEP HOP swinging the arms FORWARD and BACKWARD (individual's tempo).
TEACHING SUGGESTIONS	Practice SCHOTTISCHE to the music then STEP HOP to the music.
	Practice SCHOTTISCHE to the music adding bending and straightening.
	Practice STEP HOP swinging arms IN on the STEP HOP with the R foot, and OUT on STEP HOP with the L foot (SAY AND DO).
	Put the dance sequence together with SAY AND DO, then add music.
CHAIR DANCING	Do as described, executing steps in place.
	KICK legs on the diagonal.

Ersko Kolo
Yugoslavia

RECORD	Folk Dancer MH3020
INTRODUCTION	None
FORMATION	Circle, hands joined in "V" position—face center

PART I	IN, BACK (14); ACCENT, HOLD, STAMP, HOLD
Beat 1	Extend R heel toward center with weight on it
2	Step L foot crossing in back of R foot
3-28	Repeat beats 1-2 sideward right 13 times
29-30	Accent R foot in place
31-32	Stamp L foot
33-64	Repeat Part I, beats 1-32, moving sideward left beginning L foot

PART II	SCHOTTISCHE (FORWARD, BACKWARD, IN, OUT)
Beat 1-4	Schottische forward counterclockwise beginning R foot
5-8	Schottische backward (facing counterclockwise) beginning L foot
9-12	Schottische in to center of circle beginning R foot
13-16	Schottische out from center of circle
17-32	Repeat Part II, beats 1-16

TO SIMPLIFY	Substitute 4 walking steps for each SCHOTTISCHE.

RHYTHMIC NOTATION

PART I BEAT 1-28

X	X	X	X
R	L	R	L

REPEAT 6X

BEAT 29-32

X		X	
R		(L)	

REPEAT PART I W/OPP. FTWK.

PART II

X	X	X	X	X	X	X	X
R	L	R	R	R	L	R	L	L

REPEAT 3X

Ersko Kolo *(continued)*

LEAD-UP ACTIVITIES	Practice extending the heel FORWARD putting weight on it, then step back with the opposite foot (individual's tempo).
	Practice SCHOTTISCHE FORWARD and BACKWARD (individual's tempo).
TEACHING SUGGESTIONS	Practice IN, BACK in each direction with SAY AND DO.
	Practice the transitions (beats 29-32 and 60-64).
	Practice Part II with SAY AND DO.
	Put the parts together and add the music.
CHAIR DANCING PART I	Do in place, extending heel FORWARD.
	Substitute side to side SCHOTTISCHE for FORWARD and BACKWARD.

Fado Blanquita
Brazil-Portugal

RECORD	RCA EPA 4129 Folkraft 1173X45
INTRODUCTION	8 beats
FORMATION	Partners in single circle, hands joined
PART I	STEP HOP
Beat 1-2	Step Hop forward clockwise beginning R foot
3-16	Step Hop forward clockwise 7 times
17-32	Repeat beats 1-16 forward counterclockwise

(continued)

Fado Blanquita (continued)

BRIDGE	SWAY
Beat 1-2	Sway right
3-8	Repeat sway (left, right, left)—called a Vamp Partners face each other and take R hands (straighten arms)
PART II	SCHOTTISCHE (figure 8)
Beat 1-12	Schottische 3 times travelling clockwise in top half of a figure 8 beginning R, L, R foot
13-24	Schottische 3 times holding L hands with corner (travelling counterclockwise in bottom half of figure 8)
25-48	Repeat Part II, beats 1-24, with same two people
BRIDGE	SWAY
Beat 1-8	Sway right, left, right, left facing center
PART III	JUMP, KICK, JUMP, KICK; JUMP, JUMP, HOLD, HOLD; (REPEAT); IN, HOLD, 2, HOLD; 3, HOLD, KICK, HOLD; OUT, HOLD, 2, HOLD; 3, HOLD, TOUCH, HOLD
Beat 1	Jump
2	Hop R foot kicking L foot in toward center
3	Jump
4	Hop L foot kicking R foot in
5	Jump
6	Jump turning 1/2 to right
7-8	Hold
9-16	Repeat Part III, beats 1-8, facing away from center
17-22	Step R, L, R foot in toward center
23-24	Extend L foot toward center
25-30	Step L, R, L foot out away from center
31-32	Touch R foot out away from center
33-64	Repeat Part III, beats 1-32
RHYTHMIC **NOTATION**	

PART I

X	X	X	X	REPEAT 7X
R	R	L	L	

VAMP

X		X		REPEAT
R		L		

Fado Blanquita (continued)

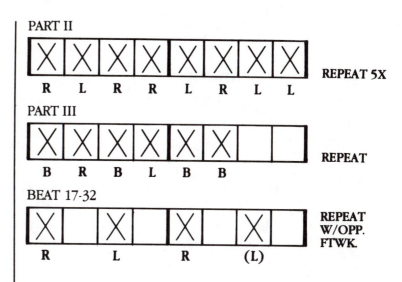

PART II

X	X	X	X	X	X	X	X
R	L	R	R	L	R	L	L

REPEAT 5X

PART III

X	X	X	X	X	X		
B	R	B	L	B	B		

REPEAT

BEAT 17-32

X		X		X		X	
R		L		R		(L)	

REPEAT W/OPP. FTWK.

LEAD-UP ACTIVITIES

Practice STEP HOP (individual's tempo).

Practice SCHOTTISCHE (individual's tempo).

Practice JUMP, KICK alternating feet (individual's tempo).

Practice IN, 2, 3, KICK; OUT, 2, 3, TOUCH (individual's tempo).

TEACHING SUGGESTIONS

Practice Part I with SAY AND DO and add the music.

Have students face partners and identify corner who is now back-to-back with each person. Take partner's hand and WALK the top half of the figure 8 then L hand to corner and WALK the bottom half. Change to SCHOTTISCHE steps with SAY AND DO.

Do Parts I and II including the Bridge with SAY AND DO and add the music.

Practice Part III with SAY AND DO.

Do the entire dance to the music.

CHAIR DANCING PART I and II

Do in place.

PART III

Do without the TURN.

Dance may be executed in wheelchairs.

Frunza
Romania

RECORD	NOROC Vol. I Romanian Folk Dances *Haj La Joc*
INTRODUCTION	32 beats
FORMATION	Circle, hands joined

PART I	SIDE/BACK (7); STEP/STEP, STEP
Beat 1	Step R foot slightly sideward right
&	Step L foot crossing in back of R foot
2-7	Repeat beat 1 & six times
8	Step R, L, R foot in place
9-16	Repeat Part I, beats 1-8, sideward left clockwise beginning L foot

PART II	CHERKESSIYA; SCHOTTISCHE
Beat 1-2	Cherkessiya beginning R foot facing center
3	Step R foot in
&	Step L foot out
4	Step R foot next to L foot
&	Hop R
5-8	Repeat beats 1-4 beginning L foot
9-16	Repeat Part II, beats 1-8

RHYTHMIC NOTATION

PART I

X X	X	X X	X	X X	X	X X	X
X	X	X	X	X	X	X	X
RL	RL	RL	RL	RL	RL	RL	RLR

REPEAT W/OPP. FTWK.

PART II

X	X	X	X	X	X	X	X
X	X	X	X	X	X	X	X
RL	RL	RL	RR	LR	LR	LR	LL

REPEAT

Frunza (continued)

LEAD-UP ACTIVITIES	Practice SIDE/BACK in each direction (individual's tempo).
	Practice SCHOTTISCHE in place alternating feet (individual's tempo).
	Practice CHERKESSIYA (individual's tempo).
	Practice ACCENT, 2, 3, 4; ACCENT, 2, 3, HOP in place alternating feet, then change to CHERKESSIYA; SCHOTTISCHE (individual's tempo).
TEACHING SUGGESTIONS	Practice SIDE/BACK with SAY AND DO.
	Do Part I using the hands in an alternating thigh PAT in order to practice the sequence and the transition rhythmically. Substitute the feet (SAY AND DO).
	Practice Part II with SAY AND DO (CHERKESSIYA; IN, OUT, STEP, HOP).
	Do the entire dance with SAY AND DO, then add music.
CHAIR DANCING	
PART I	Substitute small steps almost in place.
PART II	Do as in the dance.

Ken Yovdu
Thus Shall They Perish
Israel

RECORD	Israeli Music Foundation LP 5/6
INTRODUCTION	32 beats
FORMATION	Short lines, hands held

PART I	SIDE, CLOSE, SIDE, HOLD; BRUSH, HOP, CLOSE, HOLD; SIDE, CLOSE, SIDE, HOLD; JUMP, HOP, STAMP, HOLD
Beat 1	Step R foot sideward right
2	Step L foot next to R foot
3-4	Step R foot sideward right; hold beat 4
5	Brush L foot forward accenting heel
6	Hop R foot (L knee is bent)
7-8	Step L foot next to R foot with slight accent
9-12	Repeat beats 1-4
13	Jump turning lower body diagonally left
14	Hop L foot bringing R knee up (face center)
15-16	Lower R leg with stamp
17-32	Repeat Part I, beats 1-16
PART II	SCHOTTISCHE
Beat 1-4	Schottische forward beginning R foot (arms come forward and up)
5-8	Schottische 90° right beginning L foot (line is one behind the other, L hand brought to the shoulder)
9-12	Schottische back to starting point beginning R foot (arms lowered)
13-48	Repeat beats 1-12 (3 Schottische sequences) 3 times

RHYTHMIC NOTATION

PART I

X	X	X		X	X	X	
R	L	R		(L)	R	L	

X	X	X		X	X	X		REPEAT
R	L	R		B	L	(R)		

PART II

X	X	X	X	X	X	X	X	REPEAT 5X
R	L	R	R	L	R	L	L	

Ken Yovdu *(continued)*

LEAD-UP ACTIVITIES	Practice SCHOTTISCHE turning different directions as the HOP is executed (individual's tempo).
	Practice SIDE, CLOSE, SIDE, HOLD (individual's tempo).
TEACHING SUGGESTIONS	Practice SIDE, CLOSE, SIDE, HOLD; BRUSH, HOP, CLOSE, HOLD beginning R foot (individual's tempo then group SAY AND DO).
	Practice JUMP, HOP, STAMP, HOLD (individual's tempo) and add to SIDE, CLOSE, SIDE, HOLD beginning R foot (SAY AND DO).
	Practice Part I with SAY AND DO alternating BRUSH, HOP and JUMP, HOP.
	Practice Part II in the correct directions (individual's tempo) and then add SAY AND DO.
	Do the entire dance with SAY AND DO and then add the music.
CHAIR DANCING PART I	Do in place.
PART II	SCHOTTISCHE away from chair, SCHOTTISCHE in place, SCHOTTISCHE back toward the chair.

Korobushka
Peddler's Pack
Russia

RECORD	Folk Dancer MH 1059
INTRODUCTION	8 beats
FORMATION	Double circle, partners facing each other; man on inside
ALTERNATE FORMATION	Double line

(continued)

Korobushka (continued)

PART I	SCHOTTISCHE; SCHOTTISCHE; SCHOTTISCHE; JUMP, JUMP, JUMP, HOLD
Beat 1-4	Schottische away from center of circle; men begin L foot forward out, ladies R foot backward out
5-8	Schottische toward center of circle (men R foot backward in, ladies L foot forward in)
9-12	Repeat beats 1-4
13	Jump (men R foot in front of L foot, women opposite)
14	Jump feet slightly apart and toes in
15	Jump feet together; men click heels
16	Hold and release hands
PART II	SCHOTTISCHE; SCHOTTISCHE; STEP HOP, STEP HOP; CHANGE, 2, 3, 4
Beat 1-4	Schottische R foot sideward right; (arms are spread diagonally overhead)
5-8	Schottische L foot sideward left
9-10	Step Hop R foot toward partner (R hands held)
11-12	Step Hop L foot away from partner
13-16	Step R, L, R, L foot changing places with partners
17-32	Repeat Part II returning to own starting position on beats 29-32
NOTE	Man takes only 3 steps beats 29-32, holding beat 32.

RHYTHMIC NOTATION

PART I

X	X	X	X	X	X	X	X
L	R	L	L	R	L	R	R

X	X	X	X	X	X	X	
L	R	L	L	L	B	B	

PART II

X	X	X	X	X	X	X	X
R	L	R	R	R	L	R	L	L

X	X	X	X	X	X	X	X
R	R	R	L	L	R	L	R	L

REPEAT

Korobushka (continued)

LEAD-UP ACTIVITIES

Practice SCHOTTISCHE forward and backward (individual's tempo). Practice SCHOTTISCHE with a partner—one moves FORWARD, one BACKWARD (partner beat). Practice SCHOTTISCHE side to side (individual's tempo).

Practice STEP HOP—forward and backward (individual's tempo). Practice STEP HOP with partner—toward and away from partner (partner beat).

TEACHING SUGGESTIONS

Position the students in a double circle with partners facing or a double line with partners facing. Have the students who are facing out do 3 SCHOTTISCHES of Part I moving FORWARD, BACKWARD, FORWARD with SAY AND DO beginning L foot. Then have the students facing in do 3 SCHOTTICHES BACKWARD, FORWARD, BACKWARD with SAY AND DO beginning R foot.

Have the partners do 3 SCHOTTISCHES together with SAY AND DO (no hands held). Repeat with hands held, then "add on" the JUMP, JUMP, JUMP, HOLD.

Practice the side-to-side SCHOTTISCHE with a partner using SAY AND DO beginning R foot. "Add on" the 2 STEP HOPS, then "add on" the 4 steps to change places.

Do all of Part II with SAY AND DO. Practice the transition from Part II to Part I noting the 3 steps instead of 4 steps for the person going into the FORWARD SCHOTTISCHE.

Do the entire dance with SAY AND DO and add the music.

CHAIR DANCING

Do as described facing another person, substitute in-place steps.

Kuma Echa
Come Brother, Let's Dance
Israel

RECORD	Folk Dancer MH 1150, Tikva T-106 *Medley*
INTRODUCTION	16 beats
FORMATION	Circle facing center, hands joined
PART I	SCHOTTISCHE (IN); SCHOTTISCHE (OUT); GRAPEVINE; GRAPEVINE
Beat 1-4	Schottische R foot in toward center (raise arms)
5-8	Schottische L foot out (lower arms)
9-16	Grapevine 2 times moving sideward clockwise
17-32	Repeat Part I, beats 1-16
PART II	RUN
Beat 1-2	Run R foot, L foot forward counterclockwise
3-4	Run R foot, L foot backward counterclockwise
5-16	Repeat Part II, beats 1-4, three times
NOTE	Add a leap onto R foot on beat 3 and raise joined hands overhead.
PART III	IN, 2, 3, 4; IN, OUT, OUT, OUT; IN, OUT, OUT, OUT; IN, OUT, OUT, OUT
Beat 1-4	Run R, L, R, L foot in toward center
5	Step R foot in with accent (thrust arms in)
6-8	Step L, R, L foot out lowering arms
9-16	Repeat beats 5-8, two times

RHYTHMIC NOTATION

PART I

X	X	X	X	X	X	X	X
R	L	R	R	L	R	L	L

X	X	X	X	X	X	X	X	REPEAT
R	L	R	L	R	L	R	L	

PART II & III

X	X	X	X	REPEAT 3X
R	L	R	L	

Kuma Echa (continued)

LEAD-UP ACTIVITIES	Practice SCHOTTISCHES moving IN and OUT (individual's tempo).
	Practice GRAPEVINES moving clockwise (individual's tempo).
	Practice a running step turning to move FORWARD and BACKWARD every 2 steps (individual's tempo).
	Practice a sequence of IN, OUT, OUT, OUT (individual's tempo).
TEACHING SUGGESTIONS	Practice SCHOTTISCHE IN, SCHOTTISCHE OUT with SAY AND DO beginning R foot. "Add on" 2 GRAPEVINES moving clockwise—practice the transition from the SCHOTTISCHE to the GRAPEVINE—use individual's tempo before SAY AND DO.
	Practice Part II with SAY AND DO first as FORWARD running steps then change to the FORWARD, BACKWARD combination (individual's tempo then SAY AND DO).
	Practice Part III with SAY AND DO. Practice the transitions. Do the entire dance with SAY AND DO and add the music.
CHAIR DANCING	
PART I	Do SCHOTTISCHES away from and toward the chair. Substitute CHERKESSIYA for GRAPEVINE.
PART II	Do steps in place.
PART III	Do steps away from and toward the chair.

Road to the Isles
Scotland

RECORD	Folk Dancer MH 3003; EKS 7206, *The Whole World Dances*
INTRODUCTION	24 beats; 20 beats
FORMATION	Couples in Varsovienne position
PART I	TOUCH, BACK/SIDE; CROSS, TOUCH; BACK/SIDE, CROSS; TOUCH, TOUCH
Beat 1	Extend L heel diagonally left (women touch toe)
2	Step L foot crossing in back of R foot
&	Step R foot sideward right
3	Step L foot crossing in front of R foot
4	Extend R heel diagonally right (women touch toe)
5	Step R foot crossing in back of L foot
&	Step L foot sideward left
6	Step R foot crossing in front of L foot
7	Extend L heel diagonally left (women touch toe)
8	Extend L toe behind
PART II	SCHOTTISCHE; SCHOTTISCHE; SCHOTTISCHE; STEP/STEP, STEP
Beat 1-2	Schottische beginning L foot (couples moving side by side)
3-4	Schottische beginning R foot; on beat 4 turn 1/2 to right (clockwise) both turn same direction
5-6	Schottische beginning L foot; on beat 4 turn 1/2 to left (counterclockwise)
7-8	Step R, L, R foot

RHYTHMIC NOTATION

PART I

X	X X	X	X	X X	X	X	X
(L)	LR	L	(R)	RL	R	(L)	(L)

PART II

X X	X X	X X	X X	X X	X X	X X	X
LR	LL	RL	RR	LR	LL	RL	R

LEAD-UP ACTIVITIES

Practice BACK/SIDE CROSS (individual's tempo).

Practice SCHOTTISCHE (individual's tempo) then add TURNS on the HOP.

Road to the Isles (continued)

TEACHING SUGGESTIONS	Teach without partners until the dance is secure.
	Practice TOUCH, BACK/SIDE; CROSS, TOUCH (SAY AND DO) beginning L foot.
	"Add on" BACK/SIDE, CROSS; TOUCH, TOUCH beginning R foot (SAY AND DO).
	Do Part I with SAY AND DO and then with the music.
	Practice the SCHOTTISCHES with the TURNS and "add on" the 3 final steps (individual's tempo then SAY AND DO).
	Do the entire dance with SAY AND DO and add the music.
CHAIR DANCING	Do SCHOTTISCHES in place, omitting the TURNS.

Salty Dog Rag
U.S.A.

RECORD	Decca 27981
INTRODUCTION	16 beats
FORMATION	Partners in double circle facing counterclockwise; skater's hold
ALTERNATE FORMATION	Circle (no partners)
PART I	SCHOTTISCHE OUT; SCHOTTISCHE IN; STEP HOP; STEP HOP; STEP HOP; STEP HOP
Beat 1-2	Schottische sideward right beginning R foot
3-4	Schottische sideward left beginning L foot
5-8	Step Hop, R, L, R, L foot forward counterclockwise
9-16	Repeat Part I, beats 1-8, and turn to face partner (keep L hand-hold)

(continued)

Salty Dog Rag *(continued)*

CHORUS	SCHOTTISCHE SIDE; SCHOTTISCHE TURN; STEP HOP; STEP HOP; STEP HOP; STEP HOP
Beat 1-2	Schottische sideward right beginning R foot
3-4	Schottische with full turn left beginning L foot (release hand hold)
5-8	Step Hop R, L, R, L foot turning clockwise with partner one full turn (R forearms together)
9-16	Repeat Chorus, beats 1-8
TO SIMPLIFY	Do SCHOTTISCHE beginning L foot without the TURN.
PART II	HEEL/STEP, HEEL/STEP; HEELS OUT/HEELS IN, HEEL/UP; STEP HOP; STEP HOP; STEP HOP; STEP HOP
Beat 1	Extend R heel forward
&	Step R foot next to L foot
2	Extend L heel forward
&	Step L foot next to R foot
3	Turn heels out (weight on both feet)
&	Bring heels in
4	Extend R heel forward
&	Raise R foot in front of L foot
5-8	Step Hop R, L, R, L foot forward (counterclockwise)
9-16	Repeat Part II, beats 1-8
CHORUS **Beat 1-16**	Repeat Chorus, beats 1-16
	Alternate Part I, Chorus, Part II, Chorus
TO SIMPLIFY	Do Part I and Chorus, omit Part II.
CIRCLE DANCE	Do Parts I and II as described. Face IN on the Chorus and TURN individually.

Salty Dog Rag (continued)

RHYTHMIC NOTATION	PART I CHORUS

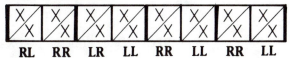

RL   RR   LR   LL   RR   LL   RR   LL

PART II

(R)R (L)L BB (R)(R) RR   LL   RR   LL

LEAD-UP ACTIVITIES	Practice SCHOTTISCHE side to side and SCHOTTISCHE TURN (individual's tempo).
	Practice STEP HOP forward (individual's tempo).
TEACHING SUGGESTIONS	Teach Part I in a circle without partners. Put the sequence together with SAY AND DO.
	Do Part I with the music.
	Teach Part II with SAY AND DO.
	Have students do both parts with a partner (partner beat).
	Practice the Chorus leaving out the TURN on the second SCHOTTISCHE (move SIDEWARD right then SIDEWARD left). Use partner beat and then SAY AND DO.
	Practice the transitions into the Chorus and back to the verse.
	Do the entire dance with SAY AND DO and then add the music.
CHAIR DANCING	Do the STEP HOPS in place.

Savila Se Bela Loza
A Vine Entwined Itself
Yugoslavia

RECORD	Folkraft 1496X45
INTRODUCTION	None
FORMATION	Broken circle or line, hands joined in "V" position
PART I	RUN (18), STEP HOP; RUN (18), STEP HOP
Beat 1-18	Run 18 steps forward right beginning R foot (feet are kicked up behind)
19-20	Step Hop R foot and turn to face left
21-40	Repeat Part I, beats 1-20, beginning L foot and end with a Step Hop L foot
	Face center
PART II	SCHOTTISCHE
Beat 1-4	Schottische sideward right beginning R foot (small steps and no swing of free leg)
5-8	Schottische sideward left beginning L foot
9-24	Repeat Part II, beats 1-8, two times

RHYTHMIC NOTATION

PART I

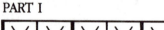

R L R L R L **REPEAT 2X**

R R **REPEAT PART I W/OPP. FTWK.**

PART II

R L R R L R L L **REPEAT 2X**

Savila Se Bela Loza (continued)

LEAD-UP ACTIVITIES	Practice side-to-side SCHOTTISCHE (individual's tempo).
	Practice running a designated number of steps then following the RUN with a STEP HOP (individual's tempo).
TEACHING SUGGESTIONS	Identify the underlying beat and do Part I with the music.
	Practice the 6 SIDEWARD SCHOTTISCHE steps with SAY AND DO.
	Do the entire dance with the music.
CHAIR DANCING PART I	Do steps in place.

Šetnja
Walking
Yugoslavia

RECORD	Folkraft 1490X45
INTRODUCTION	None or 8 beats
FORMATION	Line, leader at right; Escort hold (L hand on hip, R hand take elbow of person ahead)
PART I	FORWARD, HOLD, FORWARD, HOLD; WALK, WALK, WALK, HOLD; OUT, HOLD, OUT, HOLD; OUT, SIDE, CROSS, HOLD
Beat 1-2	Step R foot forward and hold beat 2
3-4	Step L foot forward and hold beat 4
5-6	Step R foot, L foot forward
7-8	Step R foot forward then turn so line side by side
9-10	Step L foot out and hold beat 10
11-12	Step R foot out and hold beat 12
13	Step L foot out
14	Step R foot sideward right
15-16	Step L foot crossing in front of R foot and hold beat 16; continue Part I until music accelerates
STYLE NOTE	The held beats may be changed to bounces and the steps OUT changed to reel steps, one foot behind the other.
PART II	Drop arms to "V" position. STEP HOP, STEP HOP; SCHOTTISCHE
Beat 1-4	Step Hop R foot, L foot forward
5-8	Schottische beginning R foot
9-12	Step Hop L foot, R foot out
13-16	Schottische beginning L foot (out, side, cross, hop)
NOTE	Stepping directions same as described in Part I.

Šetnja (continued)

RHYTHMIC NOTATION

PART I

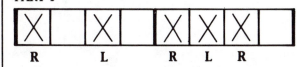

REPEAT W/OPP. FTWK.

R   L   R L R

PART II

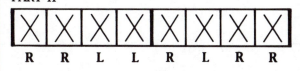

REPEAT W/OPP. FTWK.

R R L L R L R R

LEAD-UP ACTIVITIES

Practice walking in a rhythmic pattern of 1, 2, 3 &, 4 individual's tempo).

Practice STEP HOPS (individual's tempo).

Practice SCHOTTISCHES (individual's tempo).

Practice a combination of 2 STEP HOPS and 1 SCHOTTISCHE (individual's tempo).

TEACHING SUGGESTIONS

Practice Part I with SAY AND DO and add the music.

Practice STEP HOP, STEP HOP; SCHOTTISCHE pattern with SAY AND DO.

Practice OUT, HOP, OUT, HOP; OUT, SIDE, CROSS, HOP beginning L foot (individual's tempo then SAY AND DO).

CHAIR DANCING

Do steps in place moving away from and toward the chair.

Uneven
Dance Steps

Characteristic:
Movements in the sequence use the held
beat or combine divided beats with
single beats.

Bechatzar Harabbi
Israel

RECORD	Tikva T-145 *Party*
INTRODUCTION	16 beats
FORMATION	Free formation
PART I	SIDE, BACK, SIDE, CLAP; SIDE, BACK, SIDE, CLAP; UP, DOWN, UP, DOWN; UP, DOWN, UP, DOWN
Beat 1	Step R foot sideward right
2	Step L foot crossing in back of R foot
3	Step R foot sideward right
4	Clap over R shoulder
5-8	Repeat beats 1-4 to left beginning L foot
9	Step R foot on ball of foot reaching overhead with arms
10	Step L foot, bend knee slightly, bringing arms down
11-16	Repeat beats 9-10 three times turning full circle right
17-32	Repeat Part I, beats 1-16
PART II	IN, 2, 3, HOLD; OUT, 2, 3, HOLD; IN, 2, 3, HOLD; OUT, 2, 3, HOLD; SWAY, SNAP, SWAY, SNAP; TURN, 2, 3, HOLD; FORWARD, HOLD, FORWARD, HOLD; BACKWARD, 2, 3, HOLD
Beat 1-3	Step R, L, R foot in (toward facing direction)
4	Hold
5-7	Step L, R, L foot out
8	Hold
9-16	Repeat beats 1-8
17-18	Sway right, snap fingers on beat 18
19-20	Sway left, snap fingers on beat 20
21-23	Step R, L, R foot turning 1/4 turn right
24	Hold
25-26	Step L foot forward, hold beat 26
27-28	Step R foot forward, hold beat 28
29-31	Step L, R, L foot backward
32	Hold
NOTE	Each repeat of the dance begins facing new direction.

(continued)

Bechatzar Harabbi *(continued)*

RHYTHMIC NOTATION

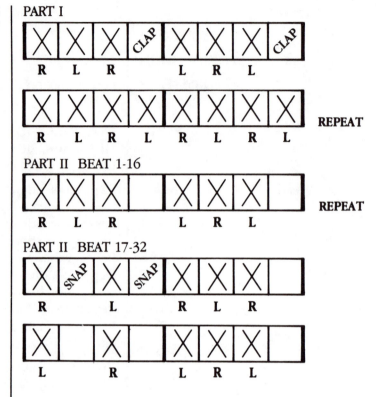

PART I

X	X	X	CLAP	X	X	X	CLAP
R	L	R		L	R	L	

X	X	X	X	X	X	X	X	REPEAT
R	L	R	L	R	L	R	L	

PART II BEAT 1-16

X	X	X		X	X	X		REPEAT
R	L	R		L	R	L		

PART II BEAT 17-32

X	SNAP	X	SNAP	X	X	X	
R		L		R	L	R	

X		X		X	X	X	
L		R		L	R	L	

LEAD-UP ACTIVITIES

Move in a SIDE, BACK pattern (individual's tempo).

Move FORWARD and BACKWARD in a pattern of WALK, 2, 3, HOLD (individual's tempo).

WALK in a rhythmic sequence of WALK, HOLD, WALK, HOLD; WALK, WALK, WALK, HOLD (individual's tempo).

Do a slow BUZZ TURN to the right (individual's tempo).

Bechatzar Harabbi (continued)

TEACHING SUGGESTIONS

Practice SIDE, BACK, SIDE, CLAP in both directions (SAY AND DO).

Do 2 patterns of SIDE, BACK, SIDE, CLAP, beginning R foot and "add on" one slow BUZZ TURN (8 beats). (Don't use arms in BUZZ TURN.)

Practice Part I (SAY AND DO).

Do IN, 2, 3, HOLD; OUT, 2, 3, HOLD twice in succession. "Add on" to the IN, OUT pattern 2 sequences of SWAY, SNAP (individual's tempo).

Do 2 patterns of SWAY, SNAP beginning R foot and "add on" 3 steps and a hold turning 1/4 right.

Do FORWARD, HOLD, FORWARD, HOLD; BACKWARD, 2, 3, HOLD.

Do Part II (SAY AND DO). Practice the transition from Part II to Part I.

SAY AND DO entire dance; then add music.

CHAIR DANCING

Substitute SIDE, CLOSE for SIDE, BACK.

Omit TURNS and step in place.

Hora Agadati
Israel

RECORD	Israeli Music Foundation LP 5/6
INTRODUCTION	16 beats
FORMATION	Single circle facing counterclockwise, hands joined
PART I	FORWARD, 2, 3, 4; JUMP, JUMP, JUMP, JUMP
Beat 1-4	Run R, L, R, L foot forward counterclockwise
5	Jump with both knees angled left
6	Jump (knees straight)
7-8	Repeat beats 5-6
9-32	Repeat beats 1-8 three times and turn to face center
PART II	HEEL, HOLD, STEP/STEP, STEP; HEEL, HOLD, STEP/STEP, STEP; JUMP, JUMP, IN, IN; OUT, OUT, STEP/STEP, STEP
Beat 1	Hop R foot and extend L heel diagonally left in
2	Hold
3-4	Step L, R, L foot in place (3 &, 4)
5-8	Repeat beats 1-4
9-10	Jump 2 times (knees angled left then straight)
11	Step L foot in toward center
12	Step R foot in with accent
13	Step L foot out away from center
14	Step R foot out
15-16	Step L, R, L foot in place
17-32	Repeat Part II, beats 1-16

RHYTHMIC NOTATION

PART I

X	X	X	X	X	X	X	X	
R	L	R	L	B	B	B	B	**REPEAT 3X**

PART II

X		X/X	X	X		X/X	X
R		LR	L	R		LR	L

X	X	X	X	X	X	X/X	X	
B	B	L	R	L	R	LR	L	**REPEAT**

Hora Agadati *(continued)*

LEAD-UP ACTIVITIES	Practice jumping angling feet diagonally left and then straight (individual's tempo).
	Combine 4 RUNS with 4 JUMPS (individual's tempo).
	Practice HOP, HOLD, STEP/STEP, STEP sequences in place (individual's tempo).
	Practice 2 JUMPS, 2 STEPS IN and 2 STEPS OUT (individual's tempo).
TEACHING SUGGESTIONS	Practice Part I with SAY AND DO.
	Practice HEEL, HOLD, STEP/STEP, STEP with SAY AND DO.
	Practice JUMP, JUMP, IN, IN, OUT, OUT (STEP L foot, R foot IN). Use SAY AND DO then "add on" the final STEP/STEP, STEP.
	Do Part II with SAY AND DO.
	Practice the transitions, Part I to Part II then back to the beginning. Add the music.
CHAIR DANCING	Do as described except execute running steps in place.

Hora Bialik
Israel

RECORD	Dancecraft LP 123301
INTRODUCTION	16 beats
FORMATION	Circle facing center, hands joined
PART I	CROSS, SIDE
Beat 1-2	Step L foot crossing in front of R foot (arms down)
3-4	Step R foot sideward right (arms up)
5-20	Repeat Part I, beats 1-4, four times
PART II	FORWARD, 2, 3, HOLD; SIDE, BACK, SIDE, HOLD
Beat 1-3	Step L, R, L foot forward counterclockwise
4	Hold and face center
5	Step R foot sideward right
6	Step L foot crossing in back of R foot
7	Step R foot sideward right
8	Hold and face counterclockwise
9-16	Repeat Part II, beats 1-8
TO SIMPLIFY	Continue to WALK FORWARD, instead of SIDE, BACK, SIDE.
PART III	IN, HOLD, IN, HOLD; CROSS, SIDE, CROSS, HOLD; OUT, HOLD, OUT, HOLD; CROSS, SIDE, CROSS, HOLD
Beat 1-2	Step L foot in toward center
3-4	Step R foot in
5	Step L foot crossing in front of R foot
6	Step R foot sideward right
7	Step L foot crossing in front of R foot
8	Hold
9-10	Step R foot out
11-12	Step L foot out
13-15	Step R foot crossing in front of L foot
14	Step L foot sideward left
15	Step R foot crossing in front of L foot
16	Hold
17-32	Repeat Part III, beats 1-16
TO SIMPLIFY	TURN body to face in the direction of steps, rather than using cross-over steps.
RHYTHMIC NOTATION	PART I

X		X	
L		**R**	

REPEAT 4X

Hora Bialik (continued)

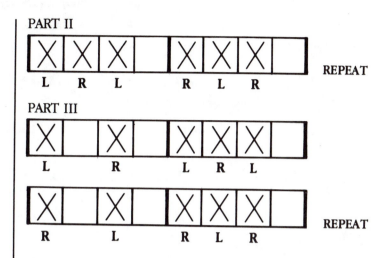

PART II

X	X	X		X	X	X		REPEAT
L	R	L		R	L	R		

PART III

X		X		X	X	X	
L		R		L	R	L	

X		X		X	X	X		REPEAT
R		L		R	L	R		

LEAD-UP ACTIVITIES

Practice CROSS, SIDE (individual's tempo).

Practice a sequence of FORWARD, 2, 3, HOLD (individual's tempo).

Practice walking in a pattern of STEP, HOLD, STEP, HOLD; STEP, STEP, STEP, HOLD (individual's tempo).

Use the imagery of a "square" and have students WALK around different size squares using different combinations of movement.

TEACHING SUGGESTIONS

Practice CROSS, SIDE beginning L foot with SAY AND DO. Practice FORWARD, 2, 3, HOLD around the circle with SAY AND DO. Practice SIDE, BACK, SIDE, HOLD and combine with FORWARD, 2, 3, HOLD beginning L foot.

Do Parts I and II with SAY AND DO and add music if desired, omitting Part III.

Practice walking the "square" with IN, HOLD, IN, HOLD; CROSS, SIDE, CROSS, HOLD; OUT, HOLD, OUT, HOLD; CROSS, SIDE, CROSS, HOLD using individual's tempo first and then SAY AND DO.

Practice the transitions from Part II to Part III and Part III to Part I.

Do the entire dance with SAY AND DO and then with music.

CHAIR DANCING PART I

Substitute L foot in front of R foot in place.

PART II

Step in place.

PART III

Do as described.

Hora Pe Gheaţa
Hora on the Ice
Romania

RECORD	Nevofoon 15005
INTRODUCTION	8 beats
FORMATION	Single circle, hands held in "W" position
PART I	FORWARD, 2, 3, 4; SIDE HOLD, SIDE HOLD; IN HOLD, OUT, 2; 3, 4, 5, STAMP
Beat 1-4	Step R, L, R, L foot forward moving counterclockwise and turn to face center
5-6	Gliding step R foot sideward right, lift L leg "skate right"
7-8	Gliding step L foot sideward left, lift R leg "skate left"
9-10	Gliding step R foot in toward center of circle, "skate in"
11-15	Step L, R, L, R, L foot out rotating the nonweightbearing foot outward on each step
16	Stamp R foot
TO SIMPLIFY	Step L, R, L, R, L foot OUT.
PART II	IN, 2, 3, HOLD; OUT, 2, 3, HOLD; IN, 2, 3, HOLD; OUT, 2, 3, HOLD
Beat 1-4	Step R, L, R foot diagonally in right and hold beat 4
5-8	Step L, R, L foot diagonally out right and hold beat 8
9-16	Repeat beats 1-8
TO SIMPLIFY	Step R, L, R, L foot IN then OUT. Do not hold beat 4 and beat 8.
RHYTHMIC NOTATION	PART I

PART I

X	X	X	X	X		X	
R	L	R	L	R		L	

X		X	X	X	X	X	X
R		L	R	L	R	L	(R)

Hora Pe Gheaţa (continued)

PART II

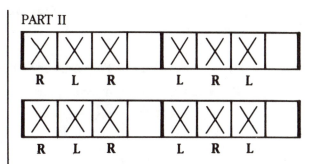

X	X	X		X	X	X	
R	L	R		L	R	L	

X	X	X		X	X	X	
R	L	R		L	R	L	

LEAD-UP ACTIVITIES

Use the imagery of a clock and skate to various numerals designated. Each time return to the center of the clock. Use R foot for numerals 1-5, L foot for 7-11.

Move IN and OUT of the circle using 4 steps IN, 4 steps OUT or 3 steps HOLD (individual's tempo). Change activity to move IN and OUT on a diagonal.

TEACHING SUGGESTIONS

Do a SIDE, HOLD, SIDE, HOLD, IN, HOLD using the clock imagery moving to the numerals 3, 9, 12 beginning R foot (individual's tempo then SAY AND DO).

"Precede" the SIDE, SIDE, IN pattern with 4 walking steps beginning R foot and "add on" OUT, 2, 3, 4, 5, STAMP. Use individual's tempo then SAY AND DO.

Do Part I with SAY AND DO.

SAY AND DO Part II using 4 steps IN and OUT if group needs the easier pattern or the authentic 3 STEPS and a HOLD.

Practice the transitions and add the music.

CHAIR DANCING PART I

Substitute steps in place for the 4 FORWARD steps.

PART II

Move away from and toward the chair.

Danish Sextur
Dance for Six Couples
Denmark

RECORD	Folk Dancer MH 1021
INTRODUCTION	4 beats, pause, upbeat
FORMATION	Six couples in a circle, numbered 1-6 clockwise around the circle
PART I	SLIDE
Beat 1-16	Slide 16 steps clockwise around the circle (six couples with hands held)
CHORUS	TWO-STEP; IN, IN; TWO-STEP; OUT, OUT
Beat 1-2	Two-Step in beginning R foot (couples 1 and 4)
3-4	Step L foot, R foot in
5-6	Two-Step out beginning L foot
7-8	Step R foot, L foot out
5-12	Couples 2 and 5 begin Chorus on beat 5 as couples 1 and 4 are starting out
9-16	Couples 3 and 6 begin Chorus on beat 9 as couples 2 and 5 are starting out
17-48	Grand right and left all the way around circle using 16 Two-Steps
TO SIMPLIFY	WALK 4 steps IN and 4 steps OUT and use a WALK in the Grand right and left.
PART II	SLIDE (women)
Beat 1-16	Women slide 16 steps clockwise once around circle, join hands in center
CHORUS	Repeat Chorus, beats 1-48
PART III	SLIDE (men)
Beat 1-16	Men slide 16 steps clockwise twice around circle, join hands in center
CHORUS	Repeat Chorus, beats 1-48
PART IV	BUZZ TURN
Beat 1-16	Partners buzz turn clockwise (shoulder-waist) position
CHORUS	Repeat Chorus, beats 1-48
PART V	SLIDE
Beat 1-16	Repeat Part I, beats 1-16

Danish Sextur (continued)

RHYTHMIC NOTATION	PART I & V

CHORUS BEAT 1-8

REPEAT W/OPP. FTWK.

GRAND RIGHT AND LEFT

REPEAT 7X

LEAD-UP ACTIVITIES	Practice the SLIDE; add a circle formation (individual's tempo).
	Practice the Grand right and left (WALK through).
	Practice the TWO-STEP FORWARD and BACKWARD (individual's tempo).
	Practice a TWO-STEP plus 2 WALKS (FORWARD and BACKWARD).
TEACHING SUGGESTIONS	Practice each of the verses in sequence using circles of 6 couples.
	Practice the Chorus with a partner TWO-STEP (IN) IN, IN; TWO-STEP (OUT) OUT, OUT.
	Do the Chorus in circles of 6 couples and add the Grand right and left.
	Do the entire dance with the music.
CHAIR DANCING	May be modified for wheelchairs.

Hashual
The Fox
Israel

RECORD	Tikva T-98 *Dance with Rivka*
INTRODUCTION	Pickup, plus 16 beats
FORMATION	Open circle, no hands held
PART I	FORWARD, 2, 3, 4; FORWARD, 2, 3; GRAPEVINE; CROSS, SIDE, SIDE, BRUSH
Beat 1-4	Step R, L, R, L foot forward counterclockwise, 3 claps with beats 3 &, 4
5-7	Step R, L, R foot forward counterclockwise
8-11	Grapevine counterclockwise beginning L foot crossing in front of R foot
12	Step L foot crossing in front of R foot and turn to face center
13	Step R foot sideward right
14	Step L foot sideward left
15	Brush R foot in
16-29	Repeat Part I, beats 1-14 (brush is omitted)
PART II	TWO-STEP, TWO-STEP; TWO-STEP, TWO-STEP; ACCENT, OUT, OUT, OUT; OUT, OUT, OUT, OUT
Beat 1-2	Two-Step in toward center beginning R foot (R arm in beat 1)
3-4	Two-Step in beginning L foot (L arm in)
5-8	Repeat beats 1-4
9	Accent R foot next to L foot (clap hands in front)
10-16	Step L, R, L, R, L, R, L foot out (arms make a circle overhead and down to sides)
17-32	Repeat Part II, beats 1-16
RHYTHMIC NOTATION	PART I

X	X	X	X	X	X	X
R	L	R	L	R	L	R

X	X	X	X	X	X	X
L	R	L	R	L	R	L (R)

REPEAT
OMIT
LAST BEAT

Hashual *(continued)*

PART   II

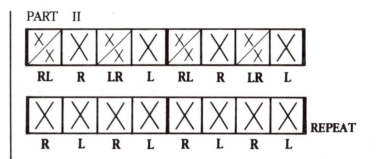

LEAD-UP
ACTIVITIES

Practice GRAPEVINE (individual's tempo).

Practice moving from walking steps to GRAPEVINES (individual's tempo).

Practice quick TWO-STEPS (individual's tempo).

TEACHING
SUGGESTIONS

Practice CROSS, SIDE, SIDE, BRUSH, beginning L foot first with individual's tempo, then with SAY AND DO.

"Precede" CROSS, SIDE, SIDE, BRUSH with a GRAPEVINE, beginning L foot (individual's tempo and then SAY AND DO).

"Precede" GRAPEVINE; CROSS, SIDE, SIDE, BRUSH with 7 WALKS (individual's tempo, then SAY AND DO).

Do Part I with SAY AND DO (note the BRUSH is omitted on the repeat). Add the CLAPS later.

Practice 4 TWO-STEPS toward the center (IN) with SAY AND DO.

Practice an accented step IN beginning R foot and 7 steps moving OUT backward with SAY AND DO.

Do Part II with SAY AND DO.

Practice the entire dance with SAY AND DO, then add the music.

CHAIR DANCING

Do as described substituting in-place steps for walking steps in Part I.

Hora Hassidit
Israel

RECORD	Hed-Arzi MN581
INTRODUCTION	8 beats
FORMATION	Single circle facing center, hands joined
PART I	GRAPEVINE; CROSS, SIDE; SIDE, SIDE; GRAPEVINE; SWAY, HOLD; SWAY, HOLD
Beat 1	Step L foot crossing in front of R foot
2	Step R foot sideward right
3	Step L foot crossing in back of R foot
4	Step R foot sideward right
5	Step L foot crossing in front of R foot
6	Step R foot sideward right
7-8	Step L foot, R foot as sideward Camel Roll (describe small "c" with hips)
9-12	Repeat beats 1-4
13-14	Step L foot swaying left (reach up and to the left with the arms)
15-16	Step R foot swaying right (reach up and to the right with the arms)
17-48	Repeat Part I, beats 1-16, two times
PART II	FORWARD, 2; 3, 4; STEP/STEP, STEP; STEP/STEP, STEP
Beat 1-4	Run L, R, L, R foot forward counterclockwise
5-8	Do 2 quick Two-Steps turning left to face clockwise beginning L foot
9-12	Run L, R, L, R foot forward clockwise
13-16	Repeat beats 5-8 turning right to face counterclockwise
17-32	Repeat Part II, beats 1-16
	IN, 2; 3, 4; STEP/STEP, STEP; STEP/STEP, STEP; OUT, 2; 3, 4; STEP/STEP, STEP; STEP/STEP, STEP
33-36	Run L, R, L, R foot in toward center
37-40	Do 2 quick Two-Steps in place; snap fingers on the beat
41-44	Run L, R, L, R foot out
45-48	Repeat beats 37-40

Hora Hassidit (continued)

RHYTHMIC NOTATION

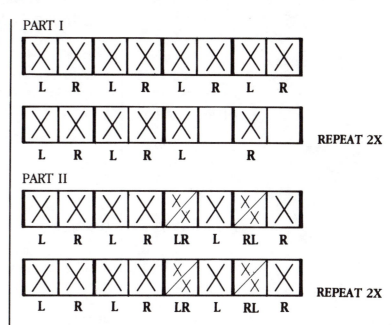

PART I

X	X	X	X	X	X	X	X
L	R	L	R	L	R	L	R

X	X	X	X	X		X	
L	R	L	R	L		R	

REPEAT 2X

PART II

X	X	X	X	X/X	X	X/X	X
L	R	L	R	LR	L	RL	R

X	X	X	X	X/X	X	X/X	X
L	R	L	R	LR	L	RL	R

REPEAT 2X

LEAD-UP ACTIVITIES

Practice GRAPEVINES (individual's tempo).

Practice transferring weight side to side (individual's tempo).

Practice quick TWO-STEPS in place turning 180° with each TWO-STEP (individual's tempo).

TEACHING SUGGESTIONS

Practice CROSS, SIDE; SIDE, SIDE (individual's tempo) develop a sideward rolling action.

Practice the above "preceding" it and "adding on" a GRAPEVINE beginning L foot.

Complete Part I with SWAY, HOLD; SWAY, HOLD, then SAY AND DO the entire part.

Practice RUN, 2; 3, 4; STEP/STEP, STEP; STEP/STEP, STEP beginning L foot first with individual's tempo and then with SAY AND DO. Substitute the 180° turn during the 2 quick TWO-STEPS.

Practice Part II with SAY AND DO.

Practice the transition from Part II to Part I then add music.

CHAIR DANCING

Substitute in-place steps where necessary.

Substitute CHERKESSIYA for GRAPEVINE.

Jambo
Hello
Africa (Ghana)

RECORD	Malayisha (reverse side of *Pata Pata*) Warner Special Products OP7500
INTRODUCTION	32 beats
FORMATION	2 circles, individuals facing one another, no hands held
ALTERNATE FORMATION	Circle

INTRODUCTION	LUNGE, NOD, NOD, NOD
Beat 1-2	Lunge diagonally right
3-4	Nod head to person diagonally right in other circle
5-6	Nod head to person opposite you
7-8	Nod head to person diagonally right
9-32	Repeat beats 1-4 three times lunging left, right, left
PART I	SIDE, HOLD, CLOSE, HOLD; SIDE, HOLD, CLOSE, HOLD; SIDE, HOLD, CLOSE, HOLD; SIDE, CLOSE, SIDE, CLOSE
Beat 1-2	Step R foot sideward right (arms raised sideward)
3-4	Step L foot next to R foot
5-12	Repeat Part I, beats 1-4, two times
13	Step R foot sideward right
14	Step L foot next to R foot
15	Step R foot sideward right
16	Step L foot next to R foot
17-32	Repeat Part I, beats 1-16
PART II	UP, TOUCH, UP, STEP; UP, TOUCH, UP, STEP; UP, TOUCH, UP, STEP; JUMP, HOLD, HOLD, HOLD
Beat 1	Raise R knee (throw head back)
2	Touch R foot next to L foot
3	Raise R knee (throw head back)
4	Step R foot next to L foot
5-12	Repeat beats 1-4 two times beginning L foot, R foot
13-16	Jump (L foot forward, R foot backward)
17-32	Repeat Part II, beats 1-16, with opposite footwork
PART III	TWO-STEP, TWO-STEP; TWO-STEP, TWO-STEP; TWO-STEP, TWO-STEP; STEP, KICK, JUMP, HOLD

Jambo *(continued)*

Beat 1-2	Two-Step L foot in place, clap beat 2
3-8	Two-Step, R, L, R foot in place, clapping on beat 2 of each Two-Step
9-12	Two-Step L foot, R foot, moving through the other circle, clap beat 2 of each Two-Step
13	Step L foot
14	Kick R foot turning 180° left
15-16	Jump with feet apart
17-32	Repeat Part III, beats 1-16, returning to place
CIRCLE DANCE	Dance as the outside circle.

RHYTHMIC NOTATION

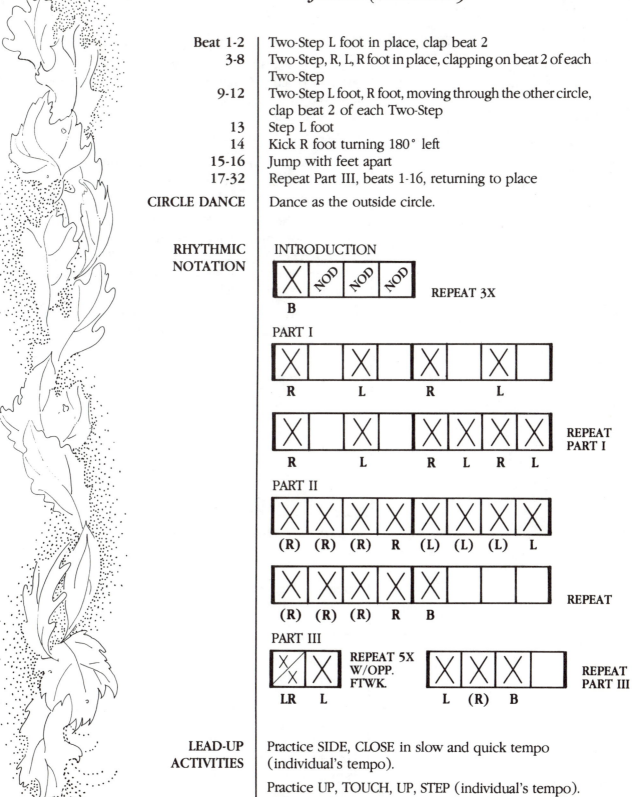

INTRODUCTION

B — REPEAT 3X

PART I
R   L   R   L

R   L   R L R L — REPEAT PART I

PART II
(R) (R) (R) R (L) (L) (L) L

(R) (R) (R) R B — REPEAT

PART III
LR L   REPEAT 5X W/OPP. FTWK.   L (R) B — REPEAT PART III

LEAD-UP ACTIVITIES	Practice SIDE, CLOSE in slow and quick tempo (individual's tempo).
	Practice UP, TOUCH, UP, STEP (individual's tempo).
	Practice TWO-STEPS in place and moving (individual's tempo).

(continued)

Jambo (continued)

TEACHING SUGGESTIONS	Teach the dance first as a single circle dance.
	Begin with Part I leaving the Introduction to last. Have students practice 3 SIDE, CLOSE steps at a slow tempo followed by 2 SIDE, CLOSE steps at quick tempo (SAY AND DO).
	Do Part II with SAY AND DO.
	Teach the STEP, KICK, JUMP, HOLD so students understand the turning direction. Have students practice with individual tempo and then with group SAY AND DO.
	"Precede" the STEP, KICK, JUMP, HOLD with 2 TWO-STEPS IN beginning L foot and then "precede" with 4 TWO-STEPS in place beginning L foot. Have students practice this sequence moving IN then OUT—first use individual's tempo and then SAY AND DO.
	Learn the Introduction and do the entire dance with SAY AND DO and then add the music.
CHAIR DANCING	Do steps in place.
	Omit the TURN, Part III.

Makedonikos Horos
Greece (Macedonia)

RECORD	Songs of Macedonia SOM-11
INTRODUCTION	4 beats
FORMATION	Open circle or lines, hands joined in "W" position
PART I	FORWARD, 2; 3, 4; SIDE, LIFT; SIDE, LIFT
Beat 1-4	Step R, L, R, L foot forward moving counterclockwise and turn to face center
5	Step R foot sideward right
6	Lift L foot in front of R leg
7	Step L foot sideward left
8	Lift R foot in front of L leg
NOTE	Music will change after 16 repetitions of Part I at which time Part II should be started.

Makedonikos Horos (continued)

PART II	OUT, OUT; SIDE/CLOSE, SIDE; IN/CLOSE, IN
Beat 1	Step R foot out diagonally right
2	Step L foot out diagonally right
3	Step R foot sideward right
&	Step L foot next to R foot
4	Step R foot sideward right
5	Step L foot in diagonally right
&	Step R foot next to L foot
6	Step L foot in diagonally right
PART III	Repeat Part II preceding beats 1, 3, and 5 with a HOP (when music changes)

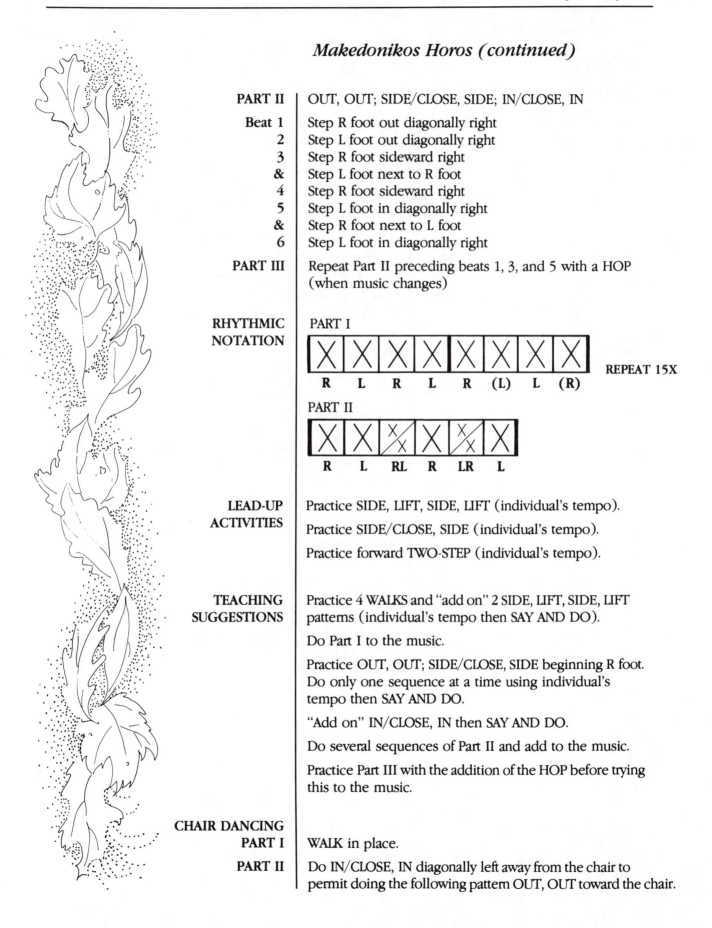

RHYTHMIC NOTATION

PART I

X X X X X X X X   **REPEAT 15X**

R L R L R (L) L (R)

PART II

X X X/X X X/X X

R L RL R LR L

LEAD-UP ACTIVITIES	Practice SIDE, LIFT, SIDE, LIFT (individual's tempo).
	Practice SIDE/CLOSE, SIDE (individual's tempo).
	Practice forward TWO-STEP (individual's tempo).
TEACHING SUGGESTIONS	Practice 4 WALKS and "add on" 2 SIDE, LIFT, SIDE, LIFT patterns (individual's tempo then SAY AND DO).
	Do Part I to the music.
	Practice OUT, OUT; SIDE/CLOSE, SIDE beginning R foot. Do only one sequence at a time using individual's tempo then SAY AND DO.
	"Add on" IN/CLOSE, IN then SAY AND DO.
	Do several sequences of Part II and add to the music.
	Practice Part III with the addition of the HOP before trying this to the music.
CHAIR DANCING PART I	WALK in place.
PART II	Do IN/CLOSE, IN diagonally left away from the chair to permit doing the following pattern OUT, OUT toward the chair.

Misirlou-Kritikos
Greek-American

RECORD	EKS 7206 *The Whole World Dances;* *The World of Folk Dances* RCA 1620
INTRODUCTION	8 beats (begin dance with vocal)
FORMATION	"W" position, open circle, leader at right end
PART I	SIDE, TOUCH, BACK/SIDE, CROSS/TURN; FORWARD/CLOSE, FORWARD; BACKWARD/CLOSE, BACKWARD
Beat 1	Step R foot sideward right
2	Touch L foot in
NOTE	Women may point L foot and men bring L foot IN slapping heel on floor.
3	Step L foot crossing in back of R foot
&	Step R foot sideward right
4	Step L foot crossing in front of R foot
&	Pivot on L foot to face clockwise (one behind another)
5-6	Two-Step beginning R foot forward clockwise (moving one behind another)
NOTE	Women may point L foot against R calf on beat 6 while men HOOK L instep behind R knee.
7-8	Two-Step beginning L foot backward counterclockwise (facing clockwise); end facing center

RHYTHMIC NOTATION

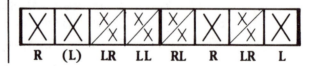

R   (L)   LR   LL   RL   R   LR   L

Misirlou-Kritikos (continued)

LEAD-UP ACTIVITIES	Practice TWO-STEP FORWARD and BACKWARD (individual's tempo).
	Practice a sequence of BACK/SIDE, CROSS (individual's tempo).
TEACHING SUGGESTIONS	Begin with the sequence BACK/SIDE, CROSS beginning L foot with SAY AND DO then "precede" with TOUCH (TOUCH, BACK/SIDE, CROSS) and practice the whole, then "precede" with SIDE and practice beats 1-4, "adding on" the 1/4 TURN at the end.
	Practice FORWARD, CLOSE, FORWARD; BACKWARD, CLOSE, BACKWARD then SAY AND DO.
	Practice the dance with SAY AND DO and then add the music.
CHAIR DANCING	Do the TWO-STEP away from and toward the chair.

Nebesko Kolo
Heavenly Circle
Yugoslavia (Serbia)

RECORD	Folk Dancer MH 1003
INTRODUCTION	None
FORMATION	Broken circle, hands joined in "V"
PART I	TWO-STEP
Beat 1-8	Two-Step 4 times forward counterclockwise beginning R foot (each Two-Step takes 2 beats)
9-16	Repeat beats 1-8 forward clockwise and turn to face center
PART II	IN, OUT, OUT, IN; IN, OUT, OUT, IN
Beat 1	Step R foot in
2	Step L foot out
3	Step R foot out
4	Step L foot in
5-8	Repeat Part II, beats 1-4
PART III	STEP/STEP, STEP; STEP/STEP, STEP; STEP/STEP, STEP; STEP/STEP, STEP; STAMP, HOLD
Beat 1-2	Step R, L, R foot in place
3-4	Step L, R, L foot in place
5-8	Repeat beats 1-4
9-10	Stamp R foot

Part II beats 1-4 are bracketed: **CHERKESSIYA**

RHYTHMIC NOTATION

PART I

X/X	X	X/X	X	X/X	X	X/X	X
RL	R	LR	L	RL	R	LR	L

REPEAT

PART II

X	X	X	X	X	X	X	X
R	L	R	L	R	L	R	L

PART III

X/X	X	X/X	X	X/X	X	X/X	X	X	
RL	R	LR	L	RL	R	LR	L	(R)	

Nebesko Kolo (continued)

LEAD-UP ACTIVITIES

Practice quick TWO-STEPS (individual's tempo).

Practice CHERKESSIYA (individual's tempo).

Practice THREES in place—STEP/STEP, STEP (individual's tempo).

TEACHING SUGGESTIONS

Practice the 8 TWO-STEPS of Part I moving counterclockwise then clockwise (individual's tempo then SAY AND DO).

Practice the 2 CHERKESSIYA steps of Part II with SAY AND DO and "add on" to Part I.

Practice the 4 THREES of Part III followed by the STAMP (individual's tempo then SAY AND DO).

Practice the transition of Part II to III and back to the beginning.

Do the entire dance with SAY AND DO and add the music.

CHAIR DANCING

Do TWO-STEPS away from and toward the chair with small steps.

Sellenger's Round
England

RECORD	RCA Victor LPM 1621
INTRODUCTION	3-chord
FORMATION	Partners in a single circle

PART I	SLIDE	
Beat 1-8	Slide 8 steps sideward clockwise	*Slipping*
9-16	Slide 8 steps sideward counterclockwise	
CHORUS	TWO-STEP, TWO-STEP; OUT, 2, 3, 4; THREE, THREE; TURN, 2, 3, 4	
Beat 1-2	Two-Step in beginning R foot	*Setting*
3-4	Two-Step in beginning L foot	
5-8	Step R, L, R, L foot out	*Back a double*
9-12	Three in place beginning R foot, L foot facing partner, leap onto the first step of each Three	*Setting to partner*
13-16	Full turn R, L, R, L foot to the right	*Turn single*
17-32	Repeat Chorus, beats 1-16	
PART II	IN, 2, 3, 4; OUT, 2, 3, 4	
Beat 1-4	Step R, L, R, L foot in	*Forward a double*
5-8	Step R, L, R, L foot out	*Back a double*
9-16	Repeat Part II, beats 1-8	
CHORUS	Repeat Chorus, beats 1-32	
PART III	FORWARD, 2, 3, TURN; FORWARD, 2, 3, TURN	
Beat 1-3	Step R, L, R foot changing places with partner; ladies moving inside clockwise and men outside counterclockwise; keep facing partner	*Siding*
4	Turn 1/2 while continuing to face partner	
5-8	Step L, R, L foot back to place along same path (keep looking at partner)	
9-16	Repeat Part III, beats 1-8	
CHORUS	Repeat Chorus, beats 1-32	
PART IV	ELBOW TURNS	
Beat 1-8	R elbow turn with partner (move apart on beats 7-8)	*Arming*
9-16	L elbow turn (move apart on beats 15-16)	
CHORUS	Repeat Chorus, beats 1-32	

Sellenger's Round (continued)

PART V	SLIDE
Beat 1-16	Repeat Part I, beats 1-6 *Slipping*
CHORUS	Repeat Chorus, beats 1-32

RHYTHMIC NOTATION

PART I

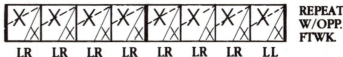

LR   LR   LR   LR   LR   LR   LR   LL

REPEAT W/OPP. FTWK.

PART II & IV

R   L   R   L   R   L   R   L

REPEAT

PART III

R   L   R   L   R   L

REPEAT

CHORUS

RL   R   LR   L   R   L   R   L

REPEAT 3X

LEAD-UP ACTIVITIES

Practice SLIDES (individual's tempo).

Practice TWO-STEPS (individual's tempo).

Practice STEP/STEP, STEP in place (individual's tempo).

Practice TURNS in 4 steps (individual's tempo).

TEACHING SUGGESTIONS

Practice the Chorus, beats 1-8, with a partner (partner beat then SAY AND DO). "Add on" the THREES with partners facing each other and then the full TURN right.

Do the entire Chorus with SAY AND DO.

Learn each of the verses repeating the Chorus after each (SAY AND DO).

Do the entire dance with SAY AND DO and then add the music.

CHAIR DANCING

Do the verses in place or away from and toward the chair.

Substitute steps in place for the TURN in the Chorus.

May be adapted for wheelchairs.

Hineh Ma Tov
How Good It Is
Israel

RECORD	Folk Dancer, MH 45-1091; Electra *Hora*
INTRODUCTION	Pickup plus 16 beats
FORMATION	Single circle, hands joined, or line with L hand at shoulder and R arm straight
CHORUS	FORWARD, 2, 3, 4; RUN/2, 3/4, 5/6, 7/8
Beat 1-4	Step R, L, R, L foot forward counterclockwise
5-8	Run 8 steps forward counterclockwise beginning R foot
9-16	Repeat Chorus, beats 1-8, and turn to face center
PART I	SIDE, OUT/CLOSE, IN, STAMP; YEMENITE, YEMENITE
Beat 1	Step R foot sideward right
2	Step L foot out away from center
&	Step R foot next to L foot
3	Step L foot in toward center
4	Stamp R foot next to L foot
5-6	Yemenite beginning R foot
7-8	Yemenite beginning L foot
9-16	Repeat Part I, beats 1-8
CHORUS	
Beat 1-16	Repeat Chorus, beats 1-16
PART II	IN/2, 3/4, 5/6, 7/8; YEMENITE, YEMENITE
Beat 1-4	Run 8 steps in, beginning R foot
5-8	Repeat Part I, beats 5-8
9-12	Run 8 steps out, beginning R foot (backing up)
13-16	Repeat Part I, beats 5-8

RHYTHMIC NOTATION

PART I

X	X	X	X	X X	X X	X X	X X		REPEAT
R	L	R	L	RL	RL	RL	RL		

PART II

X	X X	X	X	X X	X	X X	X		REPEAT
R	LR	L	(R)	RL	R	LR	L		

Hineb Ma Tov (continued)

PART III

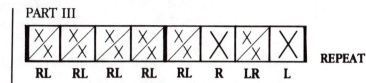

X X	X X	X X	X X	X X	X	X X	X	REPEAT
RL	RL	RL	RL	RL	R	LR	L	

LEAD-UP ACTIVITIES

Practice combinations of walking and running with RUNS executed as a divided beat (individual's tempo).

Practice YEMENITE steps (individual's tempo).

Practice 8 RUNS plus 2 YEMENITE steps.

Practice patterns of OUT/CLOSE, IN (individual's tempo).

TEACHING SUGGESTIONS

Practice 4 WALKS, 8 RUNS with SAY AND DO.

Practice 8 RUNS IN and 8 RUNS OUT (encourage small steps). "Add on" 2 YEMENITE steps after the RUNS IN and 2 YEMENITE steps after the RUNS OUT. (SAY AND DO.)

Practice SIDE, OUT/CLOSE, IN, STAMP with SAY, then SAY AND DO.

Practice "adding on" 2 YEMENITE steps to Part I, beats 1-4 (individual's tempo then SAY AND DO).

Do the dance in sequence with SAY AND DO then add the music. Be certain students understand the order of the parts.

NOTE

Part II is learned before Part I because it is easier.

CHAIR DANCING PART I

Substitute steps in place.

PART III

Use small steps away from and toward the chair.

Leor Chiyuchech
To the Light of Your Smile
Israel

RECORD	Folk Dancer MH 1151
INTRODUCTION	16 beats
FORMATION	Single circle facing center, hands joined
PART I	YEMENITE; YEMENITE; IN, OUT, CLOSE, HOLD; IN, OUT, CLOSE, HOLD
Beat 1-4	Yemenite beginning L foot
5-8	Yemenite beginning R foot
9	Step L foot in toward center (raise arms)
10	Step R foot out (lower arms)
11-12	Step L foot next to R foot
13-16	Repeat beats 9-12 with opposite footwork beginning R foot
17-32	Repeat Part I, beats 1-16, and turn to face counterclockwise
PART II	TWO-STEP; TWO-STEP; FORWARD, SIDE, BACK, SIDE
Beat 1-4	Two-Step beginning L foot forward counterclockwise (brush R foot forward on beat 4)
5-8	Two-Step beginning R foot (brush L foot forward on beat 8)
9-10	Step L foot forward and turn to face center
11-12	Step R foot sideward right (raise arms)
13-14	Step L foot crossing in back of R foot (bend knees)
15-16	Step R foot sideward right (lower arms)
17-32	Repeat Part II, beats 1-16

RHYTHMIC NOTATION

PART I

X	X	X		X	X	X	
L	R	L		R	L	R	

X	X	X		X	X	X	
L	R	L		R	L	R	

REPEAT

Leor Chiyuchech (continued)

PART II

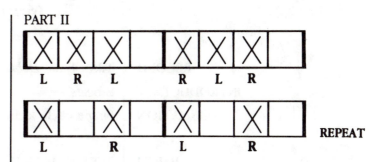

LEAD-UP
ACTIVITIES

Learn or practice YEMENITE steps (individual's tempo).

Practice slow TWO-STEPS (individual's tempo).

Practice the pattern of IN, OUT, CLOSE, HOLD (individual's tempo).

TEACHING
SUGGESTIONS

Practice 2 YEMENITE steps in sequence beginning L foot (SAY AND DO).

Practice IN, OUT, CLOSE, HOLD twice in sequence beginning L foot (SAY AND DO).

Do Part I with SAY AND DO.

Practice 2 slow TWO-STEPS moving counterclockwise beginning L foot (SAY AND DO).

Practice the pattern FORWARD, SIDE, BACK, SIDE beginning L foot moving counterclockwise (SAY AND DO).

Do Part II with SAY AND DO.

Practice the transition from Part I to Part II remembering to move counterclockwise beginning L foot.

Practice the transition from Part II to Part I with its difficult side-to-side movement pattern.

Do the entire dance with SAY AND DO and add the music.

CHAIR DANCING

Substitute in-place steps for moving steps in Part II.

Ma Na'Vu
How Beautiful Upon the Mountains
Israel

RECORD	Tikva T-100 *Debka*
INTRODUCTION	8 beats
FORMATION	Single circle facing center, hands joined
PART I	TOUCH, TOUCH, OUT/CLOSE, IN; OUT, IN, OUT/IN, TOGETHER
Beat 1	Touch R toe in, weight on L foot
2	Touch R toe sideward, weight on L foot
3	Step R foot out
&	Step L foot next to R foot
4	Step R foot in
5	Step L foot out
6	Step R foot in
7	Step L foot out
&	Step R foot in
8	Bring both feet together lowering heels
9-16	Repeat Part I, beats 1-8, with opposite footwork beginning L foot
PART II	YEMENITE; TWO-STEP
Beat 1-2	Yemenite beginning R foot then turn to face counter-clockwise
3-4	Two-Step L foot forward then turn to face center
5-16	Repeat Part II, beats 1-4, three times

RHYTHMIC NOTATION

PART I

X	X	X/X	X	X	X	X/X	X	REPEAT W/OPP. FTWK.
(R)	(R)	RL	R	L	R	LR	B	

PART II

X/X	X	X/X	X	X/X	X	X/X	X	REPEAT
RL	R	LR	L	RL	R	LR	L	

Ma Na'Vu (continued)

LEAD-UP ACTIVITIES	Practice YEMENITES (individual's tempo).
	Practice TWO-STEPS (individual's tempo).
	Practice combining 1 YEMENITE with 1 TWO-STEP (individual's tempo).
	Practice OUT/CLOSE, IN pattern (individual's tempo).
TEACHING SUGGESTIONS	Practice TOUCH, TOUCH, OUT/CLOSE, IN (SAY AND DO) then "add on" OUT, IN, OUT/IN, TOGETHER. Practice with one foot then the other.
	Do Part I with SAY AND DO.
	Practice the YEMENITE, TWO-STEP combination (individual's tempo then SAY AND DO).
	Do Part II with SAY AND DO.
	Practice the transitions from Part I to Part II and back to the beginning.
	Do the entire dance with SAY AND DO and add the music.
CHAIR DANCING PART II	Substitute in-place TWO-STEPS.

Sapri Tama
Tell Me My Innocent One
Israel

RECORD	Dancecraft LP 123301, *Dance Israel*
INTRODUCTION	12 beats
FORMATION	Individuals in lines

PART I	SWAY/SNAP, SWAY/SNAP; TURN, SNAP; YEMENITE; YEMENITE
Beat 1	Sway right
&	Snap fingers with arms high over right shoulder
2	Sway left
&	Snap fingers with arms high over left shoulder
3	Turn 1/4 right bringing feet together
4	Bend both knees (snap fingers as knees are bent)
5-6	Yemenite beginning R foot
7-8	Yemenite beginning L foot

	STEP, BEND; STEP, BEND; SIDE, CROSS; SIDE, CROSS; YEMENITE; SIDE, CROSS; SIDE, CROSS; YEMENITE
Beat 9	Step R foot sideward right
10	Bend R knee lifting L leg in front (snap fingers—hands close to body)
11	Step L foot sideward left
12	Bend L knee (repeat bend and snap as in beat 10)
13	Step R sideward right (spread arms apart)
14	Step L foot crossing in front of R foot (cross arms and snap)
15	Step R foot sideward right, spread arms apart
16	Step L foot crossing in front of R foot (cross arms and snap)
17-18	Yemenite beginning R foot
19-24	Repeat beats 13-18 sideward left beginning L foot

Sapri Tama (continued)

RHYTHMIC NOTATION

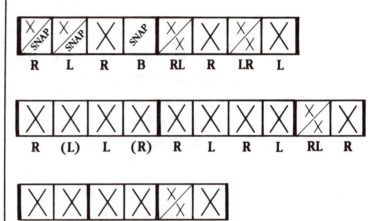

LEAD-UP ACTIVITIES

Practice YEMENITE steps (individual's tempo).

Practice SIDE, CROSS (individual's tempo).

TEACHING SUGGESTIONS

Practice SWAY/SNAP, SWAY/SNAP; TURN, SNAP (individual's tempo then SAY AND DO).

"Add on" the 2 YEMENITE steps.

Do beats 1-8 with SAY AND DO.

Practice STEP, BEND; STEP, BEND; SIDE, CROSS; SIDE, CROSS with individual's tempo and then SAY AND DO.

"Add on" the YEMENITE and SAY AND DO beats 9-18.

"Add on" the SIDE, CROSS; SIDE, CROSS; YEMENITE sideward left (SAY AND DO).

Do beats 9-24 with SAY AND DO.

Practice the transition from beat 8 to beat 9 from 12 to 13 and from the end to the beginning.

Do the entire dance with SAY AND DO and then add the music.

CHAIR DANCING

Do the steps in place omitting the 1/4 TURN.

Doudlebska Polka
Double Clap Polka
Czechoslavakia

RECORD	Folkraft F 1413; Folk Dancer MH
INTRODUCTION	8 beats
FORMATION	Partners arranged about the room
ALTERNATE FORMATION	Circle
PART I	POLKA
Beat 1-32	Polka 16 times with partner
PART II	WALK
Beat 1-32	Walk 32 steps and form a double circle; persons on left place L hands on L shoulders of persons ahead in the circle and R hands around the waist of partners; all sing "La, La, La" with the music.
PART III	CLAP/CLAP, HIT
Beat 1-32	Persons on left turn to face center and clap own hands twice then neighbors once in rhythm of 1 &, 2; the clapping sequence is executed 16 times.
	Persons on right turn to face clockwise and dance individually 16 Polka steps clockwise around the outside of the circle. At the end of the 32 beats begin the dance from the beginning with a new partner.
CIRCLE DANCE	Dance the left-hand person's part; POLKA, WALK into a circle, CLAP.
RHYTHMIC NOTATION	

POLKA

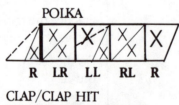

R   LR   LL   RL   R

CLAP/CLAP HIT

Doudlebska Polka (continued)

LEAD-UP ACTIVITIES	Practice GALLOP with each foot leading (individual's tempo). Add 4 GALLOPS with one foot followed by 4 with the other. Practice 2 GALLOPS with one foot then 2 GALLOPS with the other (GALLOP POLKA).
	If the group is skilled enough to learn the POLKA, review or learn the TWO-STEP then "precede" each TWO-STEP with the HOP (individual's tempo).
	Practice POLKA or GALLOP POLKA with a partner.
	Practice having everyone WALK from a scattered free formation to a circle.
	Have group stand in a circle and practice the CLAP/CLAP, HIT pattern of PART III (SAY AND DO).
TEACHING SUGGESTIONS	It is recommended that the circle dance be taught as a lead-up to the partner dance.
	Have everyone POLKA or GALLOP POLKA to the music.
	Have everyone do Part I followed by Part II with the music. Add Part III.
CHAIR DANCING	Do as described for Circle Dance.
	Substitute in-place steps.

Jessie Polka
U.S.A.

RECORD	Folkraft 1138X45 *A and E Rag*
INTRODUCTION	4 beats
FORMATION	Individual, partners, circle, line
PART I	HEEL, STEP; TOE, TOUCH; HEEL, STEP; HEEL, LIFT
Beat 1	Hop R foot extending L heel diagonally left
2	Step L foot next to R foot
3	Hop L foot extending toe diagonally backward
4	Touch R foot next to L foot
5	Hop L foot extending R heel diagonally right
6	Step R foot next to L foot
7	Hop R foot extending L heel diagonally left
8	Hop R foot lifting L foot in front of R foot (knee bent)
PART II	POLKA
Beat 1-8	Polka forward 4 times beginning with hop R foot and Two-Step L foot
TO SIMPLIFY	Change POLKAS to RUNS.

RHYTHMIC NOTATION

PART I

X	X	X	X	X	X	X	X
R	L	L	L	L	R	R	R

PART II

X	X	X	X
R	LR	LL	RL R

REPEAT

LEAD-UP ACTIVITIES	Practice 2-beat sequences of HEEL, STEP; TOE, TOUCH; HEEL, LIFT (individual's tempo).
	Practice the POLKA (individual's tempo).
TEACHING SUGGESTIONS	Have students work out the language-to-movement patterns of Part I (individual's tempo).
	Practice Part I without using HOPS at first.
	SAY AND DO Part I and "add on" 4 POLKA steps of Part II.
CHAIR DANCING	Do the sequences in place.

Jesucita en Chihuahua
Northern Mexico

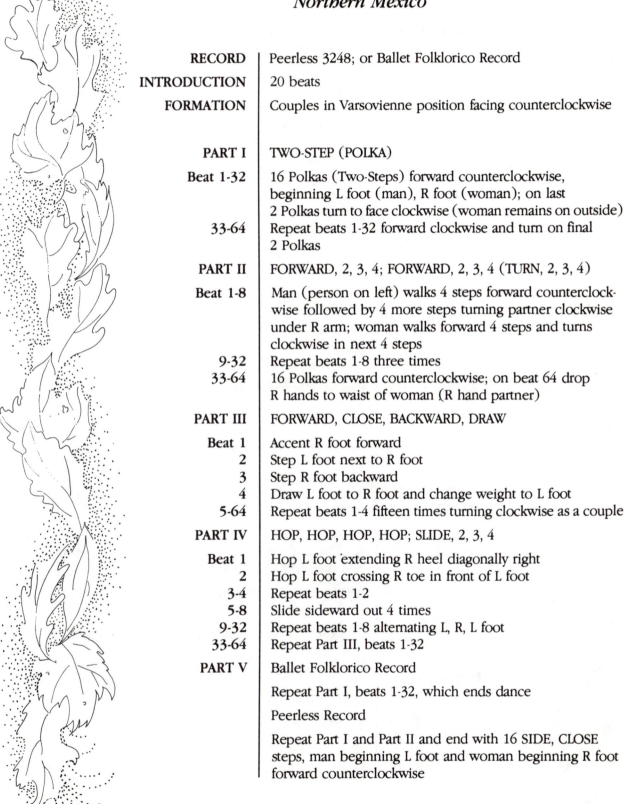

RECORD	Peerless 3248; or Ballet Folklorico Record
INTRODUCTION	20 beats
FORMATION	Couples in Varsovienne position facing counterclockwise
PART I	TWO-STEP (POLKA)
Beat 1-32	16 Polkas (Two-Steps) forward counterclockwise, beginning L foot (man), R foot (woman); on last 2 Polkas turn to face clockwise (woman remains on outside)
33-64	Repeat beats 1-32 forward clockwise and turn on final 2 Polkas
PART II	FORWARD, 2, 3, 4; FORWARD, 2, 3, 4 (TURN, 2, 3, 4)
Beat 1-8	Man (person on left) walks 4 steps forward counterclockwise followed by 4 more steps turning partner clockwise under R arm; woman walks forward 4 steps and turns clockwise in next 4 steps
9-32	Repeat beats 1-8 three times
33-64	16 Polkas forward counterclockwise; on beat 64 drop R hands to waist of woman (R hand partner)
PART III	FORWARD, CLOSE, BACKWARD, DRAW
Beat 1	Accent R foot forward
2	Step L foot next to R foot
3	Step R foot backward
4	Draw L foot to R foot and change weight to L foot
5-64	Repeat beats 1-4 fifteen times turning clockwise as a couple
PART IV	HOP, HOP, HOP, HOP; SLIDE, 2, 3, 4
Beat 1	Hop L foot extending R heel diagonally right
2	Hop L foot crossing R toe in front of L foot
3-4	Repeat beats 1-2
5-8	Slide sideward out 4 times
9-32	Repeat beats 1-8 alternating L, R, L foot
33-64	Repeat Part III, beats 1-32
PART V	Ballet Folklorico Record
	Repeat Part I, beats 1-32, which ends dance
	Peerless Record
	Repeat Part I and Part II and end with 16 SIDE, CLOSE steps, man beginning L foot and woman beginning R foot forward counterclockwise

(continued)

Jesucita en Chihuahua (continued)

RHYTHMIC NOTATION

PART I

X/X	X	X/X	X
RL	R	LR	L

REPEAT 15X

PART II & III

X	X	X	X
R	L	R	L

REPEAT 15X

PART VI

X	X	X	X	X/X	X/X	X/X	X
L	L	L	L	RL	RL	RL	R

REPEAT

LEAD-UP ACTIVITIES

Practice TWO-STEP (Mexican Polka)—individual's tempo then partner beat.

Practice 4 steps FORWARD then TURN clockwise 4 steps (individual's tempo then partner beat with R hand person turning and L hand person continuing WALK).

Practice FORWARD, CLOSE, BACKWARD, CLOSE in place then turning right (individual's tempo).

Practice 4 HOPS and 4 SLIDES (individual's tempo).

TEACHING SUGGESTIONS

Practice Parts I and II with partners (SAY AND DO then add music).

Practice Part III without the addition of the stylistic ACCENT and DRAW then add those features (partner beat then SAY AND DO).

Practice Part IV with partner (partner beat then SAY AND DO).

Do the entire dance with SAY AND DO and add music.

CHAIR DANCING

PART I | Do in place.

PART II | Do steps away from and toward the chair.

PART III | Do as described without turning.

PART IV | Do as described.

Appendices

Appendix A:
Rhythmic Competency Analysis Test

The **Rhythmic Competency Analysis Test** is designed to assess an individual's ability to perform a movement task to an underlying beat of music. The test is presented in three levels of increasing difficulty. The same piece of music is used for each level of the test. Students are tested individually in a location away from other children or adults where the tester and the student will be alone and uninterrupted or distracted.

Use a tape recorder and two cassette tapes of musical selections with a strong steady beat. One musical selection should have a metronome beat of approximately 132 (♩ = 132) and the other selection should have a metronome beat of approximately 120 (♩ = 120). Both the student and the tester should be seated. Put students at ease with friendly, relaxed conversation.

Step 1. To introduce the test, ask the student to play follow-the-leader with you. Lead the student through a sequence of patting the thighs for a minimum of 8 beats then patting the top of the head for a minimum of 8 beats. Use a tempo that is different from the tempo of the musical selections you have chosen for the test.

Step 2. To test the student's understanding of the task, ask him or her to be the leader. Suggest that the student pat the top of the head so you can follow his or her lead. Encourage definite movements, large enough to be easily assessed for beat accuracy.

Step 3. Explain to the student that you are going to play some music and that he or she should listen for the beat and use both hands to pat the top of the head in time to the beat. If necessary, describe *beat* with a word the students will understand, such as *pulse, heartbeat, walking beat, steady beat.* Begin the tape of the first musical selection (with the metronome beat of approximately 132) beyond the musical introduction.

Step 4. Ask the student to pat the top of the head and then the tops of the shoulders one after the other ("head, shoulders, head, shoulders . . ."). Be certain the student understands your instructions. (Demonstrate if necessary but not to the same tempo as the music.) Begin the test music again and have the student respond to the beat with this two-movement coordination task.

Step 5. Ask the student to stand up and walk to the beat as you play the music. Again, be certain to begin the tape beyond the musical introduction. (Use the same test music as before.)

Step 6. Play the second musical selection (metronome beat of 120) and have the student walk to this music also. This step is necessary for test accuracy in the event the first tempo matched the student's natural internal tempo.

Scoring. The test is scored on a scale from "0" to "2." A "0" is given to those students who cannot do the task to the steady beat of music (matching beat and movement accurately). A "1" is given to those students who are successful some of the time, but are inconsistent in their matching response. A "2" is given to those students who are totally successful with the task, matching the steady beat accurately.

Modification for older students (grade 4 and above). The test is the same as described above with these exceptions:

1. Step 1 is modified so that the tester only pats the legs and asks the subject to follow (omit patting the head).

2. The students are not asked to be the leader in the pretest sequence since it is assumed they will understand the directions after following the tester. Thus, Step 2 is omitted.

3. Step 3 is modified so that the student pats the legs instead of the head.

4. Step 4 is omitted.

Appendix B:
Rhythmic Coordination
Screening Test

The **Rhythmic Coordination Screening Test*** is a follow-the-leader test which is administered without music and is designed to predict an individual's ability to identify a steady beat of music—to possess a **basic level of rhythmic competency**. The test may be administered in a one-to-one testing situation, to small groups of students (3-4), or to an entire class. It should be noted that persons who are on the borderline of competency may not be identified if the entire class is screened at once. No special equipment is needed.

If more than one individual is tested at the same time, provide sufficient space for individuals to spread their arms sideward. The tester and student(s) should be seated. The student(s) are instructed to follow the motions that the tester is executing. (If a large group is being assessed, the tester will need to stand up in order to be visible.)

Step 1. Pat the thighs with both hands simultaneously saying "PAT, PAT . . . ." Do the thigh pat at least eight times using the language until you see that all the students are following your movements accurately.

Step 2. Alternate the movement of your hands as you pat the thighs. Do *not* use the words "right" and "left," but continue chanting "PAT, PAT . . ." if necessary. Repeat this alternate movement until learners seem to be comfortable. Before moving on to step 3, indicate that a change is going to occur.

Step 3. Pat the thighs once with both hands followed by one hand clap. Say "PAT, CLAP, PAT, CLAP . . ." simultaneously with the movements. Repeat this step at least eight times. Before going on to the next step indicate to the students that you are going to move on just prior to the change. (Note: "KNEES, SHOULDERS"—touching knees then shoulders—may be substituted for the "PAT, CLAP." Be certain to use both hands simultaneously.)

Step 4. Snap the fingers once with the arms spread apart then clap the hands once (for persons who cannot snap, encourage the spreading apart of the arms without a snap). Say "SNAP, CLAP, SNAP, CLAP . . ." simultaneously with the motions. Repeat this step at least eight times. Before going on to the final step, indicate that you are going to move on

just before you do. (Note: If using "KNEES, SHOULDERS" in Step 3, do "OUT, IN" in step 4—arms thrust OUT and then IN—hands to shoulders.)

Step 5. PAT the thighs once with both hands, CLAP once, SNAP the fingers once with the arms spread apart, CLAP once. Say "PAT, CLAP, SNAP, CLAP . . ." simultaneously with the motions. Do "KNEES, SHOULDERS, OUT, IN." Do this step at least eight times.

Evaluation. Persons who cannot coordinate Step 5 after two or three repetitions possess low levels of rhythmic competency.** Students who cannot coordinate Step 5 will have difficulty walking to a steady beat of music. Persons who finally succeed after several repetitions may be able to walk to a steady beat of music but will lack sufficient coordination to succeed with organized movement and dance sequences. Persons who are successful on the first or second repetition can be expected to match a steady beat in a walking pattern and perform other simple movement and dance sequences to music. These students recognize and are secure with beat.

Special directions for the tester:

- Face the students.

- Do not stop once the test has begun. Proceed from one step to the next without interruption.

- Be certain to begin each step with the single word that describes the movement executed (e.g., PAT, CLAP, OUT, IN).

- Keep the movements slow enough for beginners; a metronome beat of approximately 100 beats per minute (♩ = 100) is a good tempo to use.

- Assess the students' ability to follow the movements *exactly as executed.*

---

*The test has been administered to hundreds of individuals ranging from eight year olds to senior citizens.

**The tester may note the beginnings of the rhythmic coordination difficulty in students by Step 3 or Step 4. Students may come in late or may completely reverse the pattern the tester is using.

Locomotor Movement I*

Big Circle Dance   *USA (Novelty)*   99
Cherkessiya (simplified)   *Israel*   221
Count 32   *USA (Novelty)*   100
Djurdjevka Kolo   *Yugoslavia*   102
Fjäskern   *Sweden*   103
Haya Ze Basadeh (simplified)   *Israel*   104
Irish Stew   *USA (Novelty)*   106
La Raspa (simplified)   *Mexico*   107
Les Saluts   *French Canadian*   109
Little Shoemaker (circle)   *USA (Novelty)*   110
Seven Jumps (simplified)   *Denmark*   112
Sneaky Snake   *USA (Novelty)*   114
Te Ve Orez   *Israel*   115
Troika   *Russia*   116
Two-Part Dance   *USA (Novelty)*   118
Yankee Doodle   *USA (Novelty)*   119
Zigeunerpolka   *Germany*   120

Locomotor Movement II

Áis Giórgis   *Greece*   123
Ajde Noga Za Nogama   *Yugoslavia (Croatia)*   125
Alley Cat*   *USA (Novelty)*   126
Amos Moses   *USA (Novelty)*   128
Apat-Apat*   *Philippines*   130
Bannielou Lambaol   *France (Brittany)*   132
Bele Kawe*   *Africa*   134
Chiotikos   *Greece*   136
Close Encounters*   *USA (Novelty)*   138
Cumberland Square*   *England*   140
Debka Daluna   *Israel (Arab)*   142
Dimna Juda   *Macedonia*   144
Dučec*   *Yugoslavia*   145
Entertainer*   *USA (Novelty)*   147
Erev Shel Shoshanim   *Israel*   150
Ersko Kolo (simplified)   *Yugoslavia*   266
Good Old Days*   *USA (Novelty)*   152
Hasapikos   *Greece*   154
Hora Medura (simplified)   *Israel*   234
Instant Success   *USA (Novelty)*   156
İşte Hendek   *Turkey*   159
Kendimé   *Turkey*   161
Körtanc   *Hungary*   162
Limbo Rock*   *USA (Novelty)*   164
Man in the Hay*   *Germany*   166
Plješkavac Kolo*   *Yugoslavia*   168

Popcorn*   *USA (Novelty)*   170
Pravo Horo   *Bulgaria*   172
Spanish Coffee   *USA (Novelty)*   174
Tant' Hessie*   *South Africa*   176
Tipsy*   *USA (Novelty)*   178
Twelfth St. Rag*   *USA (Novelty)*   180
Ugros*   *Hungary*   182
Ve David*   *Israel*   185
Zemer Atik   *Israel*   186

Locomotor Movement III

Alunelul   *Romania*   189
Bossa Nova   *USA (Novelty)*   191
Bulgarian Dance #1   *Bulgaria*   194
Hole in the Wall   *England*   196
Hora Pe Gheaţa   *Romania*   294
Hot Pretzels   *USA (Novelty)*   199
Hustle   *USA (Novelty)*   200
Jamaican Holiday*   *USA (Novelty)*   202
Joe Clark Mixer   *USA (Novelty)*   204
Mexican Mixer*   *Mexico*   207
Pata Pata   *USA (Novelty)*   208
Sham Hareh Golan   *Israel*   210
Tanko Bushi   *Japan*   212
Toi Nergis   *Armenia*   214
Tsakonikos   *Tsakonia, Peloponnesos, Greece*   216
Vranjanka   *Yugoslavia (Macedonia)*   218

Even Dance Steps

CHERKESSIYA
   Cherkessiya   *Israel*   221
   Ciocarlanul   *Romania*   223
   Mechol Hagat   *Israel*   224

GRAPEVINE
   Armenian Misirlou   *Armenia*   226
   Corrido   *Mexico*   227
   Debka Le Adama   *Israel*   229
   Dimna Juda Mamo   *Yugoslavia (Macedonia)*   230
   Dirlada   *Greece*   232
   Hora Medura   *Israel*   234
   Mayim   *Israel*   236
   Romanian Hora   *Romania*   238

---

*No right or left foot is specified for any of the **Locomotor Movement I** dances. In addition, dances in **Locomotor Movement II** and **III** that do not require use of right or left foot are marked with an asterisk.

Appendix D:
Suggested Lesson Sequence for a Beginning Folk Dance Unit for Older Students*

> **Age:** Junior or senior high school to adult (including senior citizens)
>
> **Length of class:** 45 minutes to 1 hour
>
> **Prerequisite Experiences:**
> - Students possess a basic level of rhythmic competency (see *Chapter II*).
> - Students possess basic comfort with movement (see *Chapter III*).
> - Students have had opportunities to participate successfully in rhythmic movement sequences (see *Chapter IV*).

This lesson sequence is based on my firm belief that beginning students (including older students) must experience a broad base of locomotor movement experiences before moving on to more difficult folk dance steps and patterns. Therefore, the lesson sequence includes **Locomotor Movement I, II, and III** activities, but does not include **Even and Uneven Dance Steps.** The lesson sequence covers ten class periods. Upon completion of the sequence, students will be ready for **Even and Uneven Folk Dance Steps.** Those teachers who have time for more lessons can refer to the section in *Chapter V* on introducing **Even** and **Uneven Dance Steps** to beginners, as well as to *Appendix C, Dances by Level of Difficulty* for specific dances.

Each dance mentioned here is described in *Part Two* of this book. Since each of those descriptions includes lead-up activities and teaching suggestions, I will not repeat that information here.

Lesson 1
- Exercise warm-up (students seated): Use movements which will determine the rhythmic competency of your students (see *Chapter II*). Ask students to walk around the room to their own internal beat and tempo. Suggest changes in tempo (walk faster, slower); direction (walk backward, sideward); level of the body (walk tall, short, wide); and intensity (walk with heavy steps, light steps). *Chapter III* contains additional suggestions of this nature.
- *Two-Part Dance (Blackberry Quadrille):*
  Part I: Walk (use a different movement each repeat).
  Part II: Ask students to execute stationary non-locomotor arm movements (use a different one each time). (Note: This dance should be done without an organized formation, unless you need to exert control over the group by using a circle.)
- *Big Circle Dance (Circle Follow the Leader)*
  Have the group copy you in visual follow-the-leader sequence. If the students experience difficulty, add aural cues.
- *Cherkessiya* (simplified version)
- *Les Saluts*
- *Doudlebska Polka* (modify to circle variation using the GALLOP in **Part I**)
- *Count 32* (modify **Part II** to IN, 2, 3, 4; OUT, 2, 3, 4 twice)
- *Troika*

Lesson 2
- Exercise warm-up: Use rhythmic coordination sequences with the arms. Use different music than used in first lesson, such as *Rakes of Mallow*
- *Two-Part Dance:*
  Part I: Suggest locomotor movements (walking different ways, jumping, hopping)
  Part II: Suggest nonlocomotor movements (arm sequences)
- *Big Circle Dance:* Use different music than in first lesson, such as *Little Shoemaker*
- Review: *Count 32, Troika*
- New: *Fjäskern* (circle modification version); teach the "TOUCH, TOUCH, TOUCH, STEP" to be used in the next dance; *Djurdjevka Kolo; Te Ve Orez* (use the circle variation or the authentic formation and dance)
- Review: *Doudlebska Polka*

---

*Although the teaching sequence I outline in *Chapter V* can be used with any age group (age eight on), I offer the suggestions here especially for those teachers who are working with adolescents and adults.

Lesson 3

- Rhythmic warm-up: *Big Circle Dance* (add sequences found in dances such as the "TOUCH, TOUCH, TOUCH, STEP")
- Review: *Fjäskern, Djurdjevka Kolo*
- New: *Alley Cat* (follows "TOUCH, TOUCH, TOUCH, STEP" movement sequence used in *Djurdjevka Kolo*)
- Review: *Te Ve Orez*
- New: *Bele Kawe* (simplified version), *Cumberland Square*

Lesson 4

- Rhythmic warm-up: Requests (2) from a list of the dances which have been taught and reviewed
- Review: *Alley Cat*
- New: Introduce the rhythmic pattern "1, 2, 3 &, 4" by exploring different ways to move using this rhythm; *Limbo Rock; Plješkavac Kolo* (same "1, 2, 3 &, 4" rhythmic pattern used in *Limbo Rock*)
- Review: *Bele Kawe, Cumberland Square*
- New: *Close Encounters* (begin with partner from *Cumberland Square* or teach the circle dance modification)

Lesson 5

- Rhythmic warm-up: Use 2-beat alternating arm sequences (see LEVEL V, *Chapter II*); *Big Circle Dance*, include 2-beat and alternating 2-beat foot patterns (see *Chapter V*, Locomotor Movement I dances)
- Requests (2)
- Review: *Limbo Rock, Plješkavac Kolo, Close Encounters*—teach partner version if circle dance was taught in preceding lesson
- New: Introduce 4-beat movement sequences (see *Chapter V*, Locomotor Movement II dances); *Kendimé, Ugros*
- Request (1)

Lesson 6

- Rhythmic warm-up

- Requests (2)
- Review: *Kendimé, Ugros*
- New: *Hora Medura* (simplified version); *Twelfth St. Rag* (use simplified version in Part II)
- Request (1)

Lesson 7

- Rhythmic warm-up
- Requests (2)
- Review: *Hora Medura* (continue with simplified version); *Twelfth St. Rag* (continue with simplified version)
- New: *Bannielou Lambaol* (teach only the foot pattern); *Popcorn*
- Request (1)

Lesson 8

- Rhythmic warm-up
- Requests (2)
- Review: *Bannielou Lambaol* (add the arms); *Popcorn*
- New: *Istę Hendek* (teach without the variation); *Hasapikos* (teach Part I and II variations)
- Request (1)

Lesson 9

- Rhythmic warm-up
- Request (2)
- Review: *Istę Hendek* (do not add the variations); *Hasapikos* (do additional variations if the group is doing well with those presented in the preceding lesson)
- New: *Alunelul, Pata Pata* (teach without the arm pattern)

Lesson 10

- Rhythmic warm-up
- Review: *Alunelul; Pata Pata* (add the arms)
- Requests: Finish this last class with all requests which have been planned with the class in advance

Folkraft
10 Fenwick Street
Newark, New Jersey 07114
(201) 243-8700

Folk Dancer Record Service
P.O. Box 201
Flushing, New York 11352
(212) 784-7404

Worldtone Music, Inc.
230 Seventh Avenue
New York, New York 10011
(212) 691-1934

Festival Records
2769 West Pico Blvd.
Los Angeles, California 90006
(213) 737-3500

Ed Kremers
161 Turk
San Francisco, California 94102
(415) 775-3444

High/Scope Press*
600 North River Street
Ypsilanti, Michigan 48197
(313) 485-2000

---

*The Educational record is available only through this source.

Glossary of Rhythmic Movement and Folk Dance Terms

Language-to-Movement Terms

Basic Locomotor Movements

HOP A transfer of weight from one foot to the *same* foot. Executed with an even beat. May be done in place or proceed in any direction. (If the hopping foot is changed, a leap is performed.)

JUMP A transfer of weight from one or both feet to *both* feet. Executed with an even beat. May be done in place or proceed in any direction.

LEAP A transfer of weight from one foot to the other foot. Both feet are off the floor in the transfer. Greater height or distance is used than in the run. Executed with an even beat. May proceed in any direction.

RUN A transfer of weight from one foot to the other foot. Both feet are off the floor momentarily before the transfer of weight. Executed with an even beat which often is faster than the beat used for the walk. May proceed in any direction.

WALK A transfer of weight from one foot to the other foot. One foot always is in contact with the floor. Executed with an even beat which allows the same amount of time between each step. May proceed in any direction.

Basic Locomotor Movement Combinations

GALLOP A forward or backward movement. One foot steps then the other foot closes; the step takes more time than the close (uneven rhythm). The same foot always leads. The easiest of the basic locomotor combinations.

SKIP A combination of a step and a hop executed in an uneven rhythm. Same rhythmic pattern as the gallop and slide. The time interval of the hop is shorter than the step. The skip may proceed in any direction. The leading foot changes with each skip.

SLIDE A sideward gallop. Same rhythmic pattern as the gallop. The same foot leads sideward followed by a close of the opposite foot. The side step takes more time than the close (uneven rhythm).

Other Movement Terms

BUZZ TURN A movement in which partners, using the shoulders-waist or social dance position, turn 360° in a forward direction with a series of steps using divided beats. The right foot leads.

CAMEL ROLL A movement from the forward foot to the backward foot to the forward foot again. The hips describe a movement in the shape of a "C."

CHARLESTON STEP (simplified) A step forward, a forward kick of the free leg, a step backward from the kick, and a touch of the free leg backward.

DO-SA-DO A partner movement in which partners move toward one another, pass back to back, and then move backward to place (begins with partners passing right shoulders).

ELBOW SWING A partner movement in which partners hook elbows and walk, run or skip around in a forward direction, turning 360°.

FIGURE EIGHT A series of steps which describe the floor pattern of an "8."

GRAND RIGHT AND LEFT Partners face each other and begin to move around the circle in opposite directions giving right hands to each other, then alternating left and right hands with each person in turn.

HORSE TROT A "leaping" movement in which the legs bend and reach forward for each new step.

PARTNER BEAT Two persons move together with the same tempo.

RIGHT HAND STAR Dancers move in a forward direction clockwise with right hands joined in the middle.

SCISSORS KICKS A forward or backward kicking movement of the legs in which the kicks occur in sequence.

SIDEWARD CAMEL ROLL Feet step from side to side and hips move in a "C" from side to side.

Language-to-Dance Vocabulary

Weight Transfer Terms

ACCENT A forceful step on the designated foot.

BACK A step on the designated foot crossing in back of the other foot.

BACKWARD A step on the designated foot moving away from the facing direction (clockwise or counter-clockwise) around a circle or one behind the other in a line.

CHANGE A step on the designated foot to begin a change of partners or change of places between two people.

CLOSE   A step on the designated foot to bring it next to the other foot. May occur in any direction.

CROSS   A step on the designated foot crossing in front of the other foot.

FORWARD   A step on the designated foot moving in the facing direction (clockwise or counterclockwise) around a circle or one behind the other in a line.

IN   A step on the designated foot toward the center of a circle or in the facing direction when standing side by side in a line.

OUT   A step on the designated foot away from the center of a circle or away from the facing direction when standing side by side in a line.

SHUFFLE   A step from one foot to the other maintaining contact with the floor.

SIDE   A step on the designated foot perpendicular to the facing direction. Dancers are facing center in a circle or side by side in a line.

SKATE   A step on the designated foot which slides the foot against the floor.

STEP   A weight transfer to the designated foot in place (next to the other foot).

SWAY   A step on the designated foot sideward with a movement of the upper body in the same direction.

SWIVEL   The toes and heels move sideward either together (toes then heels) or toes of one foot and heels of the other in an alternating motion.

TOGETHER   A step on the designated foot without lifting the other foot. Weight now is on both feet.

TURN   A step on the designated foot which moves the body clockwise or counterclockwise 90° or 180° with a single weight transfer or a step which begins a multi-step rotation (90°, 180° or 360°).

Nonweight Transfer Terms

BEND   A motion of the supporting leg toward the floor as the knee bends.

BOUNCE   A movement of one or both heels which raises and lowers them to the floor. May be thought of as a jump or hop which doesn't leave the floor.

BRUSH   A motion of the designated foot against the floor.

CHUG   A movement of the supporting leg (generally backward) with the foot kept in contact with the floor.

CLICK, HEEL CLICK   A forceful motion of the designated foot against the other foot while it is on the floor or in the air.

DIG   A forceful motion of the designated foot to the floor with the front part of the foot contacting the floor.

DRAW   A movement which slides the free foot along the floor up to the supporting foot.

HEEL   A motion of the designated heel against the floor.

HIT   A motion of one or two hands to the foot or to the partner's hands.

HOOK   A motion of the designated foot against the back of the supporting knee causing the knee to bend.

KICK   A motion of the designated leg in front, back or to the side of the body involving a straightening of the knee.

LIFT   A motion of the designated leg in front of the body involving a bent knee. The lower leg is angled in front of the supporting leg.

PIVOT   A motion of the designated foot against the floor which turns the body to face a new direction.

SLAP   A forceful motion of the whole foot against the floor executed with the leg straight out from the body.

SNAP   A snapping motion of the fingers of one of both hands.

STAMP   A forceful motion of the designated foot against the floor.

TOE   A motion of the designated toes against the floor.

TOUCH   A motion of the designated toes or heel against the floor.

UP   A motion of the designated leg in front of the body begun by raising the knee.

Dance Steps*

CHERKESSIYA   IN, OUT, OUT, IN

GRAPEVINE   CROSS, SIDE, BACK, SIDE

GRAPEVINE PATTERN   SIDE, CROSS, SIDE, BACK or SIDE, BACK, SIDE, CROSS

POLKA   HOP/FORWARD,** CLOSE, FORWARD

SCHOTTISCHE   WALK, WALK, STEP, HOP

STEP HOP   STEP, HOP

THREE   FORWARD,** 2, 3, REST

TWO-STEP   FORWARD,** CLOSE, FORWARD, REST

YEMENITE   SIDE, SIDE, CROSS, REST

---

*The dance steps are illustrated in *Chapter V.*
**BACKWARD, IN, OUT may be substituted.

Nonpartner Formations

BROKEN CIRCLE   Dancers are arranged in a single circle with one place in which the hands are not joined, thus establishing a leader.

CIRCLE   Dancers are arranged in a single circle with or without hands joined.

FREE FORMATION   Dancers are scattered around the dance space in a random pattern.

LINE   Dancers stand side by side. Line may be short with three to five dancers or long with one leader.

OPEN CIRCLE   Dancers are arranged in circle formation except no hands are joined during the dance.

Partner Formations

DOUBLE CIRCLE (PARTNERS FACING EACH OTHER)   Partners are arranged around a circle. Outside partner faces toward the center (IN) and inside partner faces away from the center of the circle (OUT).

FRONT BASKET   Dancers stand in a circle or line and spread their own arms sideward in front of the persons on either side. Hands are joined with persons one beyond the dancer on each side. The underneath arm corresponds to the traveling direction. (If the basket moves right the right arm is under.)

HEADS   The two sets of partners in a square set who face each other across the set; one set of "heads" has their backs to the musical source. (See *Square set* illustration.)

LONGWAYS SET, CONTRA LINE   Partners are in a double line facing each other or facing the head of the set.

REVERSE BASKET   Same as FRONT BASKET with hands joined in back of the dancer on each side. The arm on top corresponds to the traveling direction.

SIDES   The two sets of partners in a square set who face each other and are not HEADS. (See *Square set* illustration.)

SINGLE CIRCLE   Partners stand side by side in a single circle facing toward the center or around the circle.

SQUARE SET   Eight persons (four couples) are arranged so that one couple is on each side of a square facing the center.

STAR   Four or more persons all join right or left hands in the middle of their circle.

Group Formations and Hand-Holds

ESCORT HOLD   Dancers are side by side or diagonally forward of one another. The hand in the moving direction hooks the bent elbow of the person ahead. The other hand is at the waist, elbow bent, with the back of the hand on the hip. Occasionally the escort hold requires dancers to be very close together in which case the arm in the moving direction is underneath the neighbor's arm.

LINE AND CIRCLE "T" (SHOULDER HOLD)   Arms are extended sideward at shoulder level to the near shoulders of the dancer on either side. Elbows are straight. Right arms are in back and left arms in front.

"V" (KOLO HOLD)   Hands are joined with arms down. The left palm faces to the rear (OUT) and the right palm faces to the front (IN). The left palm is on top.

"W"   Hands are joined at shoulder level with elbows bent. The right hand supports the neighbor's left hand. A convenient way to form this hand-hold is to take the "V" position as described and raise the arms.

Partner Positions and Hand-Holds

DOUBLE SHOULDER   This modification of the shoulder-waist position is used when two males or two females are partners. Dancers hold each other's shoulders.

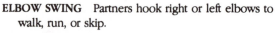

ELBOW SWING   Partners hook right or left elbows to walk, run, or skip.

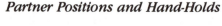

ISRAELI TURN *Partners stand with right hips adjacent to one another. Right arms are extended in front of partner, holding the partner at the waist. Left arms are held high.*

SOCIAL DANCE (CLOSED POSITION) *Partners face each other. Male holds the female's right hand in his left hand. Male's right hand holds the back of the female above the waist. The female's left hand is placed on the male's right shoulder.*

SHOULDER-WAIST *Partners face each other. Male holds the female at her waist. Female's hands are on the male's shoulders.*

VARSOVIENNE or PROMENADE *Partners are side by side with the male to the left of the female. Right hands are held at the female's right shoulder (male's right arm is straight across female's shoulders). Left hands are joined in front of the male with the female's left arm straight. (This position does not require a coed setting.)*

SKATER'S HOLD or CROSS-HAND HOLD *Partners are side by side with right hands joined in front of the right partner and left hands joined in front of the left partner. Right hands are joined on top and left hands are joined underneath. A promenade is sometimes danced in this position.*

Bibliography

Abramson, R. *Rhythm Games Book I.* New York: Music and Movement Press, 1973.

Barlin, A., and Barlin, P. *The Art of Learning Through Movement.* Los Angeles, CA: The Ward Ritchie Press, 1971.

Barrett, K. *Exploration—A Method for Teaching Movement.* Minneapolis: Burgess Publishing Co., 1977.

Boorman, J. *Creative Dance in the First Three Grades.* New York: David McKay, 1969.

Boorman, J. *Creative Dance in Grades Four to Six.* Ontario: Longman, 1971.

Boorman, J. *Dance and Language Experiences with Children.* Ontario: Longman, 1973.

Burton, E. C. *The New Physical Education for Elementary School Children.* Boston: Houghton-Mifflin Co., 1977.

Carroll, J., and Lofthouse, P. *Creative Dance for Boys.* London: MacDonald & Evans, 1969.

Clark, C. *Rhythmic Activities for the Classroom.* Dansville, NY: The Instructor Publications, Inc.

Cratty, B. *Active Learning: Games to Enhance Academic Abilities.* Englewood Cliffs, NJ: Prentice-Hall, 1971.

Findlay, E. *Rhythm and Movement.* Evanston, IL: Summy-Birchard, Co., 1971.

Fleming, G. *Creative Rhythmic Movement—Boys and Girls Dancing,* ed. 2. Englewood Cliffs, NJ: Prentice-Hall, Inc., 1976.

Froseth, J., and Weikart, P. *Movement to Music in Confined Spaces.* Chicago, IL: G. I. A. Publications, 1981.

Gallahue, D. L., Werner, P. H., and Luedke, G. C. *A Conceptual Approach to Moving and Learning.* New York: John Wiley & Sons, Inc., 1975.

Gerhardt, A. *Moving and Knowing: The Young Child Orients Himself in Space.* Englewood Cliffs, NJ: Prentice-Hall, Inc. 1973.

Gilbert, A. *Teaching the Three Rs Through Movement Experiences.* Minneapolis: Burgess Publishing Co., 1977.

Gray, V., and Percival, R. *Music, Movement and Mime for Children.* New York: Oxford University Press, 1962.

Harris, J. A., Pittman, A., and Waler, M. S. *Dance A-While,* ed. 4. Minneapolis, MN: Burgess Publishing Co., 1968.

Jacques-Dalcroze, E. *Rhythm, Music, and Education,* rev. ed. London: The Dalcroze Society, Inc., 1967.

Kraus, R. *Folk Dancing.* New York: The Macmillan Co., 1962.

Lidster, M., and Tamburini, D. *Folk Dance Progressions.* Belmont, CA: Wadsworth Publishing Co., 1965.

Logsdon, B. J., et al. *Physical Education for Children.* Philadelphia: Lea & Febiger, 1978.

Mettler, B. *Materials of Dance as a Creative Activity.* Tucson, AZ: Mettler Studios, 1973.

Movement: Physical Education in the Primary Years. London: Department of Education and Science, 1972.

Murray, R. *Dance in Elementary Education,* ed. 3. New York: Harper & Row Publishers, 1975.

Nash, G. *Creative Approaches to Child Development with Music, Language and Movement.* Port Washington, NY: Alfred Publishing Co., 1974.

Russell, J. *Creative Movement and Dance for Children,* rev. ed. Boston: Plays, Inc. 1975.

Schurr, E. *Movement Experiences for Children.* Englewood Cliffs, NJ: Prentice-Hall, Inc., 1975.

Viltis (a magazine of Folklore and Folk Dance). P. O. Box 1226, Denver, Colorado 80201.

Weikart, P. *Movement to the Musica Poetica.* St. Louis, MO: Magnamusic-Baton, Inc. 1981.

Werner, P., and Burton, E. *Learning Through Movement.* St. Louis: C. V. Mosby Company, 1979.

Winters, S. J. *Creative Rhythmic Movement for Children of Elementary School Age.* Dubuque, Iowa: William C. Brown Co., 1975.

Index of Dances
Arranged Alphabetically

Subject Index